TWENTIETH CENTURY VIEWS

The aim of this series is to present the best in
contemporary critical opinion on major authors,
providing a twentieth century perspective on
their changing status in an era of profound
revaluation.

Maynard Mack, *Series Editor*
Yale University

YEATS

YEATS

A COLLECTION OF CRITICAL ESSAYS

Edited by

John Unterecker

15641

A SPECTRUM BOOK

Prentice-Hall, Inc., *Englewood Cliffs, N. J.*

The poetry of Yeats is used by kind permission of Mrs. W. B. Yeats, The Macmillan Company, and A. P. Watt & Son.

Current printing (last digit):

12 11 10 9 8 7 6 5 4 3

LIBRARY OF CONGRESS CATALOG CARD NO.: 62-19408

Printed in the United States of America

97191-C

Preface

The principle of selection of these essays about Yeats has been a simple one: I have included the best work I could find. For though the range is from very general commentary, such as that found in Hugh Kenner's "The Sacred Book of the Arts," to such intricate material as that presented in Curtis Bradford's "Yeats's Byzantium Poems: A Study of Their Development," my concern has been always: Is the essay useful to the reader who is not a specialist, the reader who is interested both in Yeats and in Yeats's poetry?

The arrangement of the essays in this collection is, however, not entirely arbitrary. Matters of general concern, Hugh Kenner's presentation of the structure of the *Collected Poems* and my own discussion of the use Yeats made of biography and "mask," are followed by examinations of two of Yeats's most persistent themes, that of the "moment of moments" and that of the artist as isolated man. Moving closer to the texts, Tindall's essay on Yeats's symbolism—particularly that in the early poems—shows how Yeats's technique parallels a larger European tradition, and Eliot's essay on Yeats's drama reveals both something of the nature of Yeats's dramatic accomplishment and the complex way in which one major poet "influences"—in this case in a negative fashion—another. Both Blackmur and Zwerdling turn to the texts themselves to discuss large areas of Yeats's mature work, while Bradford, Gordon and Fletcher show how much examination of manuscripts and of sources can contribute to a coherent reading of very difficult poems. Miss Stock's study, on the other hand, shows some of the ways in which a careful reading of Yeats's *A Vision* illuminates the late poetry. The brilliant essay by Allen Tate tentatively defines both the nature of Yeats's genius and his place in Western literature, while that by Yeats's most perceptive biographer, Mr. Ellmann, suggests something of Yeats's own final view of himself. The inclusion of W. H. Auden's eloquent poem on Yeats in a volume of critical studies needs, I think, neither justification nor explanation.

In two instances, I have regretted that lack of space made long selections impractical. Georgio Melchiori's work on visual sources of Yeats's poetry and Frank Kermode's sensitive study of Romantic elements in Yeats's work are, however, so carefully organized and so tightly presented that anything less than the full book-length texts seemed insufficient. The passages quoted here should be regarded as samples only of the excellent work by these men. Their books and others of major value to the reader interested in Yeats are listed in the bibliography at the end of this volume.

J. U.

vii

Table of Contents

Introduction

by John Unterecker

I like to visualize the proverbial man on a desert island who, having chosen Yeats over, say, Shakespeare, watches float up to his sandy shore the as-yet-uncollected *Complete Works*, twenty or so fat volumes nudging each other on—and behind them, borne perhaps on the backs of dolphins, first, the dozens of books that have already been written about Yeats, and then a long bobbing procession of dissertations, articles, and reviews, thousands, perhaps tens of thousands of them, the sum total of Yeats scholarship.

Where, in this welter, will the islander begin?

If he is wise, he will start with Yeats; if he is very wise, he will start with Yeats's poetry. For Yeats, as Hugh Kenner points out, organizes his *Collected Poems* with meticulous care. Lyric, in context, illuminates neighboring lyric; section comments on neighboring section. If my islander never gets past that initial volume, he should have a reasonably satisfying literary experience.

Even if he is a literary critic, however, he may want help on particularly difficult passages. Yeats was well aware of the critic's problem, and he did his best to make things easy for his commentator. As the reader of the *Variorum Edition* of Yeats's poems quickly notices, Yeats regularly equipped his books of poetry with prefaces and notes, revising these props whenever he rewrote or regrouped a section of poems. But the more Yeats wrote, the more help his critics seemed to need; and Yeats cheerfully set about supplying them with all sorts of material, everything from autobiography to aesthetic theory. In 1917, for instance, Yeats explained to his father his reasons for writing "a little philosophical book": "I shall publish it in a new book of verse, side by side, I think. Reviewers find it easier to write if they have ideas to write about—ideas or a narrative like that in my *Reveries*." And when Katherine Tynan recklessly published a group of his letters, Yeats's complaint was not that the publication was unauthorized but rather that he had not had a chance, "in defiance of all right conduct," to "improve" them!

What Yeats was trying to do, of course, was to make available to his public everything that good criticism ultimately uncovers. He was also doing his best to safeguard his work against inaccurate interpretation. Essays such as "The Symbolism of Poetry" and "The Philosophy of Shelley's Poetry" were intended to show how Yeats's own symbols operated and how—by conscious repetition—they reinforced each other. The autobiographical volumes were deliberately jammed with character-sketches of those friends and relatives Yeats drew on in his "personal" public poetry. *A Vision* diagrammed the master plan of the cyclical theory of history Yeats finally accepted, a theory basic to such major poems as "The Second Coming" and "Leda and the Swan," and a theory which perhaps gave his annotators more to discuss than even Yeats bargained for.

Gradually, needless to say, a sort of interaction was set up. Not only did Yeats's prose commentary provide a background for the poems, it also began to engender them. And Yeats—diligent to the end—wrote poetic explications of the prose (what else is "Ego Dominus Tuus" but a poetic version of *Per Amica Silentia Lunae?*) and poetic commentary on his own life and works ("The Circus Animals' Desertion," for instance).

What seems to have started, therefore, as secondary matter is gradually worked into a corpus of interdependent material, poetry and prose elegantly bound together. Certainly from the time of the *Collected Edition* of 1908, when he told his publisher that chronology would have to be abandoned in favor of theme, Yeats kept constantly in mind the fact that one day a final, cohesive *Complete Works* would be assembled. Manipulating almost everything he touched to this end, he fought hard to make of life and work a grand, organic whole.

Take, for example, the way he prepared his audience for the Cuchulain figure of the plays and poems. Pleased to find scholarly support for the notion of that mythical, extroverted, passionate man as solar hero, Yeats persuaded his friend Lady Gregory to gather together as many of the scattered legends as she could, supervised her efforts to fit them into a single narrative line, wrote for her book an enthusiastic preface, adapted Lady Gregory's account to his own purposes in his dramas, pointed—in his theory of the Mask—to Cuchulain and his world as the precise opposite of and therefore the proper ideal for the modern Irishman and modern Ireland, and went on finally to hint that Cuchulain's was the mask which the introverted, sentimental, frustrated Yeats himself found most congenial and through which he would subsequently articulate a new "hardened" public art. Encouraged by assertions like these, Yeats's audience saw in Cuchulain a figure halfway between myth and allegory, an embodiment of dreams familiar to themselves as well as to Yeats. The more Yeats wrote, the more useful that figure became. Gradually, the wish-fulfillment projection took on new roles, sometimes a figure celebrated, sometimes satirized, finally humanized; for in the character's long career—the poem "The Death of Cuchullin" was published in 1892 in *United Ireland,* and the play *The Death of Cuchulain* was still being revised during the week of Yeats's last illness—Cuchulain had become as much a part of Yeats's world (and his audience's) as Maud Gonne or Lady Gregory.

He had become this familiar figure, however, by no accident; for Yeats, leaving as little as possible to chance, touched on Cuchulain over that almost-fifty-year period in poems, notes, introductions, plays, philosophical essays, historical studies, autobiography, and published letters. What we know now, from the body of his work and those works Yeats sent us to, is what we need to know when Yeats insists in the last lines of his last play that he had "thought Cuchulain" until it seemed to him that Cuchulain stood "in the Post Office/With Pearse and Connolly," until Cuchulain, in other words, merged with the modern national hero into an emblem of Irish heroic possibility. No wonder that Yeats demands at the start of the same play that every member of his audience "know the old epics and Mr. Yeats' plays about them."

It is not difficult, therefore, to see that Yeats has had one eye cocked all of the time toward my islander—first as potential reader of poetry and then as potential critic of poetry. Furthermore, there is a good chance that Yeats may also have planned to take care of that isolated man's needs if he should turn out to be potential poet—or at least student of the art of poetic composition. For not only did Yeats in both prose and poetry talk a good deal about his working methods and the working methods of those poets he admired—Shakespeare, Blake, Shelley, among a good many others—but he also kept very carefully together most of the tools of his trade, conscious or half-conscious that someday somebody would want to inspect them. These tools of his trade: diaries, files of correspondence, photograph albums, annotated books, records of dreams and waking visions, the huge piles of notebooks filled with the automatic writing which was ultimately to be reworked into the two versions of *A Vision,* and the rough drafts of poems: prose drafts, early, late, and middle drafts—almost everything, in fact, except the working memory and the musing intellect of the living artist—have already been drawn on by such scholars as Curtis Bradford, D. J. Gordon, and Richard Ellmann. Yeats, who in his three-years' work on his Blake edition had learned how valuable such material can be, seems to have saved for our inquisitive eyes everything he thought might possibly be of interest to us. (I should, in all fairness, however, point out that there was one place at which he drew the line of absolute privacy. Shortly before his death he methodically destroyed a large group of letters to Olivia Shakespear. These, returned to him at the time of her death by Ezra Pound, Yeats's friend and Mrs. Shakespear's son-in-law, Yeats wanted no one to read.)

My island student-critic-poet should, therefore, be prepared to examine everything that floats ashore; for presumably Yeats wanted him to see not just finished product but process as well. If he is lucky, all the books Yeats read and all the paintings he looked at should also sometime turn up.

He may, in fact, discover that primary materials consume so much of his time he will not have the chance ever to get the floating mass of critical material. If my man should prove everything Yeats would want him to be, he might not need any critic.

And yet, for the rest of us, there is a place for the critic. He can, first of all, sift through the heap of primary materials to point out for us that which is obvious only to the man who has been through everything. If he is a good critic, he can then suggest some of the ways in which the large framework of Yeats's design is put together and can finally go on, as Eliot, Tindall, and Melchiori do in the following essays, to show how that design relates to even larger patterns of literary and social history. He can uncover, as does D. J. Gordon, hitherto unnoticed sources for significant poems. Or, like R. P. Blackmur and Allen Tate, he can concern himself with the roots of Yeats's power, the source of significance itself.

One question, of course, has been the concern of all of Yeats's critics, the question why any man—desert islander or apartment dweller longing for a desert island—should find Yeats of really compelling interest.

The answer lies, I think, in Yeats's uncompromising integrity, an integrity both of personality and of craft.

Perhaps it is easier to see Yeats's integrity as a craftsman than his integrity as a man, for we have been trained to notice the sort of revisions he practiced in his published work. Never really content with anything he had written, he steadily doctored poems, plays, essays— even footnotes—as edition followed edition. We know, for example, of the assorted drafts of *The Wanderings of Oisin* and of *The Shadowy Waters,* of the way in which he rearranged the sequence of his poems within sections of the collected poems, of the laborious complete rewriting of *A Vision.* For Yeats felt always the tentativeness of any "finished" work. And yet, as Curtis Bradford makes clear, revision of published work only begins to hint at the extraordinary juggling of phrase and idea that takes place before the first published draft puts in an appearance.

Yeats's idea of craft was the very old-fashioned one of technique learned through long study, long practice, long experiment, technique that in final draft conceals itself in the appearance of effortless, casual speech. "A line will take us hours maybe," he points out in "Adam's Curse," "Yet if it does not seem a moment's thought,/Our stitching and unstitching has been naught." For the crucial work of the poet is composition, a nightmarishly extended process of trial and error. His work is "to articulate sweet sounds together," link them up in such a fashion that there will be no loose ends at all. He must, to expand Yeats's pun, be the articulate articulator whose intricate art is the conscious achievement of simplicity. "The common and its befitting language," he concludes in the late essay he planned as general introduction to his work, "is the research of a lifetime."

Driven by this conviction that good art is "composed" art, Yeats was always contemptuous of the sloppy expressionist who values his emotion more than the shaping of it. The bastard art this man produces, "All out of shape from toe to top," is in Yeats's eyes symptomatic of our chaotic world. Opposed to this man, the good poet must "Sing whatever is well made." As anyone knows who has stopped to examine closely any one of his poems—even the earliest ones—Yeats was lifelong a man who practiced absolute integrity of craft.

But integrity of craft alone makes no one memorable. The other kind of integrity, that of personality, jolts us into awareness.

Most of our lives are spent either telling lies or listening to them. Trained by the ad men, we accept a never-never world in which authority rests always in anyone other than ourselves, preferably in an actor in a white coat holding out to us the inviting bottle of tranquilizers, conventionally in pontificating doctor, lawyer, merchant, chief. Neither we nor these assured father-figures question anything. Like is much easier when no questions are asked. Reality is the actor in the white coat.

The honest man risks our contempt by questioning that masquerade reality. He takes the enormous risk of skepticism. And if he is a man like Yeats, he takes the even greater risk of being skeptical of our most sacred cows. (We pride ourselves in a scientific age that our scientists are skeptical—of theories long since exploded. Yeats is skeptical of science.) Because he trusts only his own observations, Yeats often seems foolish. But beneath his surface foolishness lies the sort of honesty which most of us envy and the sort of uncommercial concern for truth which most of us never dare display.

Yeats attracts us, I think, because, eloquently, he states our own unspoken doubts about our world. Mechanical progress, of which we have been so proud, is for Yeats a progress toward the junk yard; the vicious struggle for power we dignify as free enterprise is for Yeats a long stride away from aristocratic courtesy, a retrogression toward "the weasel's twist, the weasel's tooth." We live, in Yeats's eyes, in a world careening toward explosive chaos, a world in which "days are dragon-ridden, the nightmare/Rides upon sleep"; a world in which "Things fall apart; the centre cannot hold."

In such a world two things alone have value: the shaped work, art; and, more valuable, those men and women who shape, like artists, lives into ordered beauty. The job of the poet is the celebration of such persons and such things. "I say," Yeats wrote two years before his death, ". . . it is our first business to paint, or describe, desirable people, places, states of mind." These persons and places—Robert Gregory, for example, and Byzantium; or, if we want to move back earlier in Yeats's career, Maud Gonne and Innisfree; or, if we want to turn to the end of his career, Dorothy Wellesley and the "half-way house" the Chinamen of "Lapis Lazuli" climb toward—these excellent persons and places are models which can be held up for imitation; even the contemplation of them, in a world which disintegrates, can give us joy.

Because he presents for our inspection these images of order in ordered works of art, because he speaks unpopular truths about the fragmentation of our lives, Yeats more than interests, he moves us. Yet he moves us in a strange way. For by transforming the personal stuff of his own life into the woven formality of poems, he turns himself very nearly into an object. "A poet writes always of his personal life," Yeats insists; but he insists also that "he never speaks directly as to someone at the breakfast table." Distancing the personal by his formal craft, Yeats—doubly masked—looks at us through Cuchulain's cold, judging eyes. And we—islanded in ourselves—judge Yeats, if we judge him fairly, through eyes as cold, almost, as his own.

In Memory of W. B. Yeats

d. Jan. 1939

by W. H. Auden

I

He disappeared in the dead of winter:
The brooks were frozen, the airports almost deserted,
And snow disfigured the public statues;
The mercury sank in the mouth of the dying day.
What instruments we have agree
The day of his death was a dark cold day.

Far from his illness
The wolves ran on through the evergreen forests,
The peasant river was untempted by the fashionable quays;
By mourning tongues
The death of the poet was kept from his poems.

But for him it was his last afternoon as himself,
An afternoon of nurses and rumors;
The provinces of his body revolted,
The squares of his mind were empty,
Silence invaded the suburbs,
The current of his feeling failed; he became his admirers.

Now he is scattered among a hundred cities
And wholly given over to unfamiliar affections;
To find his happiness in another kind of wood
And be punished under a foreign code of conscience.
The words of a dead man
Are modified in the guts of the living.

But in the importance and noise of tomorrow
When the brokers are roaring like beasts on the floor of the
    Bourse,
And the poor have the sufferings to which they are fairly
    accustomed,
And each in the cell of himself is almost convinced of his
    freedom,
A few thousand will think of this day
As one thinks of a day when one did something slightly
    unusual.
What instruments we have agree
The day of his death was a dark cold day.

II

You were silly like us; your gift survived it all;
The parish of rich women, physical decay,
Yourself: mad Ireland hurt you into poetry.
Now Ireland has her madness and her weather
    still,
For poetry makes nothing happen: it survives
In the valley of its saying where executives
Would never want to tamper; it flows south
From ranches of isolation and the busy griefs,
Raw towns that we believe and die in; it survives,
A way of happening, a mouth.

III

Earth, receive an honored guest:
William Yeats is laid to rest.
Let the Irish vessel lie
Emptied of its poetry.

In the nightmare of the dark
All the dogs of Europe bark,
And the living nations wait,
Each sequestered in its hate;

Intellectual disgrace
Stares from every human face,
And the seas of pity lie
Locked and frozen in each eye.

Follow, poet, follow right
To the bottom of the night,
With your unconstraining voice
Still persuade us to rejoice;

With the farming of a verse
Make a vineyard of the curse,
Sing of human unsuccess
In a rapture of distress;

In the deserts of the heart
Let the healing fountain start,
In the prison of his days
Teach the free man how to
                praise.

The Sacred Book of the Arts

by Hugh Kenner

The way out is via the door, how is it no one will use this method?
—*Confucius*

I. *Catechism*

Q: In "Among School Children" we read of a "Ledaean body." Where are we to seek information about that?

A: Not from the mythological dictionary, but as everybody knows, from the poem "Leda and the Swan."

Q: And where is this poem to be discovered?

A: On the previous page.

Q: Very good. You are on the way to noticing something. Now consider the last stanza of "Among School Children." After an apostrophe to "self-born mockers of man's enterprise" we read:

> Labour is blossoming or dancing where
> The body is not bruised to pleasure soul,
> Nor beauty born out of its own despair,
> Nor blear-eyed wisdom out of midnight oil.
> O chestnut-tree, great-rooted blossomer,
> Are you the leaf, the blossom or the bole?
> O body swayed to music, O brightening glance,
> How can we know the dancer from the dance?

That "where" is by its placing in the line made very emphatic. Its gesture implies a place or a state intensely real to Yeats. Does he print lines elsewhere that might be taken as descriptive of that place or state?

A: He does; in "Colonus' Praise," after invoking "immortal ladies" who

"The Sacred Book of the Arts." From *Gnomon* (New York: Ivan Obolensky, 1958) by Hugh Kenner, pp. 9-29. Copyright © 1958 by Hugh Kenner. Reprinted by permission of Ivan Obolensky, Inc.

"tread the ground/Dizzy with harmonious sound" (which invocation of course we are meant to connect with "O body swayed to music"), he goes on,

> And yonder in the gymnasts' garden thrives
> The self-sown, self-begotten shape that gives
> Athenian intellect its mastery . . .

the self-born no longer a mocker, body and intellect thriving in unison, neither bruised to pleasure the other; and the miraculous olive-tree that, as he goes on to tell us, symbolizes that perfection, is to be connected with the domestic "chestnut-tree, great-rooted blossomer" of the famous peroration.

Q: Excellent, excellent. And now tell me where, in relation to "Among School Children," this song in praise of Colonus is to be found?

A: On the following page.

Q: You are answering today with admirable point and economy. Now tell me: were the three poems you have mentioned as bearing upon one another written, as it were, simultaneously?

A: I find by the chronology at the back of Mr. Ellmann's *Identity of Yeats* that the first was written nearly four years before the last. I notice furthermore that the arrangement of the poems in the volume we are discussing, *The Tower*, is far from chronological. "Sailing to Byzantium" (Sept. 26, 1926), with which it begins, was written *after* "Among School Children" (June 14, 1926), which is located two-thirds of the way through the book. In between there are poems dating as far back as 1919, and the volume ends with "All Souls' Night," 1920.

Q: We should be lost without these American scholars. You would say, then, that the arrangement of poems within the volume was deliberate rather than casual or merely chronological?

A: I would indeed. But wait, I have just noticed something else. In "Sailing to Byzantium," at the beginning of the book, the speaker has abandoned the sensual land of "dying generations" and is asking the "sages standing in God's holy fire" to emerge from it and be his singing-masters. At the end, in "All Souls' Night," he announces that he has "mummy truths to tell" and would tell them to some mind that despite cannon-fire from every quarter of the world, can stay

> Wound in mind's pondering
> As mummies in the mummy-cloth are wound.

In the former poem he was calling forth sages to teach him; throughout "All Souls' Night" he is calling up ghosts to hear him. Pupil has become master.

Q: How often must I enjoin precision on you? It is the land of sensual *music* he has left: bird-song, love-songs. "All Souls' Night" opens, by contrast, with the formal tolling of "the great Christ Church Bell," like the "great cathedral gong" that dissipates "night-walkers' song" in "Byzantium." Furthermore, there is a calling-up of ghosts near the beginning of the book too, in the poem called "The Tower," where he summons them not (as later) to instruct them but to ask a question. What else have you noticed?

A: Why, it gets more and more deliberate as one examines it. He began the volume by renouncing his body; he ends it in the possession of disembodied thought:

> Such thought—such thought have I that hold it tight
> Till meditation master all its parts . . .
> Such thought, that in it bound
> I need no other thing,
> Wound in mind's wandering
> As mummies in the mummy-cloth are wound.

Earlier he had expected to need the body of a jeweled bird. Through that volume, *The Tower*, runs a dramatic progression if I ever saw one. And the presence of such a progression, once it is discerned, modifies all the parts. Now I have a theory . . .

Q: Stop, you grow prolix. Write it out, write it out as an explanation that I may read at my leisure. And please refrain from putting in many footnotes that tire the eyes.

II. *Explanation*

"Among School Children," to begin with that again, is as centrifugal a major poem as exists in the language. Whoever encounters it out of the context Yeats carefully provided for it, for instance in an Anthology Appointed to be Taught in Colleges, will find himself after twenty minutes seeking out who Leda was and what Yeats made of her, and identifying the daughter of the swan with Maude Gonne (excursus on her biography, with anecdotes) and determining in what official capacity, through what accidents of a destiny sought and ironically accepted, the poet found himself doubling as school inspector. So true is this of the majority of his major poems, that the anthologists generally restrict themselves to his minor ones, his critics practice mostly a bastard mode of biography, and his exegetists a Pécuchet's industry of copying parallel passages from *A Vision* (first and second versions), from letters and diaries, from unpublished drafts, and occasionally from other poems. Even Dr.

Leavis calls his poetry "little more than a marginal comment on the main activities of his life." Occasionally someone feels that Yeats's poems need to be reclaimed for the modern critic's gallery of self-sufficient objects, and rolling up his sleeves offers to explain "Two Songs from a Play" without benefit of *A Vision*. This requires several thousand words of quasi-paraphrase. The least gesture of unannounced originality on a poet's part suffices to baffle critical presupposition completely, and the two regnant presuppositions of the mid-twentieth century—the old one, that poems reflect lives and announce doctrines, the new one, that poems are self-contained or else imperfect—are rendered helpless by Yeats's most radical, most casual, and most characteristic maneuver: he was an architect, not a decorator; he didn't accumulate poems, he wrote books.

It would have been surprising if he had not, preoccupied as he was with sacred writings. When he functioned as a critic, as in his essay on Shelley or his useful generalizations on Shakespeare, it was the oeuvre, not the fragment, that held his attention.

The place to look for light on any poem is in the adjacent poems, which Yeats placed adjacent to it because they belonged there. And the unit in which to inspect and discuss his development is not the poem or sequence of poems but the volume, at least from *Responsibilities* (1914) to *A Full Moon in March* (1935).[1] This principle is sometimes obvious enough; anyone can see that the six songs following "The Three Bushes" belong in its entourage, or that "The Phases of the Moon" incorporates the half-dozen poems appended to it. Such obvious instances are, however, slightly misleading; one is apt to think of the main poem as not quite completed, raveling out into lyrical loose ends, or not quite definitive in scope, making shift to appropriate, like a handful of minnows, lesser foci of energy that ought to have been brought within its sphere at the time of composition. In the Age of Eliot, the poet is supposed to gather his interests and impulses and discharge them utterly in a supreme opus every so often, and evades this responsibility at the price of being not quite a major poet. Those weren't the terms in which Yeats was thinking; we misread him if we suppose either that the majority of the poems are casual or that in each he was trying for a definitive statement of all that, at the time of composition, he was.

"Men Improve with the Years" looks like an attempt of this kind; it cuts off, of course, too neatly. The poet was once young, and a lover; now he is a monument, and no lady will love him. The quality of the rhetoric is impeccable, but the poem, on some acquaintance, appears to reduce itself to its mere theme, and that theme so simple-minded as to invite biographical eking out. The unspoken premise of Yeats criticism is that we have to supply from elsewhere—from his life or his doctrines—a great

[1] It isn't clear how much, if any, of *Last Poems* was arranged by Yeats himself.

deal that didn't properly get into the poems: not so much to explain the poems as to make them rich enough to sustain the reputation. It happens, however, that "Men Improve with the Years" has for context not Yeats's biography but two poems about a man who did not undergo that dubious improvement: at the climax of "In Memory of Major Robert Gregory" we read,

> Some burn damp faggots, others may consume
> The entire combustible world in one small room
> As though dried straw, and if we turn about
> The bare chimney is gone black out
> Because the work had finished in that flare.
> Soldier, scholar, horseman, he,
> As 'twere all life's epitome,
> What made us dream that he could comb grey hair? . . .

Dried straw, damp faggots; in "Men Improve with the Years" we discover a "burning youth" succeeded by water:

> A weather-worn, marble triton
> Among the streams.

Major Robert Gregory, "all life's epitome," concentrated all in an instantaneous conflagration; the speaker of "Men Improve with the Years" has advanced serially through phases one can enumerate to the condition of a statue. Statues, of course, have their immortality, their nobility of arrested gesture. Yeats isn't being picturesque in specifying the kind of statue; tritons blow their wreathèd horns, and a marble one would be puffing soundlessly at a marble trumpet, like an official Poet; not even in the open sea, but amid the fountains of Major Gregory's mother's garden. The poem isn't a small clearing in which Yeats sinks decoratively to rest, it is a counter-rhetoric to the rhetorical memorial poem. It doesn't come quite on the heels of that poem, however; between the two we hear the dry tones of the Irish Airman ("soldier, scholar, horseman") himself:

> Those that I fight I do not hate,
> Those that I guard I do not love.

Midway between Yeats's contrasting rhetorics, Gregory ("An Irish Airman Foresees His Death") hasn't a rhetoric but a style. He wasn't exhilarated by the prospect of consuming "the entire combustible world"; "a lonely impulse of delight" redeems from calculation the decision born of an explicit disenchantment:

> I balanced all, brought all to mind,
> The years to come seemed waste of breath,
> A waste of breath the years behind
> In balance with this life, this death.

Those are the words from which we pass to these:

> I am worn out with dreams:
> A weather-worn, marble triton
> Among the streams.

—the traditional sonorities, the diction ("my burning youth!"), the conventional elegances of cadence evoking (while just evading) a "literary" tradition against which is poised the next poem in the volume: "The Collar-Bone of a Hare."

> Would I could cast a sail on the water
> Where many a king has gone
> And many a king's daughter,
> And alight at the comely trees and the lawn,
> The playing upon pipes and the dancing,
> And learn that the best thing is
> To change my loves while dancing
> And pay but a kiss for a kiss.

This live rhythm quickens a remote, folkish idiom, unsonorous and wry. "Men Improve with the Years" seems in retrospect heavier than ever. In this pastoral kingdom not only are there no marble tritons (its tone has nothing in common with that of the Land of Heart's Desire where the Princess Edain was "busied with a dance"), but the newcomer's characteristic gesture is to look back through "the collar-bone of a hare" and laugh at "the old bitter world where they marry in churches" with a lunatic peasant slyness. The symbol of trivial death proffers a peephole or spyglass; it doesn't, as death is reputed to do, open vistas. You can squint with its aid at the old world, from fairyland. Yeats is trying out different arrangements of a poetic universe with the blunt fact of death in it. In the next poem he reverses the situation and rearranges the perspective. Stretched for nonchalant slumber "On great-grandfather's battered tomb," Beggar Billy sees the dancing-world: not

> the comely trees and the lawn,
> The playing upon pipes and the dancing,

but

>   a dream
> Of sun and moon that a good hour
> Bellowed and pranced in the round tower . . .
>
> That golden king and that wild lady
> Sang till stars began to fade,
> Hands gripped in hands, toes close together,
> Hair spread on the wind they made;
> That lady and that golden king
> Could like a brace of blackbirds sing.

This is the celebrated music of the spheres; and Beggar Billy decides that "great-grandfather's battered tomb" that educes such noisy and energetic visions is no place for him. So the book, having degraded its initial persona to beggardom (there are curious analogies with *Lear*) and preoccupied itself with themes and images of death until it has set the celestial boiler shop going, takes leave of this theme for a time and turns to quieter matters like the dead lovers Solomon and Sheba.

That initial persona now wants looking at. The volume we are examining, *The Wild Swans at Coole*, began not with the Gregory elegy—that is its second poem—but with "The Wild Swans at Coole" itself: an image of personal dejection ("And now my heart is sore") that uses the permanent glory of the swans to silhouette the transience attending human beings who must keep their feet on the ground and try to assimilate the "brilliant creatures" by counting them.

>   All's changed since I, hearing at twilight,
>   The first time on this shore,
>   The bell-beat of their wings above my head,
>   Trod with a lighter tread.
>
>   Unwearied still, lover by lover,
>   They clamber in the cold
>   Companionable streams or climb the air;
>   Their hearts have not grown old; . . .

"All's changed" is a mood, not a summary of presented facts; this initial poem confines itself to a wholly familiar *Angst*, a setting documented in a spare but traditional manner—

>   The trees are in their autumn beauty,
>   The woodland paths are dry—

a specified month and time of day, a poet who does and thinks and feels nothing unusual, verbs no more than inert copulas, and swans that are scarcely more than swans. We are in the presence of a mind reflecting nature and then reflecting Locke-wise upon what it reflects: tantalized— not teased, but undergoing the pangs of Tantalus—because it must undergo change while nature—the swans—remains other, "unwearied still." Though none of the great Romantics could have written it with such economy and directness, the poem remains within, say, the Coleridgean orbit of experience.

It is upon experience resignedly ordered in this plane that the brilliant death of Major Robert, the Irish Airman, impinges; he took wing like the swans; his heart has not grown old; he demonstrated that it lay within human capacity to

> consume
> The entire combustible world in one small room.
> As though dried straw.

This death and the contemplation of the poet's impotent middle age ferment and interact throughout the volume, entoiling other materials, discovering unexpected resonances in the pastoral mode ("Shepherd and Goatherd") and in the lingering end of Mabel Beardsley ("Upon a Dying Lady"), never for long oblivious of the piercing hypothesis that maximum human intensity coincides with human extinction. What is arrived at is an extinction not of the person but of his natural context. At the end of the volume October water no more mirrors a natural sky:

> On the grey rock of Cashel the mind's eye
> Has called up the cold spirits that are born
> When the old moon is vanished from the sky
> And the new still hides her horn.

The mind's eye, no longer the Newtonian optic; and that moon isn't nature's moon. Nor does the mind's eye see swans that fly away, but calls up three arresting figures—one a sphinx—observed not in placidity but in active intensity:

> Mind moved yet seemed to stop
> As 'twere a spinning-top.

> In contemplation had those three so wrought
> Upon a moment, and so stretched it out
> That they, time overthrown,
> Were dead yet flesh and bone.

The poem—and the volume—closes on a note of triumph; Yeats tells us he "arranged"—deliberate word—his vision in a song—

> Seeing that I, ignorant for so long,
> Had been rewarded thus
> In Cormac's ruined house.

The poles of this volume are its first and last poems, "The Wild Swans at Coole" and "The Double Vision of Michael Robartes," as the poles of *The Tower* are "Sailing to Byzantium" and "All Souls' Night." Between the observation of the swans and the vision of the sphinx passes the action of the book. The crisis occurs when, in "Ego Dominus Tuus" (which immediately follows the account of the Dying Lady's heroic arrogance) "Ille" [2] determines to "set his chisel to the hardest stone" and forget about the kind of self-fulfillment envisaged by people who tell us that men improve with the years. Immediately a long poem devotes itself to the moon, the faded cliché of a thousand mewling nature poets; and examining it not as they do in the Irish sky but by way of the sort of diagram one discovers in a penny astrology book, sets the stage for the double vision of Michael Robartes.

The Wild Swans at Coole is a book about death and the will. A component poem like "Men Improve with the Years" will no more pull loose from it than the "foolish fond old man" speech will pull loose from *King Lear*. It is a radical mistake to think of Yeats as a casual or fragmentary poet whose writings float on a current discoverable only in his biographable life. How much time does he not spend telling us that he has carefully rendered the mere events of his life irrelevant!

III. *Anti-Nature*

Yeats's quarrel with nineteenth century popular Romanticism encompassed more than its empty moons. He turned with increasing vehemence against a tradition that either laid streams of little poems like cod's eggs or secreted inchoate epics. Against the poet as force of nature he placed of course the poet as deliberate personality, and correspondingly against the usual "Collected Poems" (arranged in the order of composition) he placed the oeuvre, the deliberated artistic Testament, a division of that new Sacred Book of the Arts of which, Mr. Pound has recalled, he used to talk. It was as a process of fragmentation, into little people and little poems, that he viewed the history of European poetry, from the *Canterbury Tales* to the Collected Poems of, say, Lord Byron.

---

[2] "Willy," commented Ezra Pound.

If Chaucer's personages had disengaged themselves from Chaucer's crowd, forgot their common goal and shrine, and after sundry magnifications become each in turn the centre of some Elizabethan play, and had after split into their elements and so given birth to romantic poetry, must I reverse the cinematograph?

The *Canterbury Tales,* it should be recalled, isn't a bloated descant on some epic idea but, like *The Divine Comedy* or *The Wild Swans at Coole*—or *The Cantos*—a unity made by architecture out of separate and ascertainable components. And the cinematograph seemed indeed reversible:

> . . . a nation or an individual with great emotional intensity might follow the pilgrims as it were to some unknown shrine, and give to all those separated elements and to all that abstract love and melancholy, a symbolical, a mythological coherence.

This unity isn't substituted for the existing traditions of poetry, it unites them. Ireland, furthermore, might well be the chosen nation:

> I had begun to hope, or to half hope, that we might be the first in Europe to seek unity as deliberately as it had been sought by theologian, poet, sculptor, architect, from the eleventh to the thirteenth century.

For Ireland had her autochthonous mythology, and "have not all races had their first unity from a mythology, that marries them to rock and hill?" [3]

It was natural that he should inspect the practice of any discoverable forerunners, and inevitable that he should see himself as standing in the same relation to Irish folklore as Wordsworth to the English folk ballads. One of his own false starts (seduced by this parallel) had been to write ballads; Wordsworth's unreconsidered false start, it must finally have seemed to Yeats, had been to marry only himself and not his race to "rock and hill." Wordsworth had undertaken his work with an insufficient sense of hieratic dedication; for him a poet was only "a man speaking to men" (though a more than usually conscious man), not the amanuensis of revelation. That is why old age overtook not only his body but his speech. *The Prelude* is a narrative of self-discovery, in which the lesson of life, muffled by the automatic grand style, is that knowledge and experience will not synchronize.

> Hic: And I would find myself and not an image.
> Ille: That is our modern hope, and by its light

[3] Above quotations from *The Trembling of the Veil*, Book I, Ch. 23-24.

> We have lit upon the gentle, sensitive mind
> And lost the old nonchalance of the hand;
> Whether we have chosen chisel, pen or brush,
> We are but critics, or but half create,
> Timid, entangled, empty and abashed. . . .

That is the formula of Wordsworth's decline. As Yeats moved into middle age, the sole survivor of the Rhymers' Club's "Tragic Generation," the parallel between his destiny and Wordsworth's grew more insistent; had Wordsworth not in the same way survived for a quarter of a century Keats, Shelley, and Byron, the other members of the last great wave of creative force? And had he not, assuming the laureateship, turned into a "sixty year old smiling public man," moving further and further from the only time in his life when he had been alive, and lamenting over the dead imaginative vigor of his boyhood? That is the context of the defiant opening of "The Tower":

> Never had I more
> Excited, passionate, fantastical
> Imagination, nor an ear and eye
> That more expected the impossible—
> No, not in boyhood when with rod and fly,
> Or the humbler worm, I climbed Ben Bulben's back
> And had the livelong summer day to spend.

"Or the humbler worm" is a tip to the reader; it isn't Yeatsian diction but a parody of Wordsworth's. Unlike Wordsworth, Yeats the poet has passed sixty undiminished and needs no man's indulgence.

Wordsworth had developed "naturally," moving on the stream of nature; and streams run downhill. For the natural man the moment of lowest vitality is the moment of death; in the mid-eighteenth century the image of an untroubled decline into the grave fastened itself upon the imagination of England, and *"Siste viator"* was carved on a thousand tombstones. "Pause, traveller, whoever thou art, and consider thy mortality; as I am, so wilt thou one day be." The traveler came on foot, examined the inscription, and went on his way pondering, his vitality still lower than before. This was one of the odd versions of pastoral sentiment that prepared the way for Wordsworth's career of brilliance and decline; Yeats turns powerfully against it in the Goatherd's song on Major Gregory (see "Shepherd and Goatherd"), more powerfully still in the epitaph he designed for himself. The last division of his Sacred Book closes with an apocalypse, superhuman forms riding the wintry dawn,

Michelangelo electrifying travelers with his Creation of Adam, painters revealing heavens that opened. The directions for his own burial are introduced with a pulsation of drums:

> Ún dér báre Bén Búl bén's héad
> In DRUMcliff churchyard . . .

The mise en scène is rural and eighteenth century—the churchyard, the ancestral rector, the local stonecutters; but the epitaph flies in the face of traditional invocations to passers-by:

> Cast a cold eye
> On life, on death.
> Horseman, pass by.

Much critical ingenuity has been expended on that horseman. He is simply the designated reader of the inscription, the heroic counterimage of the footweary wanderer who was invited to ponder a *"siste viator"*;[4] the only reader Yeats can be bothered to address. And he is not to be weighed down by the realization of his own mortality; he is to defy it.

The life a counterlife, the book not a compendium of reflections but a dramatic revelation, the sentiments scrupulous inversions of received romantic sentiment; what more logical than that Yeats should have modeled the successive phases of his testament on the traditional collections of miscellaneous poems, and (as he always did when he touched a tradition) subverted the usual implications? He dreamed as a young man of creating some new *Prometheus Unbound*. One applauds his wisdom in not attempting that sort of *magnum opus,* but it was not likely that he should forget the idea of a work operating on a large scale. Each volume of his verse, in fact, *is* a large-scale work, like a book of the Bible. And as the Bible was once treated by exegetists as the self-sufficient divine book mirroring the other divine book, Nature, but possessing vitality independent of natural experience, so Yeats considered his Sacred Book as similar to "life" but radically separated from it, "mirror on mirror mirroring all the show." In "The Phases of the Moon," Aherne and Robartes stand on the bridge below the poet's tower, where the candle burns late, and in mockery of his hopeless toil expound, out of his earshot, the doctrine of the lunar wheel. It is clear that they know what he can never discover; they toy with the idea of ringing his bell and speaking

[4] Though Swift wrote, *"Abi, Viator, et imitare si poteris . . ."* which Yeats paraphrased as "Imitate him if you dare,/World-besotted traveller."

Just truth enough to show that his whole life
Will scarcely find for him a broken crust
Of all those truths that are your daily bread.

It is an entrancing idea:

He'd crack his wits
Day after day, yet never find the meaning.

But it is late; Aherne determines to pass up this satisfaction.

And then he laughed to think that what seemed hard
Should be so simple—a bat rose from the hazels
And circled round him with its squeaky cry,
The light in the tower window was put out.

Why is it put out? Because Yeats has finished writing the poem! Aherne,
Robartes, the doctrine of the phases, the baffled student, all of them, we
are meant suddenly to realize, are components in a book, and so is the
man who is supposed to be writing the book. What we see in this mirror,
the page, is reflected from that one, "life"; but the parallel mirrors face
each other, and in an infinite series of interreflections life has been ac-
quiring its images from the book only that the book may reflect them
again. The book, then, is (by a Yeatsian irony) self-contained, like the
Great Smaragdine Tablet that said, "Things below are copies," and was
itself one of the things below; a sacred book like the Apocalypse of St.
John, not like most poetry a marginal commentary on the world to be
read with one eye on the pragmatical pig of a text.

"Day after day," Yeats wrote at the end of *A Vision*, "I have sat in
my chair turning a symbol over in my mind, exploring all its details,
defining and again defining its elements, testing my convictions and those
of others by its unity. . . . It seems as if I should know all if I could
but banish such memories and find everything in the symbol." On that
occasion nothing came; the symbol was perhaps too limited. But the
conviction remains with Yeats that a book, if not a symbol, can supplant
the world; if not supplant it, perpetually interchange life with it. Nothing, finally, is more characteristic than his dryly wistful account of the
perfected sage for whom the radiance attending the supernatural copula-
tion of dead lovers serves but as a reading light:

Though somewhat broken by the leaves, that light
Lies in a circle on the grass; therein
I turn the pages of my holy book.

Faces and False Faces

by John Unterecker

The Use of Biography

Perhaps the most obvious organizational device in his work is that set of very personal references which, especially toward the end of his life, Yeats drew on in building for himself a public personality. "You that would judge me," he pointed out in "The Municipal Gallery Revisited,"

> do not judge alone
> This book or that, come to this hallowed place
> Where my friends' portraits hang and look thereon;
> Ireland's history in their lineaments trace;
> Think where man's glory most begins and ends,
> And say my glory was I had such friends.

In that part of his diary written in 1909 and published as "Estrangement" in *Dramatis Personae*, Yeats stated the same theme in cold prose: "Friendship is all the house I have."

His friends, as Yeats notes in the Preface to *The Trembling of the Veil*, another one of the autobiographies written, in part at least, as a kind of companion volume to the personal poetry, "were artists and writers and certain among them men of genius, and the life of a man of genius, because of his greater sincerity, is often an experiment that needs analysis and record. At least my generation so valued personality that it thought so." But even earlier, almost from the beginning of his career, Yeats had worked out a theory of the personal as a crucial element in poetry. Early in his twenties, he felt "we should write out our thoughts in as nearly as possible the language we thought them in, as though in a letter to an intimate friend. We should not disguise them in any way; for our lives give them force as the lives of people in plays give force to

"Faces and False Faces." From *A Reader's Guide to William Butler Yeats* (New York: The Noonday Press, 1959) by John Unterecker, pp. 7-18. Copyright © 1959 by John Unterecker. Reprinted by permission of The Noonday Press and the author.

their words." The great poets, Yeats argued, employed always "personal utterance," dramatizing—sometimes overtly—their own lives. "If I can be sincere," he used to think to himself, "and make my language natural, and without becoming discursive, like a novelist, and so indiscreet and prosaic . . . I shall, if good luck or bad luck make my life interesting, be a great poet; for it will be no longer a matter of literature at all."

His effort to capitalize on a life made interesting not only by luck but by good management gives us such great work as the poems written about Augusta Gregory's son, Robert Gregory; all those involving Maud Gonne; the poems celebrating those men—among them Maud Gonne's husband—who were executed as a result of the Easter, 1916 rising; and all that rich late autobiographical poetry, "The Circus Animals' Desertion," for instance, and "Under Ben Bulben." These poems, saved from sentimentality by a tone of impersonal evaluation, demand that the reader know at least a few facts concerning the figures they celebrate. Yeats's own stitching-together of the lives of his friends can be found in the autobiographical volumes which—in effect—provide necessary footnotes to the poems. Joseph Hone's biography fills in some of the details Yeats neglected. Yeats's *Letters*, brilliantly edited by Allan Wade, provide unofficial backstage views of the public man Yeats was constructing.

I do not mean to suggest that Yeats chose his friends with an eye to their ultimate utility as figures in a designed world which had as its central element his own figure. He loved and admired his friends and valued them not as literary material but as persons. Yet he recognized that if he were to make his art great and his life meaningful through "personal utterance," the persons he celebrated had to have or to be given enough fame to make their names household words for his readers. Dante, who stuck enemies in Hell and Beatrice in Heaven and who, in so doing, transformed biography to art, was very much in Yeats's mind as his poetry became both increasingly personal and at the same time increasingly objective.

Though Yeats linked poem to poem through reference to a great many relatives and friends, the most crucial figures form a relatively small group.

Of his relatives, an astrologer uncle, George Pollexfen, and Yeats's father, the painter John Butler Yeats, are probably most important.

Yeats's father, a meticulously careful portrait painter who, according to his son, spoiled his paintings by working far too long at them and who was never able to charge the high prices he felt his art deserved, was, though unsuccessful financially, an eloquent, stimulating conversationalist. Words, though casually spoken, were as much his medium as his son's; and Yeats's published memories of childhood are dominated by his father's fluent, sometimes overbearing, talk. John Butler Yeats preached—hours on end—a gospel of beauty and atheism, read aloud (at breakfast) all the most passionate scenes from Shakespeare, and saw to it that his son accompanied him on visits to a very wide circle of friends, almost all writers and painters. No wonder that years after his father died Yeats found himself still dreaming of him—sometimes as a stool and sometimes as the eyepiece of a telescope.

Believing firmly, as his son later, that the artist's subject matter is inextricably knotted to his life ("A man can only paint the life he has lived!") and that the greatest artist is a man passionately devoted to his friends (Shakespeare, he once wrote Yeats, must have been "very lovable and fond of his friends," and then, underlining the words, added, ". . . *he couldn't have been otherwise. How else could he have written his dramas?*"), Yeats's father drummed into his young son aesthetic principles which, at first rejecting, Yeats eventually modified into some of the most basic structural elements in his own system of aesthetics.

As late as 1921, self-exiled in New York, an old man of eighty-two, Yeats's father was still trying to shape the career of his admiring but recalcitrant son:

> . . . When is your poetry at its best? I challenge all the critics if it is not when its wild spirit of your imagination is wedded to concrete fact. Had you stayed with me and not left me for Lady Gregory, and her friends and associations, you would have loved and adored concrete life for which as I know you have a real affection. . . . The moment you touch however lightly on concrete fact, how alert you are! and how attentive we your readers become!
>
> . . . .
>
> Am I talking wildly? Am I senile? I don't think so, for I would have said the same any time these 20 or 30 years. The best thing in life is the game of life, and some day a poet will find this out. I hope you will be that poet. It is easier to write poetry that is far away from life, but it is *infinitely more exciting* to write the poetry of life—and it is what the whole world is crying out for as pants the hart for the water brook. I bet it is what your wife wants—ask her. She will know what I mean and drive it home. I have great confidence in her. Does she lack the courage to say it?

Ultimately, of course, Yeats's work did become concrete and was used, though not perhaps as his father had intended, to fit John Butler Yeats, along with John O'Leary, Standish O'Grady, Augusta Gregory, and Maud Gonne into that splendid catalogue of "Olympians," his poem "Beautiful Lofty Things."

In spite of the fact that Yeats showed little public affection for his father (who complained to his daughter Lily "I wish Willie . . . did not sometimes treat me as if I was a black beetle"), their debates over the artist's function shaped his mind, gave precision to his ideas.

One subject, however, he could not discuss with his father: that was
the occult. When the old Fenian leader John O'Leary, knowing that
Yeats's family was concerned about his investigations in mysticism, suggested that Yeats might profitably give up those investigations, Yeats's
answer was unequivocal: magic was the business of his life.

> . . . Now as to Magic. It is surely absurd to hold me 'weak' or otherwise
> because I chose to persist in a study which I decided deliberately four or
> five years ago to make, next to my poetry, the most important pursuit of my
> life. Whether it be, or be not, bad for my health can only be decided by
> one who knows what magic is and not at all by any amateur. The probable
> explanation however of your somewhat testy postcard is that you were out at
> Bedford Park and heard my father discoursing about my magical pursuits
> out of the immense depths of his ignorance as to everything that I am doing
> and thinking. If I had not made magic my constant study I could not have
> written a single word of my Blake book, nor would *The Countess Kathleen*
> have ever come to exist. The mystical life is the centre of all that I do and
> all that I think and all that I write.

If Yeats's father could not help him in this interest, his astrologer
uncle George Pollexfen could. Together they performed cabalistic experiments at Rosses Point where George had a little house in which he
spent his summers. Yeats, manipulating cards on which were drawn
colored symbols, was delighted to discover that he could evoke parallel
visions in himself, in George, and in George's second-sighted servant,
Mary Battle. Introverted, melancholy, in every respect the opposite of
Yeats's father who had once noted that even as a boy he had been attracted to George as an opposite, George Pollexfen became for Yeats an
unforgettable figure. Linking him to his father, Yeats may have formed
from their antithetical personalities one of his images of the impossible
whole man he wanted to be: an intellectual of feeling, an isolated man
whose intense friendships suggest to him patterns of order for his artistic
achievement.

Most of the men Yeats came to know well were writers and politicians,
and almost all of them—because of the nature of the world in which they
were born, Yeats later came to feel—after much promise, failed to achieve
what had seemed in their youths certain greatness. The writers Lionel
Johnson and Ernest Dowson whose dissipations destroyed them, Oscar
Wilde who was trapped by his own vanity into public disgrace, the
mystic George Russell (*AE*) who wrote no great book, Yeats felt, because
he had become a visionary saint entangled in mundane and practical
affairs, the occultist MacGregor Mathers whom fanaticism drove half-
mad, and John O'Leary (who, reduced to three Fenian disciples, cast out
one) were all, in Yeats's eyes, men whom circumstances had defeated
before their talent could perfect itself.

Only one of his friends, Yeats felt, had managed, though dying young and hounded by a public that could not value his work, to accomplish great art. That man, John Synge, Yeats recognized as an authentic genius, the only writer he could speak to freely as an equal. "We should unite stoicism, asceticism and ecstasy," Synge told Yeats in Paris. "Two of them have often come together, but the three never." Yeats, who took Synge's words to heart, could also give good advice: "I urged him to go to the Aran Islands and find a life that had never been expressed in literature, instead of a life where all had been expressed."

Yeats gathered images from which to construct his soul. And if, as he studied the men he knew, those men sometimes became transformed to images—his father to gregarious aesthetician, George Pollexfen to introverted mystic, John Synge to proud literary genius—the images of all those warring personalities were all, Yeats realized, aspects of himself. So too were the images—from which he also constructed patterns of order —of those women who are celebrated in his poetry.

Maud Gonne is, of course, the most famous of those necessary ladies. An intense, passionate nationalist; beautiful, eloquent, and domineering, she swept him off his feet when on January 30, 1889, ostensibly visiting his father with an introduction from O'Leary but actually, as Elizabeth, Yeats's younger sister noted, calling "on Willie, of course," she praised his poetry and became for him from that moment on the prototype of feminine beauty, "A Helen," a "Pallas Athene." "Her complexion was luminous, like that of apple blossom through which the light falls, and I remember her standing that first day by a great heap of such blossoms in the window." Four days after that meeting, in a letter to Ellen O'Leary, Yeats celebrated her conquest: "Did I tell you how much I admire Miss Gonne? She will make many converts to her political belief. If she said the world was flat or the moon an old caubeen tossed up into the sky I would be proud to be of her party."

Though Yeats tried hard to make himself enough of a nationalist to satisfy her thirst for revolution, though he focused his poetry on Irish themes and joined her in public meetings where "her beauty, backed by her great stature, could instantly affect an assembly," though he wrote as a vehicle for her politics and her acting *Cathleen ni Houlihan*, and though for more than thirteen years he courted her unsuccessfully (a courtship that ended only when she married Major John MacBride in 1903), his devotion, as he pointed out in *Dramatis Personae*, "might as well have been offered to an image in a milliner's window, or to a statue in a museum." And it is as a statue, in "A Bronze Head," that he finally commemorated her who, in bronze reduced to a "dark tomb-haunter," had once been a person of supernatural intensity, of gentleness, and of "wildness": ". . . who can tell/ Which of her forms has shown her substance right?"

Yeats saw her as destroyed by a kind of Irish nationalism, revolutionary and hysterical, a nationalism in his mind both modern and vulgar but which, in spite of all its shoddy trappings, created an opportunity for heroism. Because he felt she was fated by personality and her times to act out a role of tragic, unnecessary violence, he watched fascinated as she chose one of the two possible parts he felt she was doomed to play: "She had to choose (perhaps all women must) between broomstick and distaff and she has chosen the broomstick—I mean the witches' hats."

If Maud Gonne became ideal beauty wrecked in service of an unworthy cause, Olivia Shakespear, to whom Yeats had been writing when he set his heroine on that metaphorical broomstick, was woman as confidant. Yeats had first met her through her cousin Lionel Johnson in the spring of 1894. The young wife of an elderly solicitor, she found in Yeats, as he in her, a person who could discuss literature and ideas. Of his close friends the one least publicly celebrated in his poetry and in his auto-biographical prose, yet the woman perhaps most intimately known, she was one of the few persons with whom he could be completely relaxed. Though he destroyed many of his letters when they were returned to him after her death by her son-in-law, Ezra Pound, those casual gentle notes that survive show Yeats in a very different character from the aggressive figure he was laboring to make of himself. Temperamentally precisely opposed to Maud Gonne's flamboyant brilliance, Olivia Shakespear was a lovely generous woman of great human warmth. She too fit into Yeats's pattern, helped complete his personality through the affection, sympathy, and comradeship that Maud Gonne was never able to provide. When three and a half months before his own death he heard she had died, a part of his world died. "Yesterday morning I had tragic news," he wrote Dorothy Wellesley:

> Olivia Shakespear has died suddenly. For more than forty years she has been the centre of my life in London and during all that time we have never had a quarrel, sadness sometimes but never a difference. When I first met her she was in her late twenties but in looks a lovely young girl. When she died she was a lovely old woman. You would have approved her. She came of a long line of soldiers and during the last war thought it her duty to stay in London through all the air raids. She was not more lovely than distinguished—no matter what happened she never lost her solitude. . . . For the moment I cannot bear the thought of London. I will find her memory everywhere.

Maud Gonne offered Yeats subject matter for poetry, the "interesting" life he had hoped for, and Olivia Shakespear offered him repose. But Augusta Gregory gave him a time and place to work. For twenty sum-mers, from 1897 until he rebuilt his tower at Ballylee, Yeats was her guest at Coole Park where, under her sometimes strict supervision, he ate and wrote well. She served, however, as more than patron. "John Synge, I and Augusta Gregory," he wrote in "The Municipal Gallery Revisited,"

> thought
> All that we did, all that we said or sang
> Must come from contact with the soil. . . .
> We three alone in modern times had brought
> Everything down to that sole test again,
> Dream of the noble and the beggar-man.

Gathering folklore with Yeats in the peasant cottages on her estate and in the Galway neighborhood, she became for him an image of aristocratic courtesy, too well-bred not to be humble, too assured not to be simple and direct in speech. Together they planned and organized the theatre societies which eventually become the Abbey Theatre; they collaborated on plays; they worked together in furthering her nephew Hugh Lane's ill-fated Dublin picture gallery. Yeats came, especially after the death of her son Robert in the first World War, to think of himself as a kind of son adopted by her not from necessity but from choice. "She has been to me mother, friend, sister and brother. I cannot realize the world without her—she brought to my wavering thoughts steadfast nobility." He praised her extravagantly: "Her literary style became in my ears the best written by woman." "I doubt if I should have done much with my life but for her firmness and her care." Both her estate and her person seemed to Yeats a survival of an aristocratic past richer than our present, and when she died, he wrote Olivia Shakespear a letter describing "a queer Dublin sculptor" who, coming "to pay his respects," had walked through the house until he came to the family portraits: ". . . and after standing silent said 'All the nobility of earth.' I felt he did not mean it for that room alone but for lost tradition. How much of my own verse has not been but the repetition of those words."

When in the poem "Friends" Yeats honored the "Three women that have wrought/ What joy is in my days" he was trying to assign Lady Gregory, Mrs. Shakespear, and Maud Gonne precise places in that design of personality which, made public, would let him survive himself. By defining and redefining himself in terms of these people and those other men and women closest to him, Yeats felt he could reveal to his perceptive reader that "Unity of Being" at the core of his many-faceted self.

The Doctrine of the Mask

Though Yeats was of course right in believing that his genius lay in "personal utterance" he recognized that personal utterance alone could not organize a body of lyric poetry and drama into the organic structure he hoped to build. For one thing, personal utterance, as he had discovered in his earliest experiments in verse, is beset always by the danger of sentimentality which leads poetry away from that reality the poetry would deal with to various kinds of self-pity and self-deception.

His problem, therefore, was to discover a technique by which the personal could somehow be objectified, be given the appearance of impersonal "truth" and yet retain the emotive force of privately felt belief. A partial solution was the theory of the Mask which, perhaps compounded from popular psychology on one hand and occult material on the other, was used by Yeats to make public his secret selves.

We are all familiar enough with the false faces we wear in the ordinary business of life, the unreal and different persons we present to parents, teachers, employers, lovers, and tax collectors. Most of us, little concerned with truth, present still another false face to ourselves, "the real me," and live and die happy in our deception. The writer interested in reality, however, must make a more difficult decision: he must choose one as genuinely real or, if he is like Yeats, find ultimate reality not in any one of them but in their interaction.

"Reality," for Yeats, is neither to be found in that buried self which directs and orders a man's life or in its Mask, the anti-self, but in the product born of their struggle. Extroverts, Yeats felt, must flee their Masks. Introverts—painters, writers, musicians; all creative men—must recognize their own proper Masks, ideal opposites, and in trying to become those nearly impossible other selves create the dramatic tensions from which art arises.

The doctrine of the Mask erects, therefore, on the artist's personality a kind of private mythology in which the individual struggles to become that which is most unlike himself: the introvert artist puts on an extrovert Mask; the subjective man assumes the Mask of the man of action. And because mythology and history, reducing men to types, mere images, simpler figures than flesh and blood men, does offer us patterns, we can, if we will, choose our Mask from those stored up by the past. A modern introvert's Mask—say Yeats's—might in many ways resemble one of the great stone faces of myth—say Cuchulain's face, a hero striding out of the remote legendary Irish past, a man of action, great fighter and great lover.

Convinced that "every passionate man . . . is, as it were, linked with another age, historical or imaginary, where alone he finds images that rouse his energy," Yeats speculated that perhaps his doctrine of the Mask might be extended from person to country and so give direction not only to an individual but a people. "I, that my native scenery might find imaginary inhabitants, half-planned a new method and a new culture." A modern country's Mask, he felt—say Ireland's—might resemble that which is most unlike modern Ireland, the Ireland of priest, merchant, and politician, might resemble "an Ireland/ The poets have imagined, terrible and gay," might, in fact, resemble Cuchulain's Ireland, a land of reckless heroes:

> Have not all races had their first unity from a mythology, that marries them to rock and hill? We had in Ireland imaginative stories, which the uneducated classes knew and even sang, and might we not make those stories current among the educated classes, rediscovering for the work's sake what I have called "the applied arts of literature," the association of literature, that is, with music, speech, and dance; and at last, it might be, so deepen the political passion of the nation that all, artist and poet, craftsman and day-labourer would accept a common design?

This common design—this great image—was the myth-founded Mask of Ireland which, being opposite to the modern world, was the Mask for the modern world, "of all states of mind not impossible, the most difficult to that man, race, or nation." Yet if the modern Yeats, the modern Irishman, or modern Ireland chose to put it on, from that Hegelian tension of opposites a greatness might be synthesized, in the union of opposites a new kind of nation might be born:

> Nations, races, and individual men are unified by an image, or bundle of images, symbolical or evocative of the state of mind, which is of all states of mind not impossible, the most difficult to that man, race or nation; because only the greatest obstacle that can be contemplated without despair, rouses the will to full intensity. . . . I had seen Ireland in my own time turn from the bragging rhetoric and gregarious humour of O'Connell's generation and school, and offer herself to the solitary and proud Parnell as to her anti-self, buskin following hard on sock, and I had begun to hope, or to half-hope, that we might be the first in Europe to seek unity as deliberately as it had been sought by theologian, poet, sculptor, architect, from the eleventh to the thirteenth century.

In spite of the fact that his hope for an Ireland united in the contemplation of a heroic mask has not been realized, the doctrine of the Mask helped Yeats write a poetry firmer, far more intense than his early verse. Seeking to be what he was not, Yeats disciplined himself and his art to form: "I take pleasure alone in those verses where it seems to me I have found something hard and cold, some articulation of the Image, which is the opposite of all that I am in my daily life, and all that my country is." "Style, personality—deliberately adopted and therefore a mask—," Yeats decided finally, "is the only escape from the hot-faced bargainers and the money-changers."

The Moment of Moments

by Giorgio Melchiori

The idea that perfection, complete fulfilment, can be reached and held only for a moment is not only Yeats's. He merely found a new image for it, he called it the point where the gyre (the movement of human life) becomes a sphere—in the same way as for Eliot it is the point of intersection of the temporal with the timeless. Yeats made this point clearer in some notes for the revised version of *A Vision* which he wrote, Mr. Ellmann says (*The Identity of Yeats*, New York, Oxford, 1954, p. 221), in 1928: "At first we are subject to Destiny . . . but the point in the Zodiac where the whirl becomes a sphere once reached, we may escape from the constraint of our nature and from that of external things, entering upon a state where all fuel has become flame, where there is nothing but the state itself, nothing to constrain it or end it. We attain it always in the creation or enjoyment of a work of art, but that moment though eternal in the Daimon [man's projection in Eternity] passes from us because it is not an attainment of our whole being. Philosophy has always explained its moment of moments in much the same way; nothing can be added to it, nothing taken away; that all progressions are full of illusion, that everything is born there like a ship in full sail."

The passage is pregnant with ideas which were of the utmost importance to Yeats, and which are still relevant to a better understanding not only of his unsystematic system of thought, but of his never enunciated poetics, and therefore of his poetry. The statement that "all progressions are full of illusion" and that everything is born in the "moment of moments," seems to contradict Yeats's whole theory of existence as a continual conflict, a theory which he had found so concisely and strikingly expressed in Blake's one sentence: "Without Contraries is no progression." In fact Yeats (as, in his own way, Blake) recognizes that, though temporal existence is constant conflict, the final aim and achievement is to transcend such existence, to transcend the dimensions of time and space, to "stretch out" the moment (the expression comes from "The Double Vision of Michael Robartes,": "In contemplation had those three so wrought / Upon a moment, and so stretched it out / That they, time overthrown, / Were dead yet flesh and bone"). And this sense of transcendence was realized at certain isolated moments of human existence, it was the sudden revelation or vision perceived "in the creation or enjoyment of a work of art." Here Yeats was repeating a conception common to poets and mystics of all times. Blake had put it, in a famous passage, in this way:

> Every Time less than a pulsation of the artery
> Is equal in its period & value to Six Thousand Years,
> For in this Period the Poet's Work is Done, and all the Great
> Events of Time start forth & are conceiv'd in such a Period,
> Within a Moment, a Pulsation of the Artery.

Yeats alludes directly to "what Blake called 'the pulsaters [*sic*] of an artery'" in the . . . additional final passage of the introduction to the revised version of *A Vision*. Among Yeats's contemporaries, T. S. Eliot had called it the moment of incarnation "at the still point of the turning world" (*Four Quartets*); for Virginia Woolf it was "the moment of being," and, curiously enough, she described it in geometrical terms, in a famous passage of *The Waves*, the only novel of hers that Yeats read (see *Letters*, 799 and 853); Joyce's *Ulysses* was a long series of such moments of intensity, which he called "epiphanies," and Yeats was fully aware of this (see *Letters*, 651); finally D. H. Lawrence, an author that Yeats admired, expressed, e.g. in the preface to the American edition of his *New Poems* (1920), his idea of the moment of vision in violent sexual terms: it appears most strikingly in his poem "Swan," a companion piece to his "Leda" in the collection *Pansies*:

> Far off
> at the core of space
> at the quick
> of time
> beats
> and goes still
> the great swan upon the waters of all endings
> the swan within vast chaos, within the electron.

(The poem ends in a way which is vaguely reminiscent of Yeats's Leda sonnet: "the vast white bird / furrows our featherless women / with unknown shocks / and stamps his black marsh-feet on their white and marshy flesh.")

I have treated elsewhere at some length the central position that this conception of "the moment" has acquired in modern literature, in its different connotations: eminently aesthetic in Joyce and Virginia Woolf, religious in Eliot, physical in Lawrence (see the chapter "The Moment as a Time Unit in Fiction" in my book *The Tightrope Walkers*, London, Routledge & K. Paul, 1956). In the intuition of this supreme moment of fulfilment all experience is unified and rolled into one—the artist, the mystic, and the sensualist share the same feeling of fullness of life and achievement, beyond the temporal and spacial boundaries, reaching the condition that Yeats called Unity of Being. All Yeats's life had been a pursuit of this Unity of Being, to realize at this point that it can be achieved only momentarily.

In the note for the revised version of *A Vision* quoted before, Yeats said that the "moment of moments" is attained "in the creation and enjoyment of a work of art." The true nature of Yeats was that of the artist, and for such natures all problems, intuitions, and sensations are seen under the species of aesthetic experience—the experience that they naturally feel as the highest possible for man. This attitude was strengthened in Yeats by his youthful contacts with the aesthetic movement of the end of last century. Ultimately, then, Unity of Being is just the artistic creation, and his pursuit of such unity is the pursuit of art. As several critics have noted, in Yeats's late poetry Unity of Being is frequently symbolized by physical union. In his early writings love, especially in its physical manifestations, was treated very warily. Eros presides over the mystical ecstatic dance in "Rosa Alchemica"—but he is merely an abstraction, a symbol of that fusion of Paganism and Christianity and the Orphic mysteries which occupied Yeats's thoughts at the time; if there is a sensual element in the story it has to be looked for in the dance itself. A clearer hint at the possibility of identifying religion, and therefore the supernatural, with sexual love, is contained in the unpublished novel written in the Nineties, *The Speckled Bird*, the hero of which ". . . was going to the East now to Arabia and Persia, where he would find among the common people so soon as he had learnt their language some lost doctrine of reconciliation; the philosophic poets have made sexual love their principal symbol of a divine love and he had seen somewhere in a list of untranslated Egyptian MSS. that certain of them dealt with love as a polthugic power . . . All the arts sprang from sexual love and there they could only come again, the garb of the religion when that reconciliation had taken place" (R. Ellmann, *op. cit.*, 52).

Here we still have Yeats the magician and the occultist, exploring the meaning he has given to religion and associating it naturally with art (his real religion). Love is mentioned only as equivalent to earthiness, in accordance with Yeats's belief in a total religious experience which included the senses as well as the brain (a conception derived directly from Blake). It is only with the poems on Solomon and Sheba ("On Woman,"

1914; "Solomon to Sheba," 1918; "Solomon and the Witch," 1918) that
sexual love becomes the symbol of the reconciliation of opposites, or at
least of an attempt at such reconciliation, at transcending the conflict
in a superior unity. But the final association of the sexual act with a
supernatural event occurs in *The Player Queen*: just because this play
is an unsuccessful work of art, it stayed longer with Yeats, who kept
pouring into it all his new thoughts and conceptions as they came into
his mind, so that now it can be considered a very revealing seminal work.
There the conjunction of the Queen with the Unicorn is described as a
"New Dispensation," the advent of a new historical cycle. This idea informs also the Leda sonnet, but as yet does not represent an escape from
the wheel of time. It is a momentary suspension, miraculous and of cosmic import, but still a new beginning, not the final peace and stillness
when, as the poet says in "Chosen," "the Zodiac is changed into a
sphere." The latter conception, that of a final escape from the wheel of
time, was reached by Yeats only slowly and laboriously. For a long period,
practically until the first version of *A Vision* was completed, he was bound
to the idea of an unending series of cycles and there are only vague hints
at the possibility of permanently transcending them. "Chosen" is perhaps
the first open statement in poetry of such a possibility, which became
clearer to his mind at that time (1926). This year was one of the richest
for his poetic production—and his poems were all based on the twin
themes of old age and sexual love. He felt physically the intensity that
informs his work of this period: on May 25 of that year he wrote to
Olivia Shakespear: "One feels at moments as if one could with a touch
convey a vision—that the mystic way and sexual love use the same means."
(*Letters*, 715)

This attitude must have become even firmer in later years when,
studying Oriental religions with the Indian Swami, Shri Purohit, he
learnt of those cults in which physical intercourse is a major element in
the mystic experience. The attribution of a metaphysical meaning to the
sexual act (as in "Chosen") was certainly important for Yeats. But if we
forget for a moment this meaning we realize that his insistence on it is
only the full affirmation of the sensual element which is inevitable in all
art—since art communicates through the senses.

The Artist in Isolation

by Frank Kermode

No one has written better than Yeats about that generation of poets who "had to face their ends when young"—about Wilde, who so admired "The Crucifixion of the Outcast," about Dowson, and Johnson, who was to become crucial to Yeats's own developing idea of isolation. When the outcast counts on being crucified, indeed savors the prospect; when, bitter and gay, he abstains from morality for fear, as Yeats put it in a late letter, of losing the indispensable "heroic ecstasy," then we know we are dealing with a tradition which has become fully, not to say histrionically, self-conscious. A movement is strong when a man like Henley throws himself into an antithetical, activist movement, to oppose it. ("To converse with him," said Wilde after Henley had thrown him out of a café, "is a physical no less than an intellectual recreation.")

If we suspect the testimony of those who were all too deeply involved, we may turn to the detached, ironical, adverbial James; who, asked by the *Yellow Book* for a story, immediately began his own investigation into the relation between the quality of the work and the estrangement of its maker. As Mr. Blackmur has said, James saw the artist as an interesting theme for fiction only in his guise as a failure. If *life* is important, why be an artist? "It's so poor—so poor! . . . I mean as compared with being a person of action—as living your works." The young artist in *The Lesson of the Master*, who is in a sense James's Callicles, may protest against this plight; but the Empedoclean Master has his answer ready:

> "What a false position, what a condemnation of the artist, that he's a mere disenfranchised monk and can produce his effect only by giving up personal happiness! What an arraignment of art!" Paul went on with trembling voice.
>
> "Ah, you don't imagine by chance that I'm defending art? 'Arraignment'

—I should think so! Happy the societies in which it hasn't made its appearance, for from the moment it comes they have a consuming ache, they have
an incurable corruption in their breast. Most assuredly the artist is in a false
position! But I thought we were taking him for granted. . . ."

The life these artists want, and which the older of them achieves at
the cost of corrupting his art, is appallingly seductive; it is represented
by the girl the young man desires and the older man marries, and by
"the life she embodied, the young purity and richness of which appeared
to imply that real success was to resemble *that,* to bloom, to present the
perfection of a fine type, not to have hammered out headachy fancies
with a bent back at an ink-stained table." Allowing for the difference of
accent, this might be Yeats speaking. A man may choose (if indeed there
is a choice) perfection of the life or of the work; and, as Yeats believed,
the latter choice meant sacrifice, self-sacrifice. Marchbanks in *Candida*
is absurd and embarrassing; but like him, the poet of the Nineties was
doomed, if not for the sake of the future for which Marchbanks was to
legislate, then simply to guarantee his lonely access to the Image.

Lionel Johnson, the friend of Yeats, was in some ways the most distinguished of these poets. Yeats's many accounts of him dwell upon those
elements in Johnson's life which he came increasingly to regard as typical.
It is of Johnson he thinks first when he considers the dissipation and
despair that are the inevitable lot of the modern artist, who must live in
a world where what Yeats called Unity of Being is impossible—a world
of division, where body and mind work separately, not moving as one,
where the artist's motive and subject is his struggle with himself. When
Yeats was young he used to write in autograph albums the famous words
of Axel (later he substituted "For wisdom is a butterfly and not a gloomy
bird of prey"). In 1899 he admiringly credited Johnson with Axel's
attitude. "He has renounced the world and built up a twilight world
instead. . . . He might have cried out with Axel, 'As for living, our
servants will do that for us.'" It was *Marius,* said Yeats, that had taught
Johnson's generation "to walk upon a rope"; for as life demanded extravagant participation, art required isolation. These men, whom he later
groups in his lunar system as "belonging by nature to the nights near the
full," made, says Yeats, what Arnold called "that morbid effort," and
"suffered in their lives because of it." Formerly there had been ways of
escape—Yeats's image for one of them is the Christian Thebaid—but
these existed no more. Johnson might brood upon sanctity, but the
Christian confessor cannot order a man not to be an artist, when "the
whole life is art and poetry." "Full of the Image, he could never have
that empty heart which calls the Hound of Heaven." And Johnson took
pleasure in his doom, and in the torment he experienced because "some
half-conscious part of him desired the world he had renounced"; he and

Dowson "had the gravity of men who had found life out and were awakening from the dream." Johnson 'fell' constantly; not only in the moral sense, but downstairs, off stools, brooding upon sanctity as he did so; but when Yeats calls him "much-falling" he almost certainly has in mind that poem so much admired by Dowson, called "Mystic and Cavalier," which is quoted in the *Autobiographies:*

> Go from me: I am one of those who fall. . . .
>
> And in the battle, when the horsemen sweep
> Against a thousand deaths and fall on sleep:
> Who ever sought that sudden calm if I
> Sought not? Yet, could not die.

That such a poem exhausts action, that art exhausts life, was a notion that haunted Yeats: "Exhausted by the cry that it can never end, my love ends," he says magnificently in *A Vision*; and the song in *Resurrection* says the same thing. Johnson drained his life away into art, looking forward, with a kind of tragic irony, to ten years on when he would be ruined, begging from his friends; but he fell once too often before the time was up. What of the artist who continues to exist, preying gloomily upon the substance of his own life? Age merely confirms his abstraction, his exclusion from ordinary vitality, by turning him into a scarecrow. Age is as hateful as the headache and the cough, the inky laborious craft— Adam's curse—whether the artist be young or old. "My first denunciation of old age," said Yeats, "I made before I was twenty." Indeed the antithesis of living man and creator was one of the root assumptions of his life and work; he drew the artist as a tragic hero, proving life by the act of withdrawing from it. He was of the great conspiracy of contemplative men, and had made his choice of "perfection of the work"; but he retained and developed a harrowing sense of the goodness of life and action, and a conviction that "real success was to resemble *that.*"

"Art is solitary man," wrote J. B. Yeats to his son, in the midst of their rich wartime correspondence. At that time, the poet was obviously unhappy about his abstinence from the exceptionally violent contemporary life of action; he had a taste for such violence, satisfied later when affable irregulars frequented Thoor Ballylee, and gunfights went on round the offices of Dublin, but in the English war he could not even play a poet's part. At such a time his father's emphasis on the proper detachment of the artist must have been agreeable. "All art is *reaction from life,*" said J. B. Yeats, "but never, when it is vital and great, *an escape.* . . . In Michelangelo's time it was not possible to escape for life was there every *minute* as real as the toothache and as terrible and impressive as the judgment day." This is a very Yeatsian formula. Yet, whatever the quality of life he has to deal with, "the poet is the antithesis of the man of action." He does not "meddle in ethics"; he is a magician, "his dreams shall have a potency to defeat the actual at every point"—this is the poet *versus* the universe of death, the world of reason.

> Art exists that man cutting himself away from nature may build in his free consciousness buildings vaster and more sumptuous than these [the "habitations of ease and comfort"] built by science; furnished too with all manner of winding passages and closets and boudoirs and encircled with gardens well shaded and with everything he can desire—and we build all out of our spiritual pain—for if the bricks be not cemented and mortised by actual suffering, they will not hold together. Those others live on another plane, where if there is less joy there is much less pain. . . . The artist . . . out of his pain and humiliations constructs for himself habitations, and if she [Nature] sweeps them away with a blow of her hand he only builds them afresh, and as his joy is chiefly in the act of building he does not mind how often he has to do it.

Here, apart from the dubious connotations of the architectural analogy, we have something close to the essence of the younger Yeats's résumé of the tradition. What, after all, is *A Vision*, but a blueprint of a palace of art, a place in the mind where men may suffer, some less and some more, where the artist explains his joy in making at the cost of isolation and suffering? The joy of building is the same thing as Yeats's brief victory, the creation of an antithesis for fate. The father admitted his intellectual debt to his son; but nobody could have restated the Romantic case so suitably to the son's purposes.

The free, self-delighting intellect which knows that pain is the cost of its joy; the licence to look inward and paint, as Blake and Palmer painted, a symbolic world; to make a magical explanation of a divine order—all this represents the victory of Coleridge, of Blake and the French; it is the heritage, delightful and tragic, to which Yeats was born. Much in his own life made him kick against the pricks; his love of aristocratic skills, of the achievements of others in the sphere of action, of his own successes in the active life. Out of this oscillation between the two states of life came the desire, natural to a magician, to tame by explaining, to answer the question, why are men different, and why are men divided? But long before Yeats ventured on his schematic explanations he had been concerned in a more general way with the justification of the ways of the artist and the defence of poetry. . . .

So certain was he that art was not "escape" that he thought of the situation the other way round: art was what you tried to escape from. The failure of Wilde to understand this was, for Yeats, something to be explained only by taking Wilde out of the ranks of the artists altogether. It was because he hated the conventional notion of "escape" that Yeats was early troubled by that dreaminess, that conscientious lack of actuality, which prevailed when he made his début; he was trying to shake it off much earlier than is usually supposed, trying to get strong, living rhythms and a language "as subtle, as complex, as full of mysterious life, as the body of a flower or of a woman." He grew suspicious of a kind of covert sensuality in this Romantic dream. We may be grateful that he did; the extension of his range, the cult of a language of organic rhythms and of great rhetorical variety, are what made him a great poet. But for all that, he never ceased to subscribe to the old doctrine that art is a kind of dream, and that to dream it well is the most difficult and exhausting of all callings. Great art unifies sense and spirit, like the body of a beautiful woman, or like a portrait by Titian, or like Donne's Elizabeth Drury; but the age was unpropitious, the available method faulty and in need of revision. The tradition is not to be sacrificed; all that is potent and valid in it is to be preserved, though in a new form.

In *A Vision*, Yeats wrote of "an early conviction of mine that the creative power of the lyric poet depends upon his accepting some of a few traditional attitudes, lover, sage, hero, scorner of life"; and as early as *The Celtic Twilight* he describes a Symbolist vision, of apes eating jewels in hell, which contains the elements of what later became a powerful and immediate impulse. "I knew that I saw the Celtic Hell, and my own Hell, the Hell of the artist, and that all who sought after beautiful and wonderful things with too avid a thirst, lost peace and form, and became shapeless and common." Here, in embryo, is the story of the cost to the artist of what Yeats, in an early essay entitled "Poetry and the Tradition," calls his unique "continual and self-delighting happiness"; it turns the dedicated, however pretty their plumage, into old scarecrows, and excludes them from life. Hanrahan, of whom the poet was to speak again in the isolation of the Tower,—"leave Hanrahan, / For I need all his mighty memories"—is tricked into leaving the dance of life, just as he was coming to where comfort was. Later he composed a great curse on old age; he had been touched by the Sidhe—a Yeatsian figure for the dedication, voluntary or no, of the artist—and had to pay the cost. The poet is not like the others. Joy makes him free for his task of stitching and unstitching, of labor at the higher reality of the imagination. But this labor is what ruins life, makes the body shapeless and common. Solitude grows with what Yeats calls the growing absorption of the dream; the long series of indecisive victories, "intellectual recreations of all that exterior fate snatches away," increase it further and torment the poet. His fate is a ruined life, intermittently illuminated by the Image. Poets and artists, says Yeats in *Per Amica Silentia Lunae*, "must go from desire to weariness and so to desire again, and live for the moment when vision comes like terrible lightning, in the humility of the brutes." Tormented by the necessary failure of his life, appalled in conscience or in vanity, he can say, "I suffered continual remorse, and only became content when my abstractions had composed themselves into picture and dramatization." This content is impermanent; the poet is thus perpetually divided against himself. Hence the distinction Yeats makes "between the perfection that is from a man's combat with himself and that which is from a combat with circumstance." Behind it lies the hopeless anger of an artist in love with action, with life. This occupied Yeats incessantly, and it is hardly too much to say that it informs most of his later poetry as well as his universal history, which is, virtually, an attempt to make all history an explanation of why the modern artist is isolated.

The Symbolism of W. B. Yeats

by *William York Tindall*

Dedicating his *Symbolist Movement in Literature* to William Butler Yeats, Arthur Symons called his Irish friend "the chief representative of that movement in our country." Symons makes it plain that Yeats belongs not to the French symbolist movement but rather to a general European movement of which the French are leaders. Later critics have been less accurate. C. M. Bowra in his *Heritage of Symbolism* (1943) takes it for granted that Yeats is heir to the French; and Edmund Wilson in *Axel's Castle* (1931), searching for connections to support his thesis, went so far as to invent a meeting between Yeats and Mallarmé. Joseph Hone, also accepting Yeats as an heir to the French, asserts in his biography *W. B. Yeats* (1943) that Yeats was familiar with the *Hérodiade* of Villiers de l'Isle Adam, an assertion which would carry more weight if Mallarmé had not written it and if Yeats had been familiar with it. These critics, whose confusions suggest only that the matter is confusing, may be forgiven for their desire to impose cause, effect, and order upon something that seems to deny these satisfactions.

Yeats was a symbolist. That much is clear. But it is also clear that his knowledge of French was so slight that he was unable to read the difficult poems to which he is supposed to be indebted. His French, which he picked up here and there without much benefit of schooling, was adequate for translating Ronsard's sonnet "When You Are Old" (1893), unless, of course, Yeats took the poem from an English version. "Ephemera" (1889) resembles Verlaine's *Colloque Sentimental*. Ronsard and Verlaine, however, are comparatively simple, and neither could have become the basis for a system of symbolism such as Yeats was to devise.

The case for *Axel* by Villiers de l'Isle Adam is stronger. Probably between 1890 and 1892 Yeats read this play slowly and laboriously, for, as he says, his French was very poor. "That play seemed all the more pro-

"The Symbolism of W. B. Yeats." (Revised 1962.) First published in *Accent*, V (Summer 1945), pp. 203-212. A different version of the essay appears in *Forces in Modern British Literature, 1885-1956* (New York: Vintage Books, Inc., 1956) by William York Tindall. Copyright © 1947, 1956 by William York Tindall. Reprinted by permission of the author, Alfred A. Knopf, Inc., and *Accent*.

found," he adds in the Preface he wrote for an English translation of *Axel* in 1925, "because I was never quite certain that I had read a page correctly." On February 26, 1894, he went to Paris to see the production of *Axel* at the Théâtre Montparnasse in company with Maud Gonne, who assisted his memory by explaining the words of the actors. She also helped him through the almost surrealist obscurities of Jarry's *Ubu Roi* at the symbolist Théâtre de l'Oeuvre in 1896. On his return from Paris in 1894 Yeats reviewed *Axel* in the April *Bookman* as part of the spiritual reaction of his time against science, externality, and the realism of Zola and Ibsen. Yeats saw no hope of a London production of this transcendental play, for the public was ready only for Pinero and Jones. The reading of *Axel* had a lasting effect upon Yeats as his short stories "Rosa Alchemica" and "Out of the Rose" demonstrate. And his symbolic play *The Shadowy Waters* (1900) is a translation of *Axel* into nautical terms.

Aside from *Axel* and a number of treatises on the occult, there is no available evidence that Yeats read anything in French. But he was acquainted with the plays of Maeterlinck in English translation. These plays were produced in English on the London stage, starting with *L'Intruse*, January, 1892, and continuing with the others through the Nineties; and from 1892 on, his plays were translated and published in London almost as soon as they were published in France. Casual references from as early as 1894 in Yeats' essays and reviews show his acquaintance with Maeterlinck; and in the September, 1897, *Bookman* he reviewed Sutro's translation of *Aglavaine et Selysette*. Although he was less enthusiastic about Maeterlinck's plays and essays than he was about *Axel*, he regarded them as almost equally significant rebellions against the external. He was fascinated with Maeterlinck's repeated symbols of mysterious intruders, lighthouses, and wells in the woods.

With the other symbolists he was less familiar. In 1894, visiting Verlaine in the Rue St. Jacques, Yeats spoke with him in English—"for I had explained the poverty of my French." They talked of *Axel* and of Maeterlinck. The article in *The Savoy* (April, 1896) that tells about this visit is concerned with Verlaine's character and life, to the neglect of his poetry in which, except for the problematical "Ephemera," Yeats never displayed much interest. When he met the English-speaking Stuart Merrill in Paris, they talked not about poetry but about politics and socialism toward which both Merrill and Yeats temporarily inclined. But at this time perhaps Merrill undertook the translation into French of three of Yeats' poems. Maud Gonne and William Sharp conducted Yeats among the French during the Nineties; and in later years Iseult Gonne, Maud's daughter, took their place. It was she who kept Yeats up to date, reading and translating for him the poems of Claudel, Péguy, and Valéry, none of whom had the slightest effect on his work, although in 1938 he remarked that only Valéry's denial of immortality prevented him from placing the "Cimetière Marine" [sic] among his sacred books.

These contacts with France were inconsiderable, but Yeats managed to supplement them during the late Nineties through his friendship with Arthur Symons, his next door neighbor in the Temple and fellow member of the Rhymers' Club. As Symons wrote his translations from Verlaine and Mallarmé, he read them to Yeats. Yeats was particularly impressed, he tells us in his *Autobiography,* with Symons' selection from Mallarmé's *Hérodiade,* which increased his own inclination toward an art separated from "everything heterogeneous and casual," from circumstance and character, in other words, toward a poetry as unlike that of the Victorians as possible but like the self-contained, socially isolated, and integrated poetry of Mallarmé. Those translations, Yeats continues, "may have given elaborate form" to the latter verses of his *Wind Among the Reeds* (1899); and he will never know, he adds, how much his theory and practice owe to these translations. It is possible, as Yeats suggests, that the verses of Symons had these effects, but it must be remembered that Symons' translation from *Hérodiade* is not a good one and that any elaborateness communicated by it is from Symons, not Mallarmé. The case for theory, however, is a stronger one; for it must be supposed that Symons, who understood theories of Mallarmé, talked as much as he read, and that Yeats must have acquired some knowledge at second hand of symbolic intentions. Moreover, having read *The Symbolist Movement in Literature* when it appeared in 1899, Yeats based his essay "The Symbolism of Poetry" (1900) partly upon what he had learned. "When sound, and colour, and form are in a musical relation . . . to one another," Yeats says in this essay, "they become as it were one sound, one colour, one form, and evoke an emotion that is made out of their distinct evocations and yet is one emotion." This is Mallarmé by way of Symons. That phrase about the trembling of the veil of the temple which Yeats was continually quoting comes from the *Divagations* (1897) of Mallarmé. Since this book, if not this phrase, is difficult, Yeats received it, no doubt, from Symons, who had sat on Tuesdays at the feet of the master.

A man who cannot read Mallarmé cannot be affected by Mallarmé. But it is unnecessary to look to him or to any Frenchman for the symbolism of William Butler Yeats, who was a symbolist poet long before he had heard of the French. He based his symbolism upon the poetry of Blake, Shelley, and Rossetti and, above all these, upon the occult. In 1886, under the spell of Mme. Blavatsky, Yeats joined the Dublin Lodge of the Theosophical Society. Two years later he joined in London the Order of the Golden Dawn, a Rosicrucian and Kabalistical society, whose leader, MacGregor Mathers, maintained connections with the similar order of Stanislas de Guaita in Paris. From the works of Mme. Blavatsky,

Yeats learned that Anima Mundi, a reservoir of all that has touched mankind, may be evoked by symbols. From Swedenborg, he received the doctrine of correspondences, from Eliphas Lévi the doctrine of magical incantations and symbols which have power over spiritual and material reality, and from Boehme the similar doctrine of signatures. The Emerald Tablet of Hermes Trismegistus informed him that things below are as things above. And the symbolic ritual of the Rosicrucians confirmed these ideas. A rebel against the world of matter, Yeats learned that all material things correspond to concepts in the world of spirit, and that through the use of material objects as magical symbols the adept may call down disembodied powers. The essay "Magic" (1901) expresses his conviction that the great memory of nature "can be evoked by symbols." Like Baudelaire, who had read Swedenborg before him, Yeats became a poetic visionary. Like Rimbaud, who had followed Eliphas Lévi, Yeats became a "magus," a master of magic who through poetic symbols and trances could surprise reality in its lair. Although he had never heard of Baudelaire or Rimbaud during his reading of Lévi and Swedenborg, Yeats belonged with these poets to the great transcendental movement of the nineteenth century. He naturally turned to the same supernatural sources. Material reality became for him as for them a chaos of symbols through which a poet could deal indirectly with spiritual orders. The example of Blake, also an occultist, taught Yeats the use in poetry of magical symbols; the poems of Shelley, which he carefully analyzed, confirmed his symbolic system. Like Blake, Baudelaire, and Rimbaud, Yeats saw the poet as magus and priest but as poet before magus and priest. Knowing what he was about, he went to the occult in the first place to discover, if he could, the laws of the imagination, to find ways of inducing trance and vision through which he could confront the inner and higher realities he needed, and to find images or symbols for his poetry.

By 1890, before he learned about the French symbolists, he had been writing symbolic poems for several years. When Symons and others told him about the French poets, Yeats welcomed them as fellow travellers on the road he was following, as fellow transcendentalists and occultists who had, like Blake and Shelley, hit upon symbolism as the only possible way to express what they had experienced. It is notable that, aside from professional occultists and Huysmans, the only Frenchmen whom Yeats read were Maeterlinck, who was a kind of theosophist, and Villiers, who was also a student of Eliphas Lévi and of the Rosicrucians. Occult considerations led Yeats to the laborious reading of *Axel*. It was probably MacGregor Mathers, the Rosicrucian, who introduced him to this congenial play.

To see how congenial it was a synopsis is necessary. This play concerns the well-born Sara, a novice in a nunnery, who has read a collection of Rosicrucian works carelessly left around in the convent library. As she stands before the archdeacon in her bridal robes about to take the veil, she is overcome with longing for a more spiritual life and for a treasure she has also read about. Seizing an axe and assuming a fierce demeanor, she locks the archdeacon in a tomb, climbs out of a window, and departs. Meanwhile, Count Axel of Auersperg, living in exile from the world in his very Gothical castle in the Black Forest, pursues Rosicrucian studies, attempts the "Great Work" of alchemy, and practices magic according to the precepts of Eliphas Lévi, under the supervision of Master Janus, an adept. Indifferent to the world of matter, from which he desires to detach himself for the sake of perfection, Axel refuses to hunt for the treasure buried somewhere on his premises. He speaks eloquently of Hermes Trismegistus, Paracelsus, and the Magi. During an interminable conversation with Master Janus, however, he suddenly renounces his spiritual aims and decides to use his magic to secure the treasure. Descending into the vaults beneath the very Gothical castle, he comes upon Sara, who has already discovered the treasure. She shoots him. Enchanted by her cruelty and her shape, he covers himself in her long hair and breathes the spirit of dead roses. He proposes that they take the treasure and have a good time in Paris, Kashmir, Heliopolis, London. But she shows him her cruciform dagger and her faded rose (the Rosy Cross), which are the symbol and "correspondence" of her belief, her soul, and the nature of things. He is moved. Therefore, in expiation of their passing infidelity to the spirit of the Rosy Cross, and in contempt of the world and of love, they resolve to die, and die. The spiritual allegory, filled with symbols of castle, lamp, treasure, and the like, immediately became one of Yeats' "sacred books," surpassing even *Prometheus Unbound* in his esteem. It is easier to see why it should have appealed to a member of the Order of the Golden Dawn than why it should have appealed to the most symbolical Frenchman.

The symbols of Yeats' early poems, like those of Villiers and of Lévi, are occult in character. From Mme. Blavatsky he learned that the great memory of nature preserves the legends of all nations and that one may get into touch with Anima Mundi through symbols drawn from Irish legends, the symbolic characters of Oisin or Aengus, for example, or the hound with one red ear, the white deer with no horns, or the island in the sea. But equally characteristic are his arbitrary occult symbols of rose, cross, lily, bird, water, tree, moon, and sun, which he could find in the Kabalistic, Theosophical, and the other profound works which constituted the greater part of his reading. The two trees in his poems of that name are the Sephirotic tree of life of the Kabala and the tree of knowledge. The "Powers" of his poem "The Poet Pleads with the Elemental Powers" are Mme. Blavatsky's elemental spirits, the "Immortal Rose" is the Rosicrucian flower, and the "Seven Lights" are the seven planets and the astral light of theosophy. The "Ineffable Name" of "To Some I Have

Talked with by the Fire" is the Kabalistical *Shem Hamphorasch* or Jehovah, whose unspeakable four-lettered name in Hebrew characters admits of seventy-two combinations, as Yeats, practicing with the Kabalists in Paris, knew by experience. These symbols differ from those ordinarily employed by the French, being traditional, systematic, more arbitrary and definite in outline. But although they are first of all magical symbols, hence impersonal, as used by Yeats they become as personal, reverberating, and mysterious as the symbols of the less systematic French.

Of these early symbols the rose is the most complex. Most of the rose poems are to be found in *The Rose* (1893), written in his first enthusiasm after reading Axel with its Rosicrucian roses. But as a member of the Order of the Golden Dawn Yeats had no need to pilfer *Axel,* for the symbolic ritual of his society centered upon the rose and cross. Although this society was secret, the details of its ritual have been revealed; for Aleister Crowley, a member, violating dreadful vows, exposed the ritual of the Order at great length in the September, 1909, and March, 1910, numbers of *The Equinox,* a magazine which he edited. This ritual, which has escaped the attention of critics, does much to make Yeats' poetic symbolism clear.

The novices of the Golden Dawn were confronted with the Sephirotic tree of life, the seven planets, the sphinx, and the symbols of the four elements. Candidates of the fourth grade who were called "Unicorns from the Stars" (a phrase which Yeats took as the title for one of his plays) learned the doctrine of correspondences between microcosm and macrocosm. At one point in their spiritual development they were permitted to inhale the perfume of a rose. But only the higher initiates were admitted to the secret of the Rose of Ruby and the Cross of Gold, "the fadeless Rose of Creation and the immortal Cross of Light" or life itself, ecstasy and suffering, and union with God. Light, fire, the color red symbolized, as in Zoroaster, the highest good. In the vault of initiation there was a rose on the ceiling, a rose with a cross on the floor; and the vault was lit with the ray of a luminous rose. Father Christian Rosenkreutz, about whom Yeats wrote an essay, was regarded as the founder of the society; and the symbols of dagger, cup, and rose, which appear in Yeats' diagram of the Great Wheel, were conspicuous in the ritual. Even "Hodos Camelionis," which makes its appearance in Yeats' *Autobiography* as "Hodos Chameliontos," occurs in the course of this awful ceremony.

But to return to the symbol of the rose in Yeats' poems and stories: it is even more complex than this ritual would imply, for Yeats, personal as well as occult, used the rose to mean more than Father Christian Rosy Cross or MacGregor Mathers intended. In "The Rose of Peace" the rose means earthly love as it does in a popular song; but the rose of "The Rose of the World" is more complicated, meaning on one level transient earthly love and beauty and on another eternal love and beauty. "The Rose of Battle," more occult, symbolizes God's side in the battle of spirit against matter or what inspires occultists and those who have failed of earthly love in their endless battle with the materialists. Here the rose is a refuge from earthly love. Wearing this militant rose of ruby and intellectual flame as the symbol of his life and hope, the Rosicrucian knight of the story "Out of the Rose" wages God's wars against outer order and fixity. The rose in "To the Rose upon the Rood of Time," as the title of the poem implies, is the Rosicrucian rose but it is also the power of the creative imagination and occult philosophy too, which, Yeats fears, may remove him so far from the present world that he will cease to be a poet. A similar fear plagues the hero of the story "Rosa Alchemica," an adventure in spiritual alchemy in which the rose as in Eliphas Lévi means the "Great Work" of transmuting matter into spirit. Taken to the headquarters of the Order of the Alchemical Rose where adepts ceremoniously dance with spirits who wear black lilies in their hair, the hero joins the terrible dance. On the dancing floor, to increase his terror, is a great cross and on the ceiling a rose. The acting version of *The Shadowy Waters* has a passage on the rose and cross as a symbol of the union of body and soul, life and death, sleep and waking. More and more Yeats feared the isolation of spirit from matter as he had feared the isolation of matter from spirit. With these fears the rose came to mean what he called "unity of being" or the integration and harmony of self, world, and spirit. These meanings are present in the rose or around it, but they are not all that it suggests because from each context comes reverberations enriching the symbol as it in turn enriches its context. The value of a symbol, said Yeats, is this richness or indefiniteness of reference which makes it far more mysterious and potent than allegory with its single meaning. A hundred men, he continued, would advance a hundred different meanings for the same symbol; for "no symbol tells all its meaning" to any man.

These interpretations of symbolism and of the power of the imagination, which was the same thing to him, are to be found in his edition of Blake's *Prophetic Books* (1893), in his essays on Shelley, "Symbolism in Painting," and "The Autumn of the Body," and in his introduction to *A Book of Images* (1898) by W. T. Horton, a fellow adept. The symbol, says Yeats in the last of these essays, gives "dumb things voices, and bodiless things bodies."

The Wind Among the Reeds (1899) does exactly this. Reviewing this book, Arthur Symons hailed it as a triumph of symbolist indirection. Through the swooning, luscious diction, the musical, individual rhythms, the harmonies and overtones, and the interaction of many traditional but mysterious images each poem becomes the symbol of an unstated idea or mood. Although Yeats employed description and statement more lavishly than the French were accustomed to do, this book is closer in feeling and method to the works of the French symbolists than any other which appeared in England in the Nineties. It resembles these works not because it is indebted to them but because, coming from the same revolt against matter and surface, it is parallel to them.

Some of the plays of William Butler Yeats resemble those of the French symbolist stage not only because they are also transcendental reactions against the realistic stage but because he had Villiers and Maeterlinck in mind when he wrote them. The debt of *The Shadowy Waters* to Villiers is clear. *The Countess Kathleen* (1892), however, which has all the atmosphere of Maeterlinck, was written before Yeats knew of him. It is difficult to say what part of Yeats' other plays comes from the French and what from the so-called Celtic twilight or the English romantic tradition.

The poems of *The Wind Among the Reeds* and the earlier poems owe part of their richness and depth to something apart from the conscious use of occult symbols and wavering rhythms. Like Rimbaud, Yeats had discovered a way to evade the interference of his intellect and to explore his unconscious in search of symbols. Rimbaud had done this by a systematic derangement of the senses through drugs, fatigue, and depravity. Yeats, who was far too prudent for such excesses, found in the occult a way of doing the same thing. Inclined by nature to waking visions and trances in which he saw wonderful things, Yeats found that through the use of ritual and hypnotic symbols he could enjoy deeper and more effectual trances in which new images swam before his eyes, Magic, by putting his active intellect to sleep, permitted him to secure for his poems the wealth of his unconscious. Naturally he tried to give these floating images an occult value, but this did not prevent them from carrying with them to his poems, whatever his conscious intention, the richness of man's deepest reality. Like Rimbaud, then, and with the aid of Rimbaud's tutor, Eliphas Lévi, Yeats discovered a poetic territory which had been neglected in England except by occasional madmen since the time of William Blake. Yeats differs from Rimbaud, however, in the formal, conscious patterns he forced upon his images.

In the second part of *The Wandering of Oisin* (1889) Yeats tells of his hero's battle on an island in the sea with an elderly demon who keeps a lady in a cave. This episode, Yeats told Katherine Tynan, came to him in a kind of vision, which plagued him night and day, and left him in a state of collapse. "Under the guise of symbolism," he told her, "I have said several things to which I only have the key." The story, he continued, was for the common reader who would remain unaware of the symbolism, yet "the whole poem is full of symbols." Aware that these unconscious symbols would bear neither an occult nor a legendary explanation, Yeats seems in this letter to Katherine Tynan, written long before Freud commences his study of such symbols, to apprehend some part of their significance in his life with father.

From his interest in semi-conscious vision, Yeats was led by his occult interests to examine his dreams for their occult meaning and for poetic themes and images. "The Cap and Bells" (1899) is, he assures us, a dream recorded exactly as he dreamed it. Here the images of queen, garment, hair, cap and bells, door, window, and the colors of red and green would have interested Dr. Freud, who loved the literary exploitations of the unconscious.[1] Yeats says in a note that this poem meant much to him, but, as with all symbolic poems, its meaning was never twice the same. Dr. Freud could have delivered him from these ambiguities. The first two stanzas of "The Song of Wandering Aengus" (1899) are obviously another dream, which is rationalized in the third stanza. The change of fish into girl is dream material. The images of wand, stream, berry, and fire are from man's sleeping consciousness. But the sun, moon, and apple of the third stanza are conscious occult symbols meaning intellect, imagination, and the tree of good and evil. Aengus was introduced afterwards to impart an Irish significance to the mysterious and lovely poem.

After 1900 Yeats' poetry became older, plainer, and more classical until in its "lofty severe quality" it came to resemble the poetry of Baudelaire. Feeling left the surface and vibrated beneath it. Far from following Baudelaire, still further from following Jean Moréas and Henri de Régnier who had turned to a kind of hardness before him, Yeats was responding bitterly to circumstance and self. The satiric and occasional poetry of the 1910 period, however, appeared symbolist to George Moore, who was unable to get Paris out of his head. In *Vale* Moore speaks of a poem Yeats wrote about a house. "What house?" Moore asks. "Mallarmé could not be darker than this," and he adds, Yeats and Mallarmé, had they ever met, would have "got on famously." But Moore, as usual, was exaggerating. The only indirection or obscurity of "Upon a House Shaken by the Land Agitation" is Yeats' failure to mention Coole Park.

After 1917 Yeats returned more or less to symbolism, retaining nobility of tone and classical surface. With this return came greater obscurity. Dissatisfied with the Golden Dawn, Yeats announced in *A Vision* (1925) an occult system of his own. One of the daemons who had dictated this system to Mrs. Yeats informed her husband of its purpose: "We have come," he said, "to give you metaphors for poetry." Yeats used them in many of the poems he wrote between 1917 and 1935, but although these images belong to a private system, they are more public than those he had used in the Nineties.

Some of the later poems, such as "The Double Vision of Michael Robartes," which refers to the first and fifteenth phases of the moon, are unintelligible without reference to *A Vision,* which Yeats wrote to help readers through poems like this. "Byzantium" remains an enigma even

[1] See Morton Irving Seiden: "A Psychoanalytical Essay on William Butler Yeats," *Accent,* spring, 1946.

with the help of *A Vision* and of several explications; for although it has
every appearance of unity, and although such images as the dome are
readily intelligible, other images and their connections and references
are as obscure as those of Mallarmé. In Yeats such privacy is uncommon.
Although "Leda and the Swan" springs from the system, it has an easy
surface and an emotional impact which permit the unsubtle reader to
enjoy it. Like those of Mallarmé, this poem, however, is symbolist in the
sense that the manifest level is there to suggest unstated themes: the
union of matter and spirit, of god and man, of Dove and Virgin, and all
the cycles of history which begin with these unnatural conjunctions. In
like manner "The Saint and the Hunchback," which has a dramatic,
comprehensible level, implies three attitudes toward life symbolized by
the saint, the hunchback, and Alcibiades, the last of whom stands for
that aristocratic wholeness toward which Yeats aspired.

"The Delphic Oracle upon Plotinus," a gay, preposterous, and very
successful poem, filled with mysterious overtones, concerns the philosopher Plotinus, swimming through boisterous waves toward a shore where
Plato, Minos, Pythagoras, Rhadamanthus, and the choir of love await
him. This poem seems to be not only symbolist but surrealist. As the
title suggests, however, the author is not Yeats but the Delphic oracle,
who composed the poem in Greek a long time ago. Using Stephen
MacKenna's translation (in his edition of Porphyry's *Life of Plotinus*),
Yeats in turn translated MacKenna's English into poetry. I give part of
the Latin version by Marcilio Ficino because it is plainer to more people
than the original Greek and because, unlike MacKenna's version, it is
not copyrighted:

> *Aurei generis magni jovis ubi agitant*
> *Minos et Rhadamanthus fratres: ubi justus*
> *Aeacus: ubi Plato, sacra vis: ubi pulcher*
> *Pythagoras, et quicunque chorum statuerunt amoris . . .*

By suppressing much and by selecting such beauties as the "golden race"
and the "choir of love," Yeats made of this indifferent stuff the stuff of
poetry. As for its meaning, the Delphic oracle, according to Porphyry,
intended her symbols to imply the journey of Plotinus through the
chaos of time and death to the Elysian fields. Her symbols of sea and
island attracted Yeats, whose unconscious had persistently offered them
to him; also, like Milton, Yeats was unable to resist the richness of
polysyllabic names, especially those of Pythagoras and Plotinus, who were
among his favorite adepts. No doubt the swimming of Plotinus toward
his shore had a very personal significance to Yeats, not unlike that of
the voyage to Byzantium, to the island of Innisfree, or to the Land of
Youth.

These symbolic poems, which seem at first so French, owe little or nothing to the French. But many of the later poems, "Among School Children," for example, and "Sailing to Byzantium," have a tight logical structure and a dependence upon statement rarely found in French symbolist verse. Until the very end where the symbols of chestnut tree and dancer represent unity of being, "Among School Children" is classical in method, not symbolist. Its difficulties are those of any compressed, coherent whole of thought and feeling. "Golden-thighed," which glimmers so strangely in the sixth stanza, is only a classical epithet applied to Pythagoras by Plutarch in the life of Numa Pompilius.

Yeats' poems are rarely as transcendental as they seem. Whatever their occult bearing, they are also personal and worldly. In his most dramatic poems, those on Aengus or on the saint and hunchback for instance, Yeats had his own problems in mind. Whatever his romantic contempt of the world, it was never as thorough as that of Mallarmé, who saw the world merely as a store of symbols for something else. Even in his Rosicrucian days Yeats wanted to reconcile world and spirit and to integrate himself with world and spirit. His symbols, like his mask, gave him a way to do this. By their triple reference to self, world, and spirit they achieve on the aesthetic plane a unity of being impossible in life.

Yeats

by T. S. Eliot

The generations of poetry in our age seem to cover a span of about
twenty years. I do not mean that the best work of any poet is limited to
twenty years: I mean that it is about that length of time before a new
school or style of poetry appears. By the time, that is to say, that a man is
fifty, he has behind him a kind of poetry written by men of seventy, and
before him another kind written by men of thirty. That is my position
at present, and if I live another twenty years I shall expect to see still
another younger school of poetry. One's relation to Yeats, however, does
not fit into this scheme. When I was a young man at the university, in
America, just beginning to write verse, Yeats was already a considerable
figure in the world of poetry, and his early period was well defined. I
cannot remember that his poetry at that stage made any deep impression
upon me. A very young man, who is himself stirred to write, is not
primarily critical or even widely appreciative. He is looking for masters
who will elicit his consciousness of what he wants to say himself, of the
kind of poetry that is in him to write. The taste of an adolescent writer
is intense, but narrow: it is determined by personal needs. The kind of
poetry that I needed, to teach me the use of my own voice, did not exist
in English at all; it was only to be found in French. For this reason the
poetry of the young Yeats hardly existed for me until after my enthusiasm
had been won by the poetry of the older Yeats; and by that time—I mean,
from 1919 on—my own course of evolution was already determined.
Hence, I find myself regarding him, from one point of view, as a contemporary and not a predecessor; and from another point of view, I can
share the feelings of younger men, who came to know and admire him
by that work from 1919 on, which was produced while they were
adolescent.

Certainly, for the younger poets of England and America, I am sure

"Yeats." The first annual Yeats Lecture, delivered to the Friends of the Irish Academy
at the Abbey Theater, Dublin, in 1940. Subsequently published in *Purpose*. From *On
Poetry and Poets* (New York: Farrar, Straus, and Cudahy, Inc., 1957) by T. S. Eliot, pp.
295-308. Copyright © 1957 by T. S. Eliot. Reprinted by permission of Farrar, Straus,
and Cudahy, Inc. and Faber & Faber Ltd.

that their admiration for Yeats's poetry has been wholly good. His idiom was too different for there to be any danger of imitation, his opinions too different to flatter and confirm their prejudices. It was good for them to have the spectacle of an unquestionably great living poet, whose style they were not tempted to echo and whose ideas opposed those in vogue among them. You will not see, in their writing, more than passing evidences of the impression he made, but the work, and the man himself as poet, have been of the greatest significance to them for all that. This may seem to contradict what I have been saying about the kind of poetry that a young poet chooses to admire. But I am really talking about something different. Yeats would not have this influence had he not become a great poet; but the influence of which I speak is due to the figure of the poet himself, to the integrity of his passion for his art and his craft which provided such an impulse for his extraordinary development. When he visited London he liked to meet and talk to younger poets. People have sometimes spoken of him as arrogant and overbearing. I never found him so; in his conversations with a younger writer I always felt that he offered terms of equality, as to a fellow worker, a practitioner of the same mystery. It was, I think, that, unlike many writers, he cared more for poetry than for his own reputation as a poet or his picture of himself as a poet. Art was greater than the artist: and this feeling he communicated to others; which was why younger men were never ill at ease in his company.

This, I am sure, was part of the secret of his ability, after becoming unquestionably the master, to remain always a contemporary. Another is the continual development of which I have spoken. This has become almost a common place of criticism of his work. But while it is often mentioned, its causes and its nature have not been often analysed. One reason, of course, was simply concentration and hard work. And behind that is character: I mean the special character of the artist as artist—that is, the force of character by which Dickens, having exhausted his first inspiration, was able in middle age to proceed to such a masterpiece, so different from his early work, as *Bleak House*. It is difficult and unwise to generalize about ways of composition—so many men, so many ways—but it is my experience that towards middle age a man has three choices: to stop writing altogether, to repeat himself with perhaps an increasing skill of virtuosity, or by taking thought to adapt himself to middle age and find a different way of working. Why are the later long poems of Browning and Swinburne mostly unread? It is, I think, because one gets the essential Browning or Swinburne entire in earlier poems; and in the later, one is reminded of the early freshness which they lack, without being made aware of any compensating new qualities. When a man is engaged in work of abstract thought—if there is such a thing as wholly abstract thought outside of the mathematical sciences—his mind can mature, while his emotions either remain the same or only atrophy, and it will not matter. But maturing as a poet means maturing as the whole man, experiencing new emotions appropriate to one's age, and with the same intensity as the emotions of youth.

One form, a perfect form, of development is that of Shakespeare, one of the few poets whose work of maturity is just as exciting as that of their early manhood. There is, I think, a difference between the development of Shakespeare and Yeats, which makes the latter case still more curious. With Shakespeare, one sees a slow, continuous development of mastery of his craft of verse, and the poetry of middle age seems implicit in that of early maturity. After the first few verbal exercises you say of each piece of work: "This is the perfect expression of the sensibility of that stage of his development." That a poet should develop at all, that he should find something new to say, and say it equally well, in middle age, has always something miraculous about it. But in the case of Yeats the kind of development seems to me different. I do not want to give the impression that I regard his earlier and his later work almost as if they had been written by two different men. Returning to his earlier poems after making a close acquaintance with the later, one sees, to begin with, that in technique there was a slow and continuous development of what is always the same medium and idiom. And when I say development, I do not mean that many of the early poems, for what they are, are not as beautifully written as they could be. There are some, such as "Who Goes with Fergus?," which are as perfect of their kind as anything in the language. But the best, and the best known of them, have this limitation: that they are as satisfactory in isolation, as "anthology pieces," as they are in the context of his other poems of the same period.

I am obviously using the term "anthology piece" in a rather special sense. In any anthology, you find some poems which give you complete satisfaction and delight in themselves, such that you are hardly curious who wrote them, hardly want to look further into the work of that poet. There are others, not necessarily so perfect or complete, which make you irresistibly curious to know more of that poet through his other work. Naturally, this distinction applies only to short poems, those in which a man has been able to put only a part of his mind, if it is a mind of any size. With some such you feel at once that the man who wrote them must have had a great deal more to say, in different contexts, of equal interest. Now among all the poems in Yeats's earlier volumes I find only in a line here or there, that sense of a unique personality which makes one sit up in excitement and eagerness to learn more about the author's mind and feelings. The intensity of Yeats's own emotional experience hardly appears. We have sufficient evidence of the intensity of experience of his youth, but it is from the retrospections in some of his later work that we have our evidence.

I have, in early essays, extolled what I called impersonality in art, and it may seem that, in giving as a reason for the superiority of Yeats's later work the greater expression of personality in it, I am contradicting myself. It may be that I expressed myself badly, or that I had only an adolescent grasp of that idea—as I can never bear to re-read my own prose writings, I am willing to leave the point unsettled—but I think now, at least, that the truth of the matter is as follows. There are two forms of impersonality: that which is natural to the mere skillful craftsman, and that which is more and more achieved by the maturing artist. The first is that of what I have called the "anthology piece," of a lyric by Lovelace or Suckling, or of Campion, a finer poet than either. The second impersonality is that of the poet who, out of intense and personal experience, is able to express a general truth; retaining all the particularity of his experience, to make of it a general symbol. And the strange thing is that Yeats, having been a great craftsman in the first kind, became a great poet in the second. It is not that he became a different man, for, as I have hinted, one feels sure that the intense experience of youth had been lived through—and indeed, without this early experience he could never have attained anything of the wisdom which appears in his later writing. But he had to wait for a later maturity to find expression of early experience; and this makes him, I think, a unique and especially interesting poet.

Consider the early poem which is in every anthology, "When you are old and grey and full of sleep," or "A Dream of Death" in the same volume of 1893. They are beautiful poems, but only craftsman's work, because one does not feel present in them the particularity which must provide the material for the general truth. By the time of the volume of 1904 there is a development visible in a very lovely poem, "The Folly of Being Comforted," and in "Adam's Curse"; something is coming through, and in beginning to speak as a particular man he is beginning to speak for man. This is clearer still in the poem "Peace," in the 1910 volume. But it is not fully evinced until the volume of 1914, in the violent and terrible epistle dedicatory of *Responsibilities*, with the great lines

> Pardon that for a barren passion's sake,
> Although I have come close on forty-nine. . . .

And the naming of his age in the poem is significant. More than half a lifetime to arrive at this freedom of speech. It is a triumph.

There was much also for Yeats to work out of himself, even in technique. To be a younger member of a group of poets, none of them certainly of anything like his stature, but further developed in their limited path, may arrest for a time a man's development of idiom. Then again, the weight of the Pre-Raphaelite prestige must have been tremendous. The Yeats of the Celtic twilight—who seems to me to have been more the Yeats of the Pre-Raphaelite twilight—uses Celtic folklore almost as William Morris uses Scandinavian folklore. His longer narrative poems bear the mark of Morris. Indeed, in the Pre-Raphaelite phase, Yeats is by no means the least of the Pre-Raphaelites. I may be mistaken, but the play, *The Shadowy Waters*, seems to me one of the most perfect expressions of the vague enchanted beauty of that school: yet it strikes me—this may be an impertinence on my part—as the western seas descried through the back window of a house in Kensington, an Irish myth for the Kelmscott Press; and when I try to visualize the speakers in the play, they have the great dim, dreamy eyes of the knights and ladies of Burne-Jones. I think the phase in which he treated Irish legend in the manner of Rossetti or Morris is a phase of confusion. He did not master this legend until he made it a vehicle for his own creation of character—not, really, until he began to write the *Plays for Dancers*. The point is, that in becoming more Irish, not in subject-matter but in expression, he became at the same time universal.

The points that I particularly wish to make about Yeats's development are two. The first, on which I have already touched, is that to have accomplished what Yeats did in the middle and later years is a great and permanent example—which poets-to-come should study with reverence —of what I have called Character of the Artist: a kind of moral, as well as intellectual, excellence. The second point, which follows naturally after what I have said in criticism of the lack of complete emotional expression in his early work, is that Yeats is pre-eminently the poet of middle age. By this I am far from meaning that he is a poet only for middle-aged readers: the attitude towards him of younger poets who write in English, the world over, is enough evidence to the contrary. Now, in theory, there is no reason why a poet's inspiration or material should fail, in middle age or at any time before senility. For a man who is capable of experience finds himself in a different world in every decade of his life; as he sees it with different eyes, the material of his art is continually renewed. But in fact, very few poets have shown this capacity of adaptation to the years. It requires, indeed, an exceptional honesty and courage to face the change. Most men either cling to the experiences of youth, so that their writing becomes an insincere mimicry of their earlier work, or they leave their passion behind, and write only from the head, with a hollow and wasted virtuosity. There is another and even worse temptation: that of becoming dignified, of becoming public figures with only a public existence—coat-racks hung with decorations and distinctions, doing, saying, and even thinking and feeling only what they believe the public expects of them. Yeats was not that kind of poet: and it is, perhaps, a reason why young men should find his later poetry more acceptable than older men easily can. For the young can see him as a poet who in his work remained in the best sense always young, who even in one sense became young as he aged. But the old, unless they are stirred to something of the honesty with oneself expressed in the poetry, will be shocked by such a revelation of what a man really is and remains. They will refuse to believe that *they* are like that.

> You think it horrible that lust and rage
> Should dance attendance upon my old age;
> They were not such a plague when I was young:
> What else have I to spur me into song?

These lines are very impressive and not very pleasant, and the sentiment has recently been criticized by an English critic whom I generally respect. But I think he misread them. I do not read them as a personal confession of a man who differed from other men, but of a man who was essentially the same as most other men; the only difference is in the greater clarity, honesty and vigor. To what honest man, old enough, can these sentiments be entirely alien? They can be subdued and disciplined by religion, but who can say that they are dead? Only those to whom the maxim of La Rochefoucauld applies: "Quand les vices nous quittent, nous nous flattons de la créance que c'est nous qui les quittons." The tragedy of Yeats's epigram is all in the last line.

Similarly, the play *Purgatory* is not very pleasant, either. There are aspects of it which I do not like myself. I wish he had not given it this title, because I cannot accept a purgatory in which there is no hint, or at least no emphasis upon Purgation. But, apart from the extraordinary theatrical skill with which he has put so much action within the compass of a very short scene of but little movement, the play gives a masterly exposition of the emotions of an old man. I think that the epigram I have just quoted seems to me just as much to be taken in a dramatic sense as the play *Purgatory*. The lyric poet—and Yeats was always lyric, even when dramatic—can speak for every man, or for men very different from himself; but to do this he must for the moment be able to identify himself with every man or other men; and it is only his imaginative power of becoming this that deceives some readers into thinking that he is speaking for and of himself alone—especially when they prefer not to be implicated.

I do not wish to emphasize this aspect only of Yeats's poetry of age. I would call attention to the beautiful poem in *The Winding Stair*, in memory of Eva Gore-Booth and Con Markiewicz, in which the picture at the beginning, of:

> Two girls in silk kimonos, both
> Beautiful, one a gazelle,

gets great intensity from the shock of the later line,

> When withered old and skeleton-gaunt,

and also to "Coole Park," beginning

> I meditate upon a swallow's flight,
> Upon an aged woman and her house.

In such poems one feels that the most lively and desirable emotions of youth have been preserved to receive their full and due expression in retrospect. For the interesting feelings of age are not just different feelings; they are feelings into which the feelings of youth are integrated.

Yeats's development in his dramatic poetry is as interesting as that in his lyrical poetry. I have spoken of him as having been a lyric poet—in a sense in which I should not think of myself, for instance, as lyric; and by this I mean rather a certain kind of selection of emotion rather than particular metrical forms. But there is no reason why a lyric poet should not also be a dramatic poet; and to me Yeats is the type of lyrical dramatist. It took him many years to evolve the dramatic form suited to his genius. When he first began to write plays, poetic drama meant plays written in blank verse. Now, blank verse has been a dead meter for a long time. It would be outside of my frame to go into all the reasons for that now: but it is obvious that a form which was handled so supremely well by Shakespeare has its disadvantages. If you are writing a play of the same type as Shakespeare's, the reminiscence is oppressive; if you are writing a play of a different type, it is distracting. Furthermore, as Shakespeare is so much greater than any dramatist who has followed him, blank verse can hardly be dissociated from the life of the sixteenth and seventeenth centuries: it can hardly catch the rhythms with which English is spoken nowadays. I think that if anything like regular blank verse is ever to be re-established, it can be after a long departure from it, during the course of which it will have liberated itself from period associations. At the time of Yeats's early plays it was not possible to use anything else for a poetry play: that is not a criticism of Yeats himself, but an assertion that changes in verse forms come at one moment and not at another. His early verse-plays, including the *Green Helmet*, which is written in a kind of irregular rhymed fourteener, have a good deal of beauty in them, and, at least, they are the best verse-plays written in their time. And even in these, one notices some development of irregularity in the metric. Yeats did not quite invent a new meter, but the blank verse of his later plays shows a great advance towards one; and what is most astonishing is the virtual abandonment of blank verse meter in *Purgatory*. One device used with great success in some of the later plays is the lyrical choral interlude. But another, and important, cause of improvement is the gradual purging out of poetical ornament. This, perhaps, is the most painful part of the labor, so far as the versification goes, of the modern poet who tries to write a play in verse. The course of improvement is towards a greater and greater starkness. The beautiful line for its own sake is a luxury dangerous even for the poet who has made himself a virtuoso of the technique of the theater. What is necessary is a beauty which shall not be in the line or the isolable passage, but woven into the dramatic texture itself; so that you can hardly say whether the lines give grandeur to the drama, or whether it is the drama which turns the words into poetry. (One of the most thrilling lines in *King Lear* is the simple:

> Never, never, never, never, never

but, apart from a knowledge of the context, how can you say that it is poetry, or even competent verse?) Yeats's purification of his verse becomes much more evident in the four *Plays for Dancers* and in the two in the posthumous volume: those, in fact, in which he had found his right and final dramatic form.

It is in the first three of the *Plays for Dancers,* also, that he shows the internal, as contrasted with the external, way of handling Irish myth of which I have spoken earlier. In the earlier plays, as in the earlier poems, about legendary heroes and heroines, I feel that the characters are treated, with the respect that we pay to legend, as creatures of a different world from ours. In the later plays they are universal men and women. I should, perhaps, not include *The Dreaming of the Bones* quite in this category, because Dermot and Devorgilla are characters from modern history, not figures of pre-history; but I would remark in support of what I have been saying that in this play these two lovers have something of the universality of Dante's Paolo and Francesca, and this the younger Yeats could not have given them. So with the Cuchulain of *At The Hawk's Well*, the Cuchulain, Emer and Eithne of *The Only Jealousy of Emer*; the myth is not presented for its own sake, but as a vehicle for a situation of universal meaning.

I see at this point that I may have given the impression, contrary to my desire and my belief, that the poetry and the plays of Yeats's earlier period can be ignored in favor of his later work. You cannot divide the work of a great poet so sharply as that. Where there is the continuity of such a positive personality and such a single purpose, the later work cannot be understood, or properly enjoyed, without a study and appreciation of the earlier; and the later work again reflects light upon the earlier, and shows us beauty and significance not before perceived. We have also to take account of the historical conditions. As I have said above, Yeats was born into the end of a literary movement, and an English movement at that: only those who have toiled with language know the labor and constancy required to free oneself from such influences—yet, on the other hand, once we are familiar with the older voice, we can hear its individual tones even in his earliest published verse. In my own time of youth there seemed to be no immediate great powers of poetry either to help or to hinder, either to learn from or to rebel against, yet I can understand the difficulty of the other situation, and the magnitude of the task. With the verse-play, on the other hand, the situation is reversed, because Yeats had nothing, and we have had Yeats. He started writing plays at a time when the prose-play of contemporary life seemed triumphant, with an indefinite future stretching before it, when the comedy of light farce dealt only with certain privileged strata of metropolitan life; and when the serious play tended to be an ephemeral tract on some transient social problem. We can begin to see now that even the imperfect early attempts he made are probably more permanent literature than the plays of Shaw; and that his dramatic work as a whole may prove a stronger defense against the successful urban Shaftesbury Avenue vulgarity which he opposed as stoutly as they. Just as, from the beginning, he made and thought his poetry in terms of speech and not in terms of print, so in the drama he always meant to write plays to be played and not merely to be read. He cared, I think, more for the theater as an organ for the expression of the consciousness of a people, than as a means to his own fame or achievement; and I am convinced that it is only if you serve it in this spirit that you can hope to accomplish anything worth doing with it. Of course, he had some great advantages, the recital of which does not rob him of any of his glory: his colleagues, a people with a natural and unspoilt gift for speech and for acting. It is impossible to disentangle what he did for the Irish theater from what the Irish theater did for him. From this point of advantage, the idea of the poetic drama was kept alive when everywhere else it had been driven underground. I do not know where our debt to him as a dramatist ends—and in time, it will not end until that drama itself ends. In his occasional writings on dramatic topics he has asserted certain principles to which we must hold fast: such as the primacy of the poet over the actor, and of the actor over the scene-painter; and the principle that the theater, while it need not be concerned only with "the people" in the narrow Russian sense, must be for the people; that to be permanent it must concern itself with fundamental situations. Born into a world in which the doctrine of "Art for Art's sake" was generally accepted, and living on into one in which art has been asked to be instrumental to social purposes, he held firmly to the right view which is between these, though not in any way a compromise between them, and showed that an artist, by serving his art with entire integrity, is at the same time rendering the greatest service he can to his own nation and to the whole world.

To be able to praise, it is not necessary to feel complete agreement; and I do not dissimulate the fact that there are aspects of Yeats's thought and feeling which to myself are unsympathetic. I say this only to indicate the limits which I have set to my criticism. The questions of difference, objection and protest arise in the field of doctrine, and these are vital questions. I have been concerned only with the poet and dramatist, so far as these can be isolated. In the long run they cannot be wholly isolated. A full and elaborate examination of the total work of Yeats must some day be undertaken; perhaps it will need a longer perspective. There are some poets whose poetry can be considered more or less in isolation, for experience and delight. There are others whose poetry, though giving equally experience and delight, has a larger historical importance. Yeats was one of the latter: he was one of those few whose history is the history of their own time, who are a part of the consciousness of an age which cannot be understood without them. This is a very high position to assign to him: but I believe that it is one which is secure.

W. B. Yeats: Between
Myth and Philosophy

by R. P. Blackmur

The notes that follow are intended to make an extreme case of one aspect of Yeats's poetry. I assume that the reader is pretty familiar with the whole reach of Yeats's work and will accordingly bring my extremity back into proportion without too much irritation; for if he is familiar with Yeats he will know that Yeats combines elements any one of which is disproportionate, even incongruous, taken by itself, and that his unity —what he is taken all together—is an imaginative, a felt unity of disproportions. No poet in recent times, for example, has seemed to base his work on a system, quasi-philosophical, partly historical, and largely allegorical, both so complicated and so esoteric, as the system which Yeats worked out in the two versions of *A Vision*. With the poems which make explicit use of the machinery of that system, these notes have nothing to do, though they include both some of the most fascinating and some of the finest of Yeats's poems, and are those most often dealt with perhaps precisely because the critic is able to catch hold of them by the levers and switches of the machinery. No; here the interest is in those poems where the machinery plays the least explicit part. For with his abstract system and the poetry which it channelized on one side, there is on the other side of Yeats what is also the most concrete, the most independent, perhaps the most personal poetry, in the good sense of the word personal, of our time. One thinks of the ballads, of Burns, of Villon, and of the dramatic aspects of Dante, in looking for archetypes; but one must think of all of them together in order to build up an expectation of great imaginative generalizing power behind or under the concrete images and individual cries of which the poems are made. The system, in short, is still there, but translated back into the actual experience from which it came. How the translation was made, what the

"W. B. Yeats: Between Myth and Philosophy." From *Language as Gesture* (New York: Harcourt, Brace & World, Inc., 1953) by R. P. Blackmur, pp. 105-123. Copyright 1942 by Richard P. Blackmur. Reprinted by permission of Harcourt, Brace & World, Inc. and George Allen and Unwin Ltd.

compositional habits of the poems are, will make up our interest and the extremity of our case.

It may be risked that in dealing with the structure of poetry thought may be taken as felt assertion, irrelevant to critical analysis, but open to discussion with regard to what it permitted the poet to discover in his poems. Thought becomes metaphor, if indeed it was not already so; from a generalized assertion it becomes in each poetic instance an imaginative assertion that has to do with identity, the individual, the rash single act of creation. We seek to recover the generalized form of the assertion as a clue to what happened to it in the poetry, to find, that is, the spur of the metaphor: an operation which even if failure is an aid to understanding. It gives us something we can verbalize.

So in Yeats, we can detach certain notions which we call basic—though we may mean only that they are detachable—as clues to better reading. At the end of the first version of *A Vision*, Yeats suggests the need of putting myths back into philosophy, and in the "Dedication to Vestigia" in the same version, there is the following sentence: "I wished for a system of thought that would leave my imagination free to create as it chose and yet make all that it created, or could create, part of the one history, and that the soul's." If we take these two notions as sentiments, as unexpanded metaphors, we can understand both what drove Yeats to manufacture his complicated abstract system and the intensity of his effort to make over half of the consequent poetry as concrete as possible. He knew for himself as a poet that the most abstract philosophy or system must be *of* something, and that its purpose must be to liberate, to animate, to elucidate that something; and he knew further that that something must be somehow present in the philosophy. His system, if it worked, would liberate his imagination; and if it worked it must put those myths—the received forms, the symbolic versions of human wisdom —which were its object concretely into his system. A philosophy for poetry cannot be a rationale of meaning, but, in the end, a myth for the experience of it.

I should like to put beside these two notions or sentiments, two more. At different places in his autobiographies and in his letters to Dorothy Wellesley, Yeats quotes one or another version of Aristotle's remark that a poet should "think like a wise man, yet express himself like the common people." It should be insisted that this is a very different thing from what has been lately foisted on us as a model in the guise of Public Speech. To turn poetry into public speech is to turn it into rhetoric in the bad sense or sentimentality in the meretricious sense.

> The rhetorician would deceive his neighbors,
> The sentimentalist himself; while art
> Is but a vision of reality.

If we keep these lines—from one of Yeats's more esoteric poems—well in mind, they will explain for us much of what Yeats meant by the desire to express himself like the common people. He wanted to charge his words to the limit, or to use words that would take the maximum charge upon themselves, in such a way that they would be available to the unlearned reader, and demand of him all those skills of understanding that go without learning. We shall come to an example shortly.

The fourth sentiment that I want brought to mind here is again one found in many places in both prose and verse in Yeats's work. This is his sentiment that a poet writes out of his evil luck, writes to express that which he is not and perforce, for completion or unity, desires to be. Dante required his exile and beggary, the corruption of the Church, the anarchy of Florence, in order to write *The Divine Comedy*, with its vast ordering of emotion, its perspicuous judgment of disorder and corruption. Villon needed his harlots and his cronies at the gibbet. "Such masters—Villon and Dante, let us say—would not, when they speak through their art, change their luck; yet they are mirrored in all the suffering of their desire. The two halves of their nature are so completely joined that they seem to labor for their objects, and yet to desire whatever happens, being at the same instant predestinate and free, creation's very self." So Yeats in his chapter of autobiography called "Hodos Chameliontos"—the path of muddlement, of change, of shift from opposite to opposite. And he goes on, in language characteristic elsewhere of his regard both for his own life and his own works. "We gaze at such men in awe, because we gaze not at a work of art, but at the re-creation of the man through that art, the birth of a new species of man, and it may even seem that the hairs of our heads stand up, because that birth, that re-creation, is from terror." Lastly, in the next paragraph, there is a declaration of exactly what I want to make manifest as the effort in the dramatically phrased poems of the later years. "They and their sort," he writes, and it is still Dante and Villon, "alone earn contemplation, for it is only when the intellect has wrought the whole of life to drama, to crisis, that we may live for contemplation, and yet keep our intensity."

Now I do not believe Yeats felt all these sentiments all the time, for a man is never more than partly himself at one time, and there is besides a kind of outward buoyancy that keeps us up quite as much as the inward drive keeps us going—but I believe that if we keep all four sentiments pretty much consciously in mind we shall know very nearly where we are in the simplest and most dramatic as in the most difficult and most occult of Yeats's poems. With these sentiments for landmarks, he is pretty sure to have taken a two- or a three- or even occasionally a four-point bearing, in setting the course of a particular poem.

To say this smacks of instruments and tables, of parallel rules and compass roses. But only when the waters are strange and in thick weather are thoughts taken as instruments necessary or helpful. With familiarity the skill of knowledge becomes unconscious except in analysis, running into the senses, and all seems plain sailing. As with sailing so with poetry, the greatest difficulties and the fullest ease lie along known coasts and sounds; there is so much more in the familiar to work on with the attention, whether conscious or not. The object of these remarks is to suggest why it is appropriate to research, so to speak, the original perils of certain poems of Yeats—those in which one way or another the intellect has wrought life to drama—and thereby to jolt the reader's attention, on as conscious a level as possible, back to those aids to navigation which long practice safely ignores but which alone made the passage, in the beginning, feasible. In this figure it is the intellect, the imagination, the soul that is sailed. The poem is not the ship, the poem is the experience of sailing, the course run, of which it is possible to make certain entries. It should be insisted, though, that these entries in the log only recount and punctuate the voyage, and in no way substitute for it. The experience of sailing cannot be put in any log, in any intellectual record. There is the sea, and there is language, experienced; there is the sailing and the poetry: there are not only no substitutes for these, there is nothing so important as getting back to them unless it be to begin with them.

Let us begin then, and it is quite arbitrary to begin in this way, and to many minds will seem extreme, by conceiving that there is a play of words in the composition of poetry, which the conscious mind cannot control but of which it must take continuous stock, and which, by holding itself amenable, it can encourage or promote. Let us insist, further, that to equip himself with conscious amenities of this order is the overt training of a poet: remarking that this is one way to consider the acquisition of habits of meter, pattern, phrase, cadence, rhyme, aptitude for trope and image: adding, that without such intellectual training the poet will be quite at a loss as to means of taking advantage of the play of the words as it begins and will write wooden of demeanor, leaden of feet. Let us insist on this because Yeats himself insisted on it. Aubrey Beardsley once told Yeats—and Yeats liked to repeat it—that he put a blot of ink on paper and shoved it around till something came. This is one routine hair-raising practice of the artist of any sort: to invoke that which *had been* unknown, to insist on the apparition, to transform the possible into a vision. The artist poaches most on his resources when ad-libbing, when he meets, and multiplies, his perils with, as Yeats said, nonchalance. The rest is cribbing or criticism.

To crib is to find something from which to start—some system, some assumption, some assertion; and to criticize is only to spot the connections, to name the opposite numbers. To crib and criticize together is to get the whole thing back on a concrete or actual basis where it is its own meaning. It is in this sense that art is a realized, an intensified (not a logical or rhetorical) tautology. Art declares its whatness, its self, with such a concreteness that you can only approach it by bringing abstractions to bear, abstractions from all the concrete or actual experience you can manage to focus. That is how art attracts richness to itself and reveals its inner inexhaustibleness; that is how art becomes symbolic, how it lasts, how it is useful, how it is autonomous and automotive—how it puts its elements together so as to create a quite unpredictable self. Different accounts reach similar conclusions; all accounts bring up on the unaccountable fact of creation; this account merely emphasizes ad-libbing as a means of getting at the unaccountable, and is meant to invoke the murk—the blot of ink—in which words habitually do their work.

Yeats, as he grew older, wrote a good many of his most effective poems by ad-libbing around either some fragment of his "system" or some free assumption or assertion. Often these *donnée's* turn up as refrains. For example, the poem called "The Apparitions" works around the refrain lines:

> *Fifteen apparitions have I seen;*
> *The worst a coat upon a coat-hanger.*

The whole poem is made of three stanzas, of three couplets each, with the refrain added. The first stanza is "about" talking vaguely, implausibly, untrustingly of an apparition. The second is "about" the pleasure of talking late with a friend who listens whether or not you are intelligible. There is no "poem," there is nothing made, so far; the refrain with one repetition seems to hang fire, but there is a sense of fire to come. The blot of ink is beginning, after a move this way and that, after just *possible* movements, to turn itself into a vision; and indeed the third stanza shows itself as the product, backed or set by the first two stanzas, of the vision *and* the refrain. Put another way, the possible is pushed over the edge and into the refrain, so that the refrain is, for the instant, the limit of meaning.

> When a man grows old his joy
> Grows more deep day after day,
> His empty heart is full at length,
> But he has need of all that strength
> Because of the increasing Night
> That opens her mystery and fright.
> *Fifteen apparitions have I seen;*
> *The worst a coat upon a coat-hanger.*

The scarecrow hangs in that closet for good; nobody knows how or why, unless we say by ad-libbing around the refrain. That the refrain may in fact have come earlier and required the stanzas, or that the stanzas may in fact have searched for the refrain, makes no difference. Something has been done to the refrain by the progressive interaction between it and the stanzas that has built up a plurisignificance (to borrow Philip Wheelwright's substitute for the Empsonian term Ambiguity) that has not stopped when the poem stops. The astonishing thing is that this plurisignificance, this ambiguity, is deeper than the particular words of the poem, and had as well been secured by other words at the critical places, indeed by the opposite words, so far as superficial, single meanings go. I do not mean to rewrite Yeats; I mean to take a slightly different tack on the course he himself set, and with the same wind in my tail. Ignoring the exigences of rhyme, let us ad-lib the stanza quoted above so that instead of joy growing more deep it grows less, so that the full heart grows empty, and remark that he has need of all that room—the room of emptiness, it will be—precisely

> Because of the increasing Night
> That opens her mystery and fright.

But let us not stop there. Could not the night diminish as well as increase; could it not, for the purposes of the achieved poem, close as well as open? One tends to let poems stay too much as they are. Do they not actually change as they are read? Do they not, as we feel them intensely, fairly press for change on their own account? Not all poems, of course, but poems of this character, which engage possibility as *primum mobile* and last locomotive? Is not the precision of the poem for the most part a long way under the precision of the words? Do not the words involve their own opposites, indeed drag after them into being their own opposites, not for contradiction but for development? After such queries we can return to the poem as it is, and know it all the better so, and know that we have not altered, even tentatively, anything of its actual character by playing with what is after all merely its notation. We have come nearer, rather, to the cry, the gesture, the metaphor of identity, which as it invades the words, and whichever words, is the poem we want.

I bring up this mode of treating a poem, because Yeats more than any recent poet of great ability has written many of the sort that invite the treatment, and because it is that class of his poems which this paper proposes to treat. In these poems he is dealing with a kind of experience which is understood by the unlearned better than, as a rule, by the learned; for the learned tend to stick to what they know, which is super-

ficial, and the unlearned, who should ideally be, in Yeats's phrase for
his own ambition, as ignorant as the dawn, have their own skills of
understanding immediately available.

That this race of the unlearned, these common readers every poet
hopes for, cannot be found in a pure state, whether under the apple
tree or the lamplight, is not relevant beyond first thought. There are
no poems, only single lines or images, entirely fit for this kind of common reading. There are only poems which move in the direction of
such reading—such hearing, I would rather say; and, similarly, there
are only readers sufficiently able to rid themselves of their surface, rote
expectations to get down to their actual abiding expectations about
poetry. It was such readers as well as such poetry that Yeats had in mind
when he ended his verses rejecting the embroidered brocade of his early
work with the lines:

> For there's more enterprise
> In walking naked.

And it was the poetry which came out of that enterprise made him put
this in a letter to Dorothy Wellesley: "When I come to write poetry I
seem—I suppose because it is all instinct with me—completely ignorant."
The excitement and the difficulty of the enterprise show in another
letter: "I have several ballads, poignant things I believe, more poignant
than anything I have written. They have now come to an end I think,
and I must go back to the poems of civilisation."

To push the process one step further, it was perhaps the contemplation
of a combination of both kinds of poetry, that led him to write a month
later, with the proof sheets of *A Vision* just done, and with all the burden
of that effort, so abstract in frame and so learned in its special rash
fashion, so concrete in intention and detail, that he had begun "to see
things double—doubled in history, world history, personal history. . . .
In my own life I never felt so acutely the presence of a spiritual virtue
and that is accompanied by intensified desire. Perhaps there is a theme
for poetry in this 'double swan and shadow.' You must feel plunged as I
do into the madness of vision, into a sense of the relation of separated
things that you cannot explain, and that deeply disturbs emotion."

Yeats as a poet was indeed a double man and the drive of one half was
always encroaching upon the drive of the other half, the one richening,
quickening, anchoring, disfiguring the other, as the case might be. The
one half was always, to come back to our poem, infecting the other with
the violence and inevitability of an apparition, proof, as he wrote in
"Under Ben Bulben,"

> Proof that there's a purpose set
> Before the secret working mind:
> Profane perfection of mankind.

Let these lines be an example as well as a commentary; and let the example, before we are done, flow back into the whole poem with a kind of extra resilience for our having pulled it out taut. The lines have their prose meaning clear and immediate enough for the purposes of quotation, a meaning that brings up as something of a puzzler only, at first sight, on the word profane. Just what that word signifies here I don't know in any sense that I can communicate. But I am certain that its meanings are plural, and that neither Yeats nor his poem may have intended to apply all of them. It is one of those words which, looked at, gets ahead of all its uses and makes something unexpected of its context, as words in poetry should. As it seems to have in it the theme—that which is held in tension—of the poems I want to discuss, some of the meanings may be elaborated a little.

There are meanings over the horizon, meanings that loom, and meanings that heave like the sea-swell under the bows, and among them, when you think of them all, it is hard to say which is which, since any one gradually passes through the others. There is the traditional association of profane with Sacred and Profane Love. There is profane in the sense of violated, of common in the good sense, of racy rather than austere, of instinctive or passionate rather than inspired. There is profane in the sense of known to everybody, to the uninitiate, known in ignorance without articulation. And there is also profane in the etymological sense, still thriving in Donne, the sense which the other senses only get back to, the sense which has to do with that which is outside or before the temple; and this suggests, of course, profane in the senses of the impious, the disorderly, the random, even the wicked, the lustful: all that is anathema to the absolute or obsessed mind. To elaborate further is vain waste, for with what we have the context begins to draw the meanings in, and begins to illustrate, too, in passing, to what degree the poet using this mode of language cannot help ad-libbing, playing, with his most inevitable-seeming words: he cannot possibly control or exclude or include all their meanings.

But to return to the text. Wondering a little whether profane is not alternatively both verb and adjective, we attach it to the word perfection, enhanced or confused as we may have rendered it. Profane perfection! what is that but man's perfection outside the temple of his aspiration, the perfection from which his aspiration sprang, and yet a perfection which cannot be felt except in apposition to the temple. Let all the meanings of profane play in the nexus, here surely is the madness of vision, the "sense of the relation of separated things that you cannot explain," into which, with his double view, Yeats felt he had plunged. But we are not finished; we are not yet concrete enough. If we go back a little in the poem, and remind ourselves that Yeats is only developing his admonition to the sculptor and poet to

> Bring the soul of man to God.
> Make him fill the cradles right,

then the relatedness between profane and perfection becomes almost a matter of sensation; and indeed does become so if we now at last take the lines as they come. We see, as in the Apparitions poem, how the ad-libbing of notions and images finally works full meaning out of the final reading of profane perfection.

> Measurement began our might:
> Forms a stark Egyptian thought,
> Forms that gentler Phidias wrought.
> Michael Angelo left a proof
> On the Sistine Chapel roof,
> Where but half-awakened Adam
> Can disturb globe-trotting Madam
> Till her bowels are in heat,
> Proof that there's a purpose set
> Before the secret working mind:
> Profane perfection of mankind.

It should be noted that we have deliberately begun with two poems where the ad-libbing is for the most part done with material that may well have been derived from Yeats's system; at least it may all be found outlined in *A Vision* or in the *Autobiographies*. We have plain examples of the system affording the poet's imagination the chance to create what it chose: it gave backing, movement, situation to the intuitive assertions, and the intuitions, working backward, make the rest seem concrete. The reader will not now object, I think, if I insist that here as in the other poem all except the lines quoted separately could have as well been different, most of all could have been their own opposites without injury to the meaning which is under the lines. I believe that this is one of the freedoms of imagination consequent upon having a sufficiently complex system of reference, though I know, as Yeats knew, that there are other ways of securing similar freedom. There is that freedom, for example, which would have come had Yeats set the course of his poem according to the first of the four bearings mentioned above: had there been enough mythology put into this particular patchwork of his system to keep his invention a little nearer the minimum. Thus we can say that as it stands there is a little too much tacking to the poem. The famous sonnet to "Leda and the Swan" gives us the nearly perfect example of the fusion of mythology and system and intuitive assertion so dramatized in crisis as to provide an inexhaustible symbol in contemplation without loss of intensity. This poem I have dealt with elsewhere, and here only add that the circulating presence of the myth, like the blush of blood in the face, brings the underlying richness of meaning nearer the surface, and nearer, if you like, too, to the expectations of the learned reader, than the poems we have just examined. There is less in the meanings but curiously more in the words themselves that could have been different; which is witness that the reality of myth is much further beneath the words in which it happens to appear than mere unmoored philosophy can be.

An example halfway between the two comes to hand in the short poem called "Death," which had it been given but a situation, a place in history, and the man in it a name, would have been a myth in little.

> Nor dread nor hope attend
> A dying animal;
> A man awaits his end
> Dreading and hoping all;
> Many times he died,
> Many times rose again.
> A great man in his pride
> Confronting murderous men
> Casts derision upon
> Supersession of breath;
> He knows death to the bone—
> Man has created death.

Here lines five to nine provide out of Yeats's system the *necessary* stuffing to complete the interval between dread and hope and the supersession of breath; they both could be too readily something else and too much invite expansion in terms of Yeats's known field of reference. Yet the splendid word supersession almost makes up for them, almost removes from them their murk of facileness; for supersession, mind you, means both plain stoppage and the condition (here death) of having become superfluous. As it stands, I think it is one of those poems that tremble between on the one hand collapse and on the other hand supreme assertion. It depends on what voice you hear or say the poem in. It allows but does not itself release a great gesture.

The trouble is, generally, that not all a man wishes to write always finds for itself bodily support in existing myth, and that, too, even if it did, most readers would be insufficiently familiar with the machinery of the myth used to understand the development to which it had been pushed without the use of reference books. This has been my experience in a practical way with readers of "Leda and the Swan." The skill of nearly instinctive, deposited understanding of the classic myths has become either mechanical or muddled where it has not disappeared; and without such a skill in his reader the poet cannot use his own, and is driven inward. Specifically, the trouble with Yeats was that the system that he had been driven to invent in despite of both Christianity and rationalism, did not in actuality leave him free to create what he chose more than, say, half the time. Thus as a poet he was left in the dubious position of being unable to believe in his own system more than half the time; he was constantly coming on things which his system could not explain, and which he was yet compelled to turn into poetry.

Yeats's solution was to wipe out of his consciousness the whole middle class, the educated class, the Christian class, the rationalist class, both as subject matter and for direct audience, and write poems addressed to a double-faced class of his own creation, which luckily includes a part of us all, half peasant or fisherman or beggar, half soldier or poet, half lord and half lout. It was as if, groping for Dante's luck he had come suddenly on Villon's, but with the knowledge of Dante in his blood beating in furious aspiration and with the burning indignation of Swift blinding his eyes with light: Dante the "chief imagination of Christendom" and

> Swift beating on his breast in sibylline frenzy blind
> Because the heart in his blood-sodden breast had dragged him
>   down into mankind.

Villon's luck was enough as Yeats used it in the poems I think of— the best of the Crazy Jane poems and the best of his other three groups with a similar ballad-like surface and subterranean symbolism—Villon's luck was enough to make the hair stand up cold on end. This quality is present only in the best of these poems; in others there is a deal of aimless and irredeemable violence, or worst of all an aimlessness without violence. One can say immediately, with this discrepancy in mind, that in the successful poems the machinery is fused in the dramatized symbol, and that in the worst there is not enough machinery—whether from Yeats's system or from the general machinery of the tradition—to bring the symbolism to light, let alone dramatize it. But to say that is to make phrases too easily, and actually to ignore what we pretend to judge. Let us rather exhibit what poetic facts we can in both good and bad examples, and see whether the poems do not render judgment themselves.

There is a kind of general fact involved when in the phrase above the hair is said to stand up *cold* on end; there is a kind of coldness in the sense of remoteness about the best Yeats that we do not find either in Dante or Villon or Swift; the kind of coldness which we associate with the activities of a will incapable of remorse or compunction or humility: the kind of coldness that reverses itself only as the heat of a quarrel, the violence of assault, the fire of the merely tumescent emotions. I do not speak of the man but of the poetry, which he made, as he said, out of his antithetical self: the self which in his old age he called old Rocky Face, that *other* self for which he wrote this epitaph in a moment of rage against Rilke's warmer ideas about death—

> *Cast a cold eye*
> *On life, on death.*
> *Horseman, pass by!*

The coldness of this created self shows most, I think, in the fact that none of the human figures in his poems—most of them nameless, for to name, he thought, was to pin the butterfly—are created as individuals. They are rather types dramatized as if they were individuals. They move as all that is typical must in a separated space. There is a barrier between them and wholly individual being which is set up by the fact that they cannot ever quite overcome the abstractions from which they sprang. Thus when Yeats pushed furthest to escape from his system he was in most peril of collapsing into it, which is what fills his figures—his Crazy Jane, his Bishop, his men and women Young and Old—with the focusing force of dramatic crisis. It is his system precariously dramatized, the abstract felt as concrete: the allegorical simulacrum churned with action. The point is, the system *is* dramatized, the typical figures *are* liberated into action, however precariously, which we can and do experience as actual within their limited focus. And the curiosity is, they are liberated most, seem most nearly individuals crying out, when inspection shows they are in fact most nearly commentaries upon some notion or notions taken out of Yeats's system. Man being man and in his senses, right or wrong, even as a poet, there is vertigo in wondering whether Yeats at bottom is giving us "felt thought" or is giving us a generalized version of what he could grasp of certain fundamental, self-created symbols of love and death. Is it insight or experience that is invoked, or a third thing which is neither but reveals both?

I do not mean to be mystifying—there is enough of that in Yeats— but I find it difficult to ascribe the right quality to such lines as come at the end of the seventh poem in "A Woman Young and Old." It is a dialogue between lovers in three quatrains and a distich called "Parting," and the first ten lines in which the two argue in traditional language whether dawn requires the lover to leave, are an indifferent competent ad-libbing to prepare for the end. The stable element or

symbol is the singing bird, and it is almost a version of "The bird of
dawning singeth all night long," which indeed as a title would have
strengthened the poem. It ends:

> *She.* That light is from the moon.
>
> *He.* That bird . . .
>
> *She.*   Let him sing on,
>   I offer to love's play
>   My dark declivities.

Declivities—my dark downward slopes—seems immediately the word that
clinches the poem and delivers it out of the amorphous into form, and
does so as a relatively abstract word acting in the guise of a focus for the
concrete, delicately in syllable but with a richness of impact that develops
and trembles, a veritable tumescence in itself of the emotion wanted. Call
it lust and you have nothing, certainly not lust; call it as the poem does
and you do have lust as a theme, and life caught in the theme. But the
last two lines do not perform that feat by themselves; the situation is
needed, the bird, the dawn, the song, and the moon, perhaps the moon
most of all. The moon is all machinery, and very equivocal machinery
out of Yeats's system. To use John Ransom's terms, does the moon supply
structure to the declivities, or does the word declivities supply texture to
the moon? Or is there a kind of being set up between the two, a being
which is the created value of both? If so, and I think that this is one way
of putting it, can we not say that Yeats has created a sort of rudimentary
symbol, nameless but deeply recognizable, good in any apt repetition?
Is not that what this sort of poetry is for? In what else does its immanent
richness consist?

Yeats did the same thing again in "The Lover's Song" from *Last
Poems.*

> Bird sighs for the air,
> Thought for I know not where,
> For the womb the seed sighs.
> Now sinks the same rest
> On mind, on nest,
> On straining thighs.

The illuminating, synergizing word here, without which the rest is
nothing but maundering, is of course the word sighs; but I am afraid
it will not take analysis. Fortunately there is pertinent material from
Yeats's letters to Dorothy Wellesley. First, there is a phrase from Yeats's

introduction to *The Selected Poems of Dorothy Wellesley*, which has an incipient connection to his own poem: "in the hush of night are we not conscious of the unconceived." Next there is a letter in which Yeats describes the reproductions of pictures on one wall of his bedroom: "Botticelli's 'Spring,' Gustave Moreau's 'Women and Unicorns,' Fragonard's 'Cup of Life.' . . . The first & last sense, & the second mystery— the mystery that touches the genitals, a blurred touch through a curtain." Evidently these phrases got him going, for the next day he sent the poem quoted in a letter beginning: "After I had written to you I tried to find better words to explain what I meant by the touch from behind the curtain. This morning, this came."

In comparing this poem with "Parting," there is the important difference that here the symbolic line could ride by itself, so that if it were plausible in English to have poems of one line, "For the womb the seed sighs" would be enough, and would make its own work of application wherever apt. English poetry being what it is, we say rather that the line infects the rest of the poem with its symbolic richness. But in saying that, it should not be forgotten that it is not a situation but something as primitive as a pulse that the poem dramatizes.

If the reader objects to the ascription of such qualities as rudimentary and primitive to the symbols in these two poems, I mean them so only relatively and do not at all mean that they lack complexity. Primitive symbols like primitive languages are likely to be more complex than those in which the mind has a longer history at work. This will be clear I think if we look now at the poem called "Crazy Jane Talks With the Bishop" (the second, not the first of that name). In this poem the Bishop tells Crazy Jane she is old enough to die and had better leave off the sin of flesh, but she answers him valiantly in the flesh, ending:

> "A woman can be proud and stiff
> When on love intent;
> But love has pitched his mansion in
> The place of excrement;
> For nothing can be sole or whole
> That has not been rent."

This is like the "torn and most whole" symbolism of Eliot's *Ash Wednesday* and of much other religious poetry, but it is also like the sexual symbolism in *Lear* and in Swift's poems, and again is like some of the "lighter" sexual poems of Blake, where the lightness of the verse forms covers profound observation; indeed, it is a fusion, with something added, of all three. Beyond that, as a trope it is an enantiosis, which includes as well as expresses its own opposite. Further, and in fact, it is an enantiodromia, the shocked condition, the turning point, where a thing *becomes* its own opposite, than which there is no place at once more terrifying and more fortifying to find oneself in. Feeling and sensation and intuition and thought are all covertly at work here, and what we see is the sudden insight at the end of a long converging train.

It may be risked that this insight, this symbol, cannot be as easily "used" as those of the two poems just discussed. As there is a great deal more development of all kinds behind this stanza, so a greater stature of response is required of the reader. At first it merely makes the hair stand on end; only later it reveals itself as an object of contemplation. Neither the terror nor the strength will show, nor will they resolve themselves in full symbolic value, unless the reader gets over the shock of the passage and begins to feel, even if he does not analyze, the extraordinary plurisignativeness of the words of the verses, taken both separately and together. I doubt if even in "Sailing to Byzantium" Yeats ever packed so much into the language of his poetry. The words are fountains of the "fury and the mire in human veins." Yet none of the meanings are abstruse or require a dictionary; none of them are derived directly from Yeats's system, but come rather from the whole history of the common language of the mind, or as Yeats calls it of the soul. The reader has been long at home with all these words, yet as he reflects he will perceive that he has never known them in this particular completeness before. It was only the convention of this poem that Yeats invented; the rest was discovery of what had long since been created. The terror is in recognition, the strength in the image which compels assent: a recognition and an assent which it is the proper business of the symbolic imagination to bring about, whether as philosophy or as myth, or as the poetry of either.

Yeats commonly hovered between myth and philosophy, except for transcending flashes, which is why he is not one of the greatest poets. His ambition was too difficult for accomplishment; or his gift too small to content him. His curse was not that he rebelled against the mind of his age, which was an advantage for poetry, considering that mind, but that he could not create, except in fragments, the actuality of his age, as we can see Joyce and Mann and it may be Eliot, in equal rebellion, nevertheless doing. Yeats, to use one of his own lines, had "to wither into the truth." That he made himself into the greatest poet in English since the seventeenth century, was only possible because in that withering he learned how to create fragments of the actual, not of his own time to which he was unequal, but of all time of which he was a product.

To create greatly is to compass great disorder. Yeats suffered from a predominant survival in him of that primitive intellect which insists on asserting absolute order at the expense of the rational imagination; hence his system, made absolute by the resort to magic and astrology, which produced the tragic poetry appropriate to it. But hence, too, when the system failed him, his attempt to create a dramatic, concrete equivalent for it. If the examples we have chosen are fairly taken, he found himself ad-libbing—as most poets do—most of the time. But his ad-libbing was in the grand manner and produced passages of great and luminous poetry. He was on the right track; "Homer was his example and his unchristened heart"; and more than any man of his time he upheld the dignity of his profession and re-opened the way for those of us who have the fortitude and the ability to follow, and the scope to go beyond him, if as is unlikely any such there be. For our times are of an intolerable disorder, as we can see Yeats's were for him, and will take a great deal of compassing.

> *"I am of Ireland,*
> *And the Holy Land of Ireland,*
> *And time runs on," cried she.*
> *"Come out of charity,*
> *Come dance with me in Ireland."*

W. B. Yeats: Variations
on the Visionary Quest

by Alex Zwerdling

It is, therefore, supreme ignorance for any one to think that he can
ever attain to the high estate of union with God before he casts away
from him the desire of natural things.

St. John of the Cross

St. John's words are not intended to sum up Yeats's ideas on the
subject of the visionary quest but rather to epitomize the position which
he so strenuously opposed, particularly in his later work. They help us to
understand Yeats's important quarrel with the traditionally accepted idea
of visionary experience. As St. John suggests, the religious mind ordinarily
strives to move *toward* perfection, toward a final union with God or a
transcendent realm of spirit, and in an antinomic system of religious
belief like Christianity, this implies the logical corollary of a movement
away from "the desire of natural things," from the mortal world itself,
multitudinous, impermanent, decaying, and ultimately undesirable. It is
precisely this "necessary" corollary which Yeats could never fully accept.
The central problem of visionary experience for him, the reconciliation
of the two worlds, perfect and imperfect, grew out of his refusal to accept
the necessity of pursuing one at the expense of the other. Yeats's dis-
satisfaction with either world taken separately, his unwillingness to accept one or the other as the province of ultimate value, inspired his
attempt to reconcile the two apparently opposed realms.

This restless search for an escape from the implications of an antinomic
religious belief has been misunderstood by many of Yeats's readers. It is
a critical commonplace, for example, that in the later poetry the powerful
attraction of the mortal, physical, perishable world is seen as greater than
that of the flawless spiritual one. In reality this movement—which we

might call the rejection of the perfect—presents itself in Yeats's work from the very first, as we shall see, and yet never actually becomes powerful enough to "find," in Auden's words, "the mortal world enough."

We must trace this movement with some care in order to evaluate its importance. In Yeats's early work, the inadequacy of an independent spiritual realm is suggested most clearly by the treatment of Irish myth. The ideal world of Tir-na-n-Og, the paradise of Irish mythology and the home of the Shee or immortal fairies, was traditionally one of permanence, gaiety, and perfect bliss, a land of eternal youth and happiness. It is therefore interesting that Yeats consistently chooses incidents and characters which reveal the inadequacy of this perfect world. His most characteristic means of suggesting this is to make the "imperfect" mortal world seem highly desirable to his immortal characters. Yeats was, for example, fond of quoting a remark which George Russell ("AE") once heard "an old religious beggar" repeating: " 'God possesses the heavens, but He covets the earth—He covets the earth.' " [1]

Yeats's immortals also "covet the earth," for there is something about the mortal world, for all its limitations and imperfections, which to the flawless spiritual one seems unattainable and therefore desirable. Again and again in the early work, we find Yeats making use of this idea, as for instance in the characteristic story of the immortal fairy who snatches a mortal away to her own world. The most familiar examples which come to mind are *The Land of Heart's Desire* and *The Wanderings of Oisin*, but there are others. In a little known short story published in 1891, *Dhoya*, the pattern of the Oisin legend is reworked. Dhoya is a mortal of great strength and passion who leads a life of self-sufficient isolation for many years until an immortal fairy falls in love with him and agrees to share his mortal existence. She explains:

"Dhoya, I have left my world far off. My people—on the floor of the lake they are dancing and singing, and on the islands of the lake; always happy, always young, always without change. I have left them for thee, Dhoya, for they cannot love. Only the changing, and moody, and angry, and weary can love. . . . I left the places where they dance, Dhoya, for thee!"

Some of the stories in the 1897 collection, *The Secret Rose*, are based on a similar idea, that the people of the Shee, the "gentry" of the Irish immortal world, envy men their passions. In "The Book of the Great Dhoul and Hanrahan the Red," for instance, the fairy Cleena says to Hanrahan, "I love you, for you are fierce and passionate, and good and bad, and not dim and wave-like as are the people of the Shee." And the poem "The Host of the Air" is a variation on the story of *The Land of Heart's Desire*; here, it is O'Driscoll's bride, Bridget, who is stolen by the

[1] *The Trembling of the Veil* (London, 1922), 130.

fairies. Yeats makes clear in a note to the first edition of the collection *The Wind among the Reeds* that all of these tales merely appropriate a constant theme of Gaelic literature itself: "The old Gaelic literature is full of the appeals of the Tribes of the goddess Danu to mortals whom they would bring into their country."

Later poems and plays continue to stress the same theme. "The Grey Rock," from *Responsibilities* (1914), describes the grief of Aoife when the mortal hero she loves spurns her offer of immortality and chooses to die fighting a human battle with his king. She asks in despair,

> "Why should the faithfullest heart most love
> The bitter sweetness of false faces?
> Why must the lasting love what passes,
> Why are the gods by men betrayed?"

We can see the answer to her question in Yeats's poems, for it is man's mortality, and the way in which he squanders the precious gift of life, that gives him a kind of greatness the gods cannot possess. The point is made clearly in a poem from the same collection, "The Two Kings." Here Edain, asked to return to the immortal world by her immortal husband, spurns his offer and refuses to leave her mortal husband, the warrior Eochaid. When the former asks, uncomprehendingly, "What happiness/Can lovers have that know their happiness/Must end at the dumb stone?" Edain replies,

> "How should I love . . .
> Were it not that when the dawn has lit my bed
> And shown my husband sleeping there, I have sighed,
> 'Your strength and nobleness will pass away'? . . .
> What can they know of love that do not know
> She builds her nest upon a narrow ledge
> Above a windy precipice? . . .
> Never will I believe there is any change
> Can blot out of my memory this life
> Sweetened by death, but if I could believe,
> That were a double hunger in my lips
> For what is doubly brief."

The idea that human life is "sweetened by death" is at the heart of the paradox which is given its definitive statement in the play *The Only Jealousy of Emer* (1919). There Cuchulain, the mortal warrior-hero, rejects the woman of the Shee for "mere" humanity, and the Chorus explains,

> He that has loved the best
> May turn from a statue
> His too human breast.

And in the play *The King of the Great Clock Tower* (1934), we find the baldest answer to the question of what the immortals lack, why they descend into human life: "For desecration and the lover's night." In the words of one of Yeats's favorite poets, William Blake, "Eternity is in love with the productions of time."

It should be clear, then, that a "rejection of the perfect," with its concomitant praise of the human world of passion, is not the product of Yeats's later years but begins at the beginning of his career. It is equally misleading, however, to suggest that the movement away from perfection was more powerful in Yeats's work than the movement toward it. Certainly the "mere" mortal world was hardly the ideal state either, and few writers could have been more conscious of its imperfection than Yeats. We will see presently that the celebration of the physical world in the later poetry is never at the *expense* of the spiritual one. The problem, then, is not which to choose but how to avoid the necessity of making a choice between mortal and immortal.

Yeats found two "solutions" to this vexing problem: the first a sceptical vacillation and refusal to accept the necessity of commitment, the other an actual attempt to resolve the dichotomy. Yeats must have realized that scepticism presented a poetic problem, that in hesitating to renounce either of two contradictory worlds, his poetry was in danger of itself becoming confused, uncertain, and so robbed of its essential energy. He solved this technical problem in a technical way, by inventing a series of *personae* and using them in a kind of poetic debate. These *personae* are very distinct, dramatically conceived characters who have a clear and unambivalent point of view about the desirability of a certain way of life. The best examples are the three people involved in the story of "The Three Bushes," the lover, the lady, and the chambermaid. Each has an intense and passionate conviction despite the fact that all three are the product of a highly sceptical and "unconvinced" consciousness.

Crazy Jane is such a *persona*. She argues for the virtues of the physical life against the Christian form of spiritual experience in poems like "Crazy Jane Talks with the Bishop" and "Crazy Jane and the Bishop." Yeats uses the technique of exaggeration and caricature in these poems. The physical world is summed up in the idea of illicit sex, the spiritual in organized religion, so that the principles remain inevitably at odds. Nevertheless, they are both represented within the unified framework of one series of poems, and thus the metaphysical choice is avoided while at the same time the poetry retains its air of passionate conviction.

Yeats's *personae* are most frequently involved in a kind of debate, a natural medium for the sceptic. The method is simply to have more than one speaker, more than one point of view, represented in a single poem. "Crazy Jane Talks with the Bishop," for example, unlike "Crazy Jane and the Bishop," records a literal debate, for the Bishop is here a *persona* too, with a point of view which the poem permits him to express. Much of the later poetry exploits this technique by recording a dialogue between two or more characters about the relative value of physical and spiritual life: "Michael Robartes and the Dancer," "A Dialogue of Self and Soul," "For Anne Gregory," "Ego Dominus Tuus," and others. But if we expand the definition of "debate" a little so that it means simply the juxtaposition of opposing ideas, we can see how persistent the method actually is, for many of Yeats's poems fall into this category even though no actual verbal debate occurs: for example, "Oil and Blood," the two Byzantium poems, or "Ribh Denounces Patrick." The advantages of such a method are obvious, for a desirable ambiguity can be retained without sacrificing either clarity or the energy generated by passionate conviction.

Nevertheless, the *persona* and the debate were after all only methods; they did not resolve the vacillation in Yeats's own mind, but merely exploited it. The later poetry goes further than this by denying the necessity of an exclusive choice, by demonstrating how the soul can "attain to the high estate of union with God" *without* "casting away the desire of natural things." When one sees beyond the logically acceptable position of the inevitable conflict between one principle and its opposite, man's spiritual quest and the "desire of natural things" are seen to be simultaneous and inseparable.

The idea is succinctly stated in the last stanza of "Among School Children," in the parallel images of the chestnut tree and the dance. Here is a world where "body is not bruised to pleasure soul":

> O chestnut-tree, great-rooted blossomer,
> Are you the leaf, the blossom or the bole?
> O body swayed to music, O brightening glance,
> How can we know the dancer from the dance?

The antithesis between mortal and immortal is here stated in Platonic terms, but the answer to these rhetorical questions is clear enough: because the ideal world of forms intersects the actual world of particulars at innumerable points, the two are almost indistinguishable. We cannot "know the dancer from the dance" because they are inseparable. Most of the characters in the poem are incapable of understanding this fact: the nuns and mothers, who worship only the images of perfection; the philosopher who, like the misguided Plato, thinks "nature but a spume that plays/Upon a ghostly paradigm of things." But the true visionary, here and in the later poetry of Yeats, does not leave the actual world behind in the moment of vision. He sees *both* the tree and its form, both the dancer and the dance, in one instant of time.

The most important metaphor which Yeats uses to describe the intersection of the two worlds is that of sex, a fact which might suggest that he is praising the world of flesh at the expense of the world of spirit. That is not, however, the case. Yeats pictures sexual experience as a moment of ecstasy which takes man, in a kind of transport, out of himself. It is important to remember that before the word "ecstasy" became part of the language of the marriage manuals, it was used to describe religious experience. Yeats exploits the word in its modern ambiguity. The poem "Solomon and the Witch," for example, records such an ecstasy:

> "Last night, where under the wild moon
> On grassy mattress I had laid me,
> Within my arms great Solomon,
> I suddenly cried out in a strange tongue,
> Not his, not mine."

And in the poem "Ribh Denounces Patrick," the metaphor is reversed and the suggestion made that eternal creation is like sexual reproduction on earth:

> Natural and supernatural with the self-same ring are wed.
> As man, as beast, as an ephemeral fly begets, Godhead begets Godhead.

In Yeats's final view of the visionary, then, physical and spiritual are seen as inseparable, mutually dependent, and simultaneous. The change is recorded in the two Byzantium poems. The earlier "Sailing to Byzantium" is a "debate" which emphasizes the dichotomy between physical and spiritual very sharply. "That country" and "the holy city" are set against each other, the one a world of youth, sex, and decay, the other a world of art, religion, and the changeless. The speaker in the poem does not reconcile these two but abandons one for the other: "Once out of nature I shall never take/My bodily form from any natural thing." Although the later "Byzantium" superficially exploits the same contrast, the last stanza in particular shows that there is an essential difference. The perfect world of Byzantium and the changing world of "the fury and the mire of human veins" are not only connected literally by the constant trips of the dolphins but seen as mutually dependent on each other. Although it is true that the poem records the process whereby mortal becomes immortal, it is also true that this process is described in metaphors of eating and burning, and that the mortal world provides the necessary food and fuel to keep the immortal world alive. And it is significant that the final image of the poem is not of the eternal world, but of the world of nature which is feeding it:

> Astraddle on the dolphin's mire and blood,
> Spirit after spirit! The smithies break the flood,
> The golden smithies of the Emperor!
> Marbles of the dancing floor
> Break bitter furies of complexity,
> Those images that yet
> Fresh images beget,
> That dolphin-torn, that gong-tormented sea.

To put the matter succinctly, the idea of an actual world intersected at innumerable points by a spiritual one appealed to Yeats because it raised the actual world to an ultimate level, thus making its rejection unnecessary, while at the same time it created an opportunity for ecstatic visionary experience which did not leave man's world behind. In such a view, the actual physical world became sacred territory. Yeats felt that these ideas echoed Plotinus, the philosopher whom he read with such enthusiasm in 1926. Plotinus, he says,

> was the first to establish as sole source the timeless individuality, or daimon, instead of the Platonic Idea, to prefer Socrates to his thought. This timeless individuality contains archetypes of all possible existence whether of man or of brute. . . . Plotinus thought that we should not 'baulk at this limitlessness of the intellectual; it is an infinitude having nothing to do with number or part' (Ennead V. 7. I.) *yet it seems that it can at will re-enter number and part and thereby make itself apparent to our minds.* If we accept this idea, many strange or beautiful things become credible. . . . All about us there seems to start up a precise, inexplicable, teeming life, and *the earth becomes once more, not in rhetorical metaphor, but in reality, sacred.*[2]

This notion of the earth itself as sacred, along with the possibility that spiritual reality can "make itself apparent to our minds," appealed greatly to Yeats. It is no wonder, then, that Plotinus becomes the hero of some of the later poems and is usually contrasted with Plato, as in the two related poems "The Delphic Oracle upon Plotinus" and "News for the Delphic Oracle." In both, Plotinus is pictured as striving to reach the safe harbor of Platonic Love, a world of perfection, but still "buffeted by such seas" and with "salt blood" blocking his eyes. As in the Byzantium poems, the sea represents the physical world of passion and blood. It is therefore significant that Plotinus reaches the shore only after a passionate struggle

---

[2] *The Words upon the Window Pane* (Dublin, 1934), 32-3. Italics mine.

with the sea, while Plato and the stately "choir of Love" look on blandly from the safety of the shore.

It should be pointed out, however, that Yeats evolved this ideal of the intersection of the spiritual and actual worlds only in the work of his last fifteen or twenty years, and that the early poetry is based for the most part on the traditional dichotomy between spiritual and physical—without, as has been pointed out, always preferring the former. Unlike the visionary hero of the later Yeats, the seer of the early poetry is forced to abandon the mortal world if he wants to reach the spiritual one. The predominant symbol of spiritual reality in these poems and plays is the island, separated from the mainland and providing a kind of absolute isolation from it. We might say that there is a gradual shift in Yeats's poetry from the *goal* of the spiritual quest to the quest itself, and that metaphorically this can be seen in the later poetry in the greater use of the images of the sea and of water—symbolizing the quest—which replace the numberless islands of the early work.

An interesting example of the early ideal of the isolated island of spiritual contemplation is Yeats's plan (mentioned first in the Nineties) for a "Castle of the Heroes," to be located on an unoccupied island in Lough Key.[3] There the finest men and women could retire, very much like monks to a monastery, for spiritual contemplation, and there they might "establish mysteries like those of Eleusis and Samothrace." [4] The plan suggests the necessity of divorcing oneself completely from the actual world in order to find the spiritual one, and thus emphasizes the distinction between Yeats's early and late views. The same idea is suggested in *The Shadowy Waters*, when Forgael says that it is only "where the world ends" that the "mind is made unchanging," and finds "Miracle, ecstasy, the impossible hope." In *Where There Is Nothing* (1902), the hero insists that "We must destroy the World; we must destroy everything that has Law and Number, for where there is nothing, there is God." He has learned, he says, "that one needs a religion so wholly supernatural, that is so opposed to the order of nature that the world can never capture it." The Yeats of the Twenties and Thirties would never have accepted such a statement. As early as 1888 he was already writing to Katharine Tynan, "I have noticed some things about my poetry I did not know before, in this process of correction; for instance, that it is almost all a flight into fairyland from the real world, and a summons to that flight." [5] But many years were to pass before Yeats could combine in

[3] See Richard Ellmann, *Yeats: The Man and the Masks* (New York, 1948), 121-3.

[4] *Poems, 1899-1905* (London, 1906). These lines were not in the first version of *The Shadowy Waters*.

[5] *W. B. Yeats: Letters to Katharine Tynan*, ed. Roger McHugh (Dublin and London, 1953), 47.

his imagination the "flight into fairyland" with the real world from which the flight began.

The change in Yeats's thought can best be understood in terms of the traditional faculties of man: reason, imagination, and the passions. Ordinarily, we consider the former two the less "earth-bound," reason being often identified as "man's divine spark." In Yeats's early poetry, accordingly, much more stress is laid on the so-called higher faculties of reason and imagination. Through them (and particularly, as in the romantic poets, through the imagination at work in dreams and visions) man may reach the world of spirit. The reversal comes first in some of the poems in the 1920 collection, *Michael Robartes and the Dancer*. At this point it is the "passions" which become the higher faculty, and the link between them and visionary experience is clearly made in several poems: "Solomon and the Witch," "An Image from a Past Life," "Towards Break of Day." In the later poetry, this connection is retained, the only significant change being that human "passions" become interpreted in a more and more blatantly sexual way. At the same time, there is a complementary rejection of and exaggerated contempt for reason alone, as in the poem "A Prayer for Old Age":

> God guard me from those thoughts men think
> In the mind alone;
> He that sings a lasting song
> Thinks in a marrow-bone.

In the *Pages from a Diary Written in Ninteen Hundred and Thirty*, Yeats sees himself "set in a drama where I struggle to exalt and overcome concrete realities perceived not with mind only but as with the roots of my hair. The passionless reasoners are pariah dogs and devour the dead symbols."

We may legitimately ask why this reversal took place, why it is now man's physical and passionate life which opens the doors to the spiritual world. There is, of course, a possible biographical explanation, for the praise of physical life seems always to be connected with another theme in Yeats's later poetry, the lament for old age. In poem after poem this juxtaposition is made: "Among School Children," "The Tower," "A Prayer for Old Age," "The Wild Old Wicked Man," "Politics," and many others, including the Crazy Jane poems. "The Tower" answers the question of what connection there is between old age and the praise of physical life, for here we see that age brings with it a narrowing of the possibilities of life. "Decrepit age" has made the life of passion impossible, and one must reconcile oneself and "be content with argument and deal/ In abstract things." In a sense, then, the poems of old age continue a basic pattern established early in Yeats's work, that of longing for the unattainable and scorning the easily attainable. The only difference is that the terms have been reversed. In youth it was abstraction, wisdom, philosophy which one longed for, because they seemed so difficult to reach. In old age, on the other hand, the physical vigor which has been so prodigally wasted in youth seems much more desirable than the "wisdom" which has come.

Yet the neatness of such an explanation obscures a more important reason for the great emphasis on the value of the actual world in the late poetry. In a letter to John O'Leary written in 1892, Yeats suggests that he has made "magic"—meaning by this the cultivation of the means of discovering the spiritual world—"next to my poetry the most important pursuit of my life." [6] It is highly significant that he thus places artistic creation first, for Yeats never really changed his mind about this hierarchy. If anything, his art seemed always to become more and more demanding. And art, he came to realize, must inevitably begin with the actual physical world and cannot ever completely bypass it. During the period when Ezra Pound acted as Yeats's secretary (1913-16), Yeats asked him to go through his poetry and point out all the abstract words he could find. The number was so startling that Yeats embarked upon a systematic attempt to de-emphasize abstraction in his work. Pound convinced him that a vague "spiritual" language was the curse of the poetry of the Nineties, and that all poetry must be more strongly rooted in the actual and the physical than Yeats's had been heretofore.

Here, then, is a partial explanation of the constant insistence in the later poetry that art begins with physical reality and the actual world rather than with abstraction. To those who feel that lust and rage are not fit subjects for an old man's poetry, Yeats answers in "The Spur," "What else have I to spur me into song?" And in "Vacillation," the Heart gets the better of a dialogue with the Soul:

> THE SOUL. Seek out reality, leave things that seem.
> THE HEART. What, be a singer born and lack a theme?

Despite the attractions (such as they are) of a life of pure spirit, the artist's example must be "Homer . . . and his unchristened heart," the Homer whose theme was not salvation but "original sin." Finally, in "The Circus Animals' Desertion," the most uncompromising poem on this subject, Yeats speculates on the origin of all the spiritual images of the artist. Though they "grow in pure mind," their origin is not only in the actual world, but in the most grossly physical part of it. The "ladders" of artistic creation all lead up from "the foul rag-and-bone shop of the heart":

[6] *Some Letters from W. B. Yeats to John O'Leary and His Sister*, ed. Allan Wade (New York, 1953), 14.

Those masterful images because complete
Grew in pure mind, but out of what began?
A mound of refuse or the sweepings of a street,
Old kettles, old bottles, and a broken can,
Old iron, old bones, old rags, that raving slut
Who keeps the till. Now that my ladder's gone,
I must lie down where all the ladders start,
In the foul rag-and-bone shop of the heart.

These, then, are two possible explanations, biographical and aesthetic, for the increased emphasis on the actual world, on man's physical and passionate nature, in the later poetry of Yeats. For all that emphasis, however, it cannot be repeated too often that Yeats's celebration of the physical world in the poetry of the last years is never at the expense of the visionary goal, is never proof that the mortal world taken independently is enough. Though it is the place "where all the ladders start," it is not where they end. Only the *means* to vision had undergone an important transformation. As a result of the shift from the "higher" faculties to the "lower," true vision now seemed possible in ecstatic transcendence through, rather than apart from, the physical world. This idea of the intersection of physical and spiritual experience seemed to open a new world of visionary possibility and to resolve the self-destructive antagonism of flesh and spirit in poems like "Sailing to Byzantium."

The apparent dichotomy of mortal and immortal, then, is seen finally as potential harmony, for man "thinks in a marrow-bone" and "perceives" with "the roots of his hair." Yet at the same time, we realize with Yeats that even this is in a sense a false resolution. For though man may be able to combine physical life with spiritual truth, though it is true that visionary experience is within man's scope, the ultimate fruition is still denied to the Yeatsian seer: his "vision" does not last. We get a sense of this when Sheba, in describing her visionary experience to Solomon, suddenly realizes that it has been nothing but a momentary release from a humdrum existence: " 'Yet the world stays.' " And here is the basic problem with all of Yeats's visionaries, that, in spite of a momentary fruition, "the world stays," and the ordinary conditions of life are re-established. The very metaphor of sexual union obviously emphasizes the transience of the experience, but even in poems which do not describe "ecstasy" in strictly sexual terms, the visionary state is at best a few moments snatched from the immense flow of time, as the poem "Vacillation" suggests:

While on the shop and street I gazed
My body of a sudden blazed;
And twenty minutes more or less

> It seemed, so great my happiness,
> That I was blessèd and could bless.

Although time and eternity may occasionally intersect, Yeats's visionary is always ultimately frustrated by the reassertion of the laws of time. Even in the early "Song of Wandering Aengus" (1897), the vision of the "glimmering girl" almost instantly fades "through the brightening air," and Aengus spends the rest of his life in a fruitless search to recapture the lost vision. The frustration of the devoted visionary in the play *At the Hawk's Well* is even more complete, for here Cuchulain's search for spiritual reality is frustrated by the guardian hawks who cast a spell over him whenever the water—which represents the immortal here—rushes into the well. Yeats's visionary then, like all his other heroic men, is not a success but a failure, and it is only through the transcendence of that failure and the despair which it might bring that he becomes truly heroic.

The philosophic implications of this frustrated search for ultimate truth were described in Yeats's *A Vision*. In that book, he formulated a theory of history based upon a notion of human existence as a series of endlessly repetitive cycles. "Immortality," for man at least, was simply the necessity of rebirth after rebirth in age after age. Yeats's system is, of course, a variation of the familiar idea which Mircea Eliade has called the "myth of the eternal return," but it is essential to stress that it is not conceived as moving toward a clear terminal point and thus creating the sense of direction and meaning. Rather, existence seems to repeat itself eternally, life following upon life, civilization upon civilization, the second coming following the first, and no doubt, the third following that, and so on. What hope does such a system offer man in his search for apocalypse, for a spiritual world no longer subject to the frustrating exclusive reassertion of time?

The escape from the "wheel" of existence is, I think, stressed unduly by some interpreters of Yeats, particularly by Ellmann in his *Yeats: The Man and the Masks*.[7] It is true, as Ellmann says, that Yeats postulates an eventual release in something which he calls the "thirteenth cycle." Yet this scarcely makes his system a very optimistic one, since the knowledge of this ultimate reality is denied to man and "has kept the secret." [8] Unfortunately, "the day is far off when the two halves of man can define each its own unity . . . and so escape out of the Wheel." [9] As Yeats says in his essay on *Prometheus Unbound*, "Divinity moves outside our antinomies, it may be our lot to worship in terror."

It is clear, then, that Yeats offers no easy faith to his visionaries. But it is also clear that his last poems emphasize the supreme necessity of conquering the despair which such a gloomy view of the universe might

---

[7] See pp. 281-4.   [8] *A Vision* (London, 1937), 302.   [9] *A Vision* (London, 1925), 215.

generate. Yeats devoted much thought to the final problem of how the visionary, caught in a cyclical pattern of existence which can only minimize the meaning of his achievement, is to react to the knowledge that his own momentary vision has little meaning and no permanence in the endless repetition of human events. Despair itself is destructive and makes any kind of heroic achievement impossible. Under no circumstances, then, must the visionary hero give way to it. To an inevitably tragic situation, he perpetually sings a song of innocence rather than of weary wisdom and disillusionment.

The false "resolution" of the antithesis between mortal and immortal thus leads ultimately to an exaltation of man himself, for its pessimistic message is a test of heroic resiliency. If ultimate reality—or God—is unattainable except in rare and irregular moments of ecstatic communion, the "joyous" visionary himself becomes of supreme importance, for his heroic acceptance of the situation is at least self-generated and self-sustained. In a sense, then, Yeats's variations on the visionary quest lead him closer and closer to a position which we might call consecrated humanism, the elevation of humanity to near-Godlike status. Man's ultimate and inevitable defeat makes his refusal to surrender and his occasional triumph all the more meaningful and offers the consolation that

> Whatever flames upon the night
> Man's own resinous heart has fed.

Yeats's Byzantium Poems:
A Study of Their Development

by Curtis Bradford

I. *Background*

Yeats's interest in Byzantine art and civilization began in the Nineties and continued through his life. The first issue of "Rosa Alchemica" (1896) refers to the mosaic work at Ravenna ("mosaic not less beautiful than the mosaic in the Baptistery at Ravenna, but of a less severe beauty"),[1] work which Yeats probably saw when in 1907 he travelled in Italy with Lady Gregory. Unfortunately, Yeats has left us no account of his visit to Ravenna. A revision of "The Holy Places," final section of *Discoveries,* made for the 1912 edition of *The Cutting of an Agate,* shows that between 1906 and 1912 Yeats's knowledge of Byzantine history had increased. In 1906 he wrote of "an unstable equilibrium of the whole European mind that would not have come had Constantinople wall been built of better stone"; in 1912 this became "had John Palaeologus cherished, despite that high and heady look . . . a hearty disposition to fight the Turk." In preparation for the "Dove or Swan" section of *A Vision,* which Yeats finished at Capri in February 1925, and left virtually unchanged in the revised *A Vision* of 1937, Yeats read several books[2] about

"Yeats's Byzantium Poems: A Study of Their Development." This essay is a revision of an essay which appeared in PMLA, LXXV (March 1960), pp. 110-125. Copyright © 1960 by Curtis B. Bradford and Mrs. W. B. Yeats.

[1] The reference to "Byzantine mosaic" in the final text of "Rosa Alchemica" (*Early Poems and Stories,* New York, 1925, p. 467) is not to be found in the first edition (*The Secret Rose,* London, 1897, p. 224). Yeats added the reference while revising "Rosa Alchemica" for *Early Poems and Stories.* All manuscript material used is in the collection of Mrs. W. B. Yeats. Quotations are made by permission of Mrs. Yeats, The Macmillan Company, and A. P. Watt & Son.

[2] The following books about Byzantium are in Yeats's library: O. M. Dalton, *Byzantine Art and Archaeology;* W. G. Holmes, *The Age of Justinian and Theodora,* Vol. I; Mrs. Arthur Strong, *Apotheosis and After Life;* Josef Strzygowski, *Origin of Christian Church Art* (trans. by Dalton and Braunholtz). Yeats annotated only the Holmes, and of Holmes only the first chapter, "Constantinople in the Sixth Century," an elaborate reconstructive description of Byzantium in Justinian's time. Nearly every page of this chapter was marked. Yeats could not have derived his favorable opinion of Byzantine culture from Holmes, whose attitude toward his subject is both condescending and unfriendly. Yeats also collected reproductions of Byzantine mosaics.

Byzantine art and civilization and studied Byzantine mosaics in Rome
and Sicily. He did not return to Ravenna, being fearful of its miasmal
air. Once Byzantium had found a place in "the System," it shortly appeared in the poetry, first in "Sailing to Byzantium," and "Wisdom"
(1926-27); then changed, though not utterly, in "Byzantium" (1930).

II. *The Two Byzantiums*

From his reading and, especially, from his experience of Byzantine art
Yeats constructed Byzantium, his golden city of the imagination. The
Byzantium to which we travel in "Sailing to Byzantium" is Justinian's
city as Yeats described it in "Dove or Swan," an imagined land where
Unity of Being has permeated an entire culture. Yeats wrote three com-
ments on this poem in a manuscript book and two radio speeches.

The comment in the manuscript book is part of an account of a
séance Yeats had with a London medium, Mrs. Cooper. Since Yeats wrote
a longer and already published account of a "book test" which was part
of this séance (in a letter to Olivia Shakespear dated 27 October),[3] I
quote only a suggestive comment somewhat different from the comment
made in the letter: "I had just finished a poem in which a poet of the
Middle Ages besought the saints 'in the holy fire' to send their ecstasy."
(Transcribed from the manuscript book begun at Oxford, 7 April 1921).
The remark about "a poet of the Middle Ages" reminds us that the
"I-persona" in a poem by Yeats is sometimes a dramatization, Yeats, that
is, in a mask assumed for the duration of a poem. A knowledge of Yeats's
intention here will help us to understand the successive drafts of the
poem. In the early drafts Yeats is consciously medievalizing; the "poet
of the Middle Ages" gradually disappears until the action of the finished
poem is timeless, recurrent, eternal.

The second comment was intended for a reading Yeats made from his
poems over the BBC, Belfast, 8 September 1931. Yeats omitted both text
and comment from the final script:

> Now I am trying to write about the state of my soul, for it is right for an
> old man to make his soul, and some of my thoughts upon that subject I
> have put into a poem called "Sailing to Byzantium." When Irishmen were

[3] *Letters* (London, 1954), pp. 730-731. In dating this letter, Allan Wade supplied the
year, 1927. I think the letter was written in 1926. It will fit with the 1926 letters between the letters of 24 September and 7 December (pp. 718-719); the first complete TS
of "Sailing to Byzantium," quoted below, is dated in Yeats's hand 26 September 1926.
In October 1927, after "Sailing to Byzantium" had been printed in *October Blast*,
Yeats would not have written that he had "just finished" it. If I am right about the
date of this letter, the poem was then far from being the poem we know; it was in
the state found in the revised typescript of "Towards Byzantium."

illuminating the Book of Kells and making the jewelled croziers in the National Museum, Byzantium was the center of European civilization and the source of its spiritual philosophy, so I symbolize the search for the spiritual life by a journey to that city.

The third comment occurred in the broadcast "My Own Poetry," given from London, 3 July 1937. It concerns the golden bird:

I speak of a bird made by Grecian goldsmiths. There is a record of a tree of gold with artificial birds which sang. The tree was somewhere in the Royal Palace of Byzantium. I use it as a symbol of the intellectual joy of eternity, as contrasted with the instinctive joy of human life.

The central correlative of "Byzantium" is not Justinian's sixth century city. The prose version of the poem makes this clear. I give that as Yeats first wrote it, with a long cancelled passage.

Subject for a poem

Describe Byzantium as it is in the system towards the end of the first Christian millennium. (The worn ascetics on the walls contrasted with their [?] splendour. A walking mummy. A spiritual refinement and perfection amid a rigid world. A sigh of wind—autumn leaves in the streets. The divine born amidst natural decay.)

April 30 [1930]

In ink of a different color, hence presumably at a later time, Yeats cancelled the passage I have placed in parentheses, and wrote over it:

. . . A walking mummy; flames at the street corners where the soul is purified. Birds of hammered gold singing in the golden trees. In the harbour [dolphins] offering their backs to the wailing dead that they may carry them to paradise. [Both passages transcribed from the MS of the 1930 Diary.]

When we look in *A Vision* for a description of Byzantium near the end of the tenth century, we do not easily find it. Perhaps Yeats had in mind the concluding paragraphs of section iv of "Dove or Swan," perhaps he is there describing both Eastern and Western Europe. The thought of those paragraphs is similar to the thought of the original prose version of "Byzantium," quoted above, especially in this passage:

. . . All that is necessary to salvation is known, but as I conceive the age there is much apathy. Man awaits death and judgment with nothing to occupy the worldly faculties and is helpless before the world's disorder, and this may have dragged up out of the subconscious the conviction that the world was about to end. Hidden, except at rare moments of excitement or revelation, and even then shown but in symbol, the stream of *recurrence,* set in motion by the Galilean Symbol, has filled its basin, and seems motionless for an instant before it falls over the rim. . . . [*A Vision,* 1924, pp. 195-196]

In this later Byzantium Unity of Being is threatened, though it is miraculously restored when the symbolic dolphins carry the souls of the dead to a Yeatsean paradise, a paradise of art, art which is at once sensual and spiritual. Yeats makes this interpretation of "Byzantium" in a passage cancelled from the MS of his unpublished lecture "Modern Ireland," written for his final American lecture tour of 1932-33. He has been writing of O'Leary, to whom he has ascribed Aristotle's "magnificence." He then stops to comment on "magnificence."

Aristotle says that if you give a ball to [a] child, and if it was the best ball in the market, though it cost but sixpence, it is an example of magnificence: and style, whether in life or literature, comes, I think, from excess, from that something over and above utility which wrings the heart. (In my later poems I have called it Byzantium, that city where the saints showed their wasted forms upon a background of gold mosaic, and an artificial bird sang upon a tree of gold in the presence of the emperor; and in one poem I have pictured the ghosts swimming, mounted upon dolphins, through the sensual seas, that they may dance upon its pavements.) [Transcribed from the MS. I have placed the cancelled passage in parentheses.]

This comment, taken together with the fact that Byzantine art works break the flood of images, the bitter furies of complexity at the climax of "Byzantium," indicates that Yeats's later Byzantium, though he distinguishes it from his earlier, remains essentially the same. This sameness in difference is a characteristic stratagem with Yeats. In the development of nearly all his recurring symbols new shades of meaning will be added while the old meanings are retained.

The Drafts of "Sailing to Byzantium"

Yeats composed the drafts of "Sailing to Byzantium" in a looseleaf notebook, and he did not number his pages before he removed the sheets for filing. I have arranged the drafts in what seems to me their proper order from internal evidence, working back and forward from a typescript version of the poem corrected in Yeats's hand and dated 26 September 1926. According to his own dating of the printed poem, Yeats finished it in 1927. The MSS which precede the typescript are in pencil; those which follow it are in ink. I have reproduced the MSS as exactly as possible, except that I have normalized the spelling. An "X" in front of a line means that it has been cancelled entire; internal cancellations are lined out; then, following a slanting rule, the revised version is given. Actually Yeats wrote his revisions above, below, or at the side of the cancelled words. Passages cued in from the margins have been inserted in their proper places. I mark the end of each MS page by three asterisks. All other editorial matter, including added punctuation, has been placed between square brackets. The line numbers used follow the *Variorum Edition*. I place its number before a line when it reaches the form in which it was first printed.

[A1]

[After writing two lines of which I can certainly read only the opening words "Farewell friend," Yeats continues approximately as follows:]

    This is no country for old men—if our Lord
X Smiles
    Is a smiling child upon his mother's knees
    And in the hills ~~the old gods~~/ those—I know now
    What name to call them by—still hunt and love
    There is still a love for those that can still sing
X ~~All~~/ For all the
    Forever sing the song that [two cancelled words undeciphered] you have
        sung[4]

*   *   *

[A2]

X The young

    Here all is young, and grows young day by day
    Even my Lord smiles as upon your knees.
    Upon his mother's knees—[five words undeciphered]

    Here all is young and grows young day by day
X Even my God
X Ev
X And God himself—comes down from [two words undeciphered] and smiles

[4] When this essay was first printed, I did not know of the existence of drafts A1, 2, and 3. I first saw them in Dublin in the summer of 1960.

X God lies upon his mother's
    Even God lies upon his mother's ~~lap~~/knees
    And holds out childish hands in play
X ~~And even~~/And called the gods and we
X And those my fathers called the gods
X And even those I know
X And there are some—and I know not who they be
X ~~My~~/Called the gods, that

✳   ✳   ✳

[A3]

    All here—my God upon his mother's knees
    Holding out his infant hands in play
X The old gods ~~still~~ at their
X The gods
X Those ~~older~~/other gods

X All here—my God
X Every thing
    All in this land—~~even my God~~/my maker at his play
    Or else asleep upon his mother's knees
    Those other gods that still—I have heard say

[WBY cancels this line, experiments with other readings in the two lines printed just below, cancels them and puts stet marks under the line above.]

X And those, to whom [two words undeciphered] the mountain people say
X Make love in shadow of the twilit trees
    ~~Keep~~/Are at their hunting and their gallantries
    Under the hills as in our fathers' [?] day
    The changing colour of the hills and seas
    All that mankind think they know, being young
    Cry that my tale is told my story sung

✳   ✳   ✳

[A4]

X Now I have shipped among these mariners
X And sail south eastward toward Byzantium
X Where in the

X But now I sail among these mariners
X From things becoming to the thing become
X And sail south eastward towards Byzantium
X That I may anchored by the marble stairs
X O water that
X After a dozen storms to come

X I therefore voyage towards Byzantium
X Among these sun browned friendly mariners
X Another dozen days and we shall come
X Among the waves to where the noise of oars
X Under the shadow of its marble stairs

*   *   *

[A5]

I therefore travel towards Byzantium
Among these sun-browned pleasant mariners
Another dozen days and we shall come
Under the jetty and marble stairs
Already I have learned by spout of foam
X Creak of the sail's tackle, or of the oars
Can wake from slumber where it lies
X That fish the souls ride into paradise
That fish whereon souls ride to Paradise

X I fly from things becoming to the thing become
I fly from nature to Byzantium
Among these sunbrowned pleasant mariners
X To the gold and ivory
X I seek for gold and ivory of Byzantium

*   *   *

[A6]

Or Phidias
~~Therefore I travel~~ / Flying from nature towards Byzantium
Among these dark skinned pleasant mariners
I long for St. Sophia's sacred dome
X That I may look on painted [?] columned dome

X Statues of Phidias
X A statue by Phidias   stairs
   Mirrored in water where a glint of foam
X Proves that ~~noise~~/ the splashing
X But demonstrates that splash or creak of oar
X Proves that ~~the sudden splashing of the oar~~/ ~~creaking or~~ the splash of oars
   But demonstrates that the splash of oars
   Can ~~wake~~/startle from the slumber where it lies
   That fish that bears the soul to paradise

X That I may look on the great churches dome
X Statues of bronze over a marble stair
   For [word undeciphered] of gold and ivory marble stairs
   Mirror-like water where a glint of foam
   But demonstrates that sudden falling oars

[This whole page cancelled]

*   *   *

[A7]

X This Danish merchant on a relic swears
X That he will
X All that afflicts me, but this merchant swears
X To bear me eastward to Byzantium
   But now this pleasant dark skinned mariner
   Carries me towards that great Byzantium
X Where nothing changes
X And ageless beauty
   Where age is living [word undeciphered] to the oars
   That I may look ~~on St. Sophia's dome~~/ on the great shining dome
X On Phidias' marble, ~~or a~~/ or upon marble stairs
X Or mirroring waters where a glint
X On mirroring water, upon sudden foam
   On gold limbed saints and emperors
   After the mirroring waters and the foam
   Where the dark drowsy fins a moment rise
   Of fish, that ~~bear~~/ carry souls to paradise.

*   *   *

[A8]

X And most of all an old/ aged thought harried me
X Standing in gold on church or pedestal

X Angel visible or emperors lost in gold

  O dolphin haunted wave of flooding gold
                        might
                        fold
                        sight
                        bold

*   *   *

[A9]

  Procession on procession, tier on tier
  Saints and apostles in the gold of a wall
X As though it were God's love await
X Symbolic of God's love await my prayer
X Turn their old withered heads and wait my prayer
X Or into sea like   tier
X Or lost   wall
X As if God's love   were
X As if God's burning heart awaits my prayer
X To fill me with
  As if God's love will refuse my prayer
  When prostrate on the marble step I fall
X And cry amid my tears—
  And cry aloud—"I sicken with desire
  Though/ And fastened to a dying animal
  Cannot endure my life—O gather me
24 Into the artifice of eternity."

*   *   *

[A10]

And if it be the dolphin's back   take
                                     spring
                                     sake

28   Of hammered gold and gold enamelling
      That the Greek goldsmiths make
      And set in golden leaves to sing
      Of present past and future to come
      For the instruction of Byzantium

                    *   *   *

                         [A11]

X   If it must be the dolphin I shall take
X   And if I stride the dolphin I shall take
    The sensual shears being past I shall not take
    No shifting form of nature's fashioning
X   The shears being past but such as goldsmiths make
27 But such a form as Grecian goldsmiths make
28 Of hammered gold and gold enamelling
    At the emperor's order for his Lady's sake
    And set upon a golden bough to sing
31 To lords and ladies of Byzantium
32 Of what is past, or passing or to come

    O saints that stand amid God's sacred fire
18 As in the gold mosaic of a wall
X   Transfigure me and make me what you were
    Consume this heart and make it what you were
X   Rigid, abstracted, and fanatical
    Unwavering, indifferent, and fanatical
X   The body buried away—sick with desire
    It faints upon the road—sick with desire
    ~~Being/~~ But fastened to this dying animal
    Or send the dolphin's back and gather me
24 Into the artifice of eternity.

[WBY indicates by arrows that the order of these two stanzas is to be
reversed.]

                    *   *   *

[The first complete version of the poem, which follows, is from a
typescript.⁵]

⁵ Norman Jeffares gives an eclectic version of this typescript in *RES*, January 1946.
My versions are progressive. I print first the typed words, then, below, Yeats's revisions.
These revisions, including the date, are all in Yeats's hand. There are. two copies of
this typescript. WBY worked on the first pages of both copies, that is on stanzas I and
II, but on only one copy of page 2, that is stanzas III and IV. I transcribe the first page
that has the latest revisions and the revised second page.

[B1]

Towards Byzantium

All in this land—my Maker that is play
Or else asleep upon His Mother's knees
Others, that as the mountain people say
Are in their hunting and their gallantries
Under the hills as in our fathers' day
The changing colours of the hills and seas
All that men know, or think they know, being young
Cry that my tale is told my story sung

X   I therefore travel towards Byzantium
X   Among these sun-brown pleasant mariners
X   Another dozen days and we shall come
X   Under the jetty and the marble stair

But now these pleasant dark-skinned mariners
Carry me towards that great Byzantium
Where all is ancient, singing at the oars
That I may look in the great churches dome
On gold-embedded saints and emperors
After the mirroring waters and the foam
Where the dark drowsy fins a moment rise
Of fish that carry souls to Paradise.

O saints that stand amid God's sacred fire
18   As in the gold mosaic of a wall
Consume this heart and make it what you were
Unwavering, indifferent, fanatical
It faints upon the road sick with desire
But fastened to this dying animal
Or send the dolphin's back, and gather me
24   Into the artifice of eternity

The sensuous dream being past I shall not take
A guttering form of nature's fashioning
But rather that the Grecian smithies make
28   Of hammered gold and gold enamelling
At the Emperor's order for his lady's sake
And set upon a golden bough to sing
31   To lords and ladies of Byzantium
32   Of what is past or passing or to come.

[Below is Yeats's revision of the typescript reproduced above.]

[B2]

Towards Byzantium

Here all is young; the chapel walls display
An infant sleeping on His Mother's knees
Weary with toil Teig sleeps till break of day
That other wearied with night's gallantries
Sleeps the morning and the noon away
I have toiled and loved until I slept like these
A glistening labyrinth of leaves [;] a snail
Scrawls upon the mirror of the soul.

But now I travel to Byzantium
With many a dark skinned pleasant mariner
Another dozen days and I shall come
Under the jetty and the marble stair
And after to unwinking wisdom's home
The marvel of the world and gardens where
Transfigurations of the intellect
Can cure this aging body of defect

Transfigured saints that move amid the fire
18 As in the gold mosaic of a wall
Transform this heart and make it what you were
Unfaltering, indifferent, fanatical
It faints upon the road sick with desire
But fastened to this dying animal
Or send the dolphin's back, and gather me
24 Into the artifice of eternity

The sensuous dream being past I shall not take
A guttering form of nature's fashioning
But rather that the Grecian smithies make
Of hammered gold and gold enamelling
At the Emperor's order for his lady's sake
And set upon a golden bough to sing
31 To lords and ladies of Byzantium
32 Of what is past or passing or to come.

                                        September 26, 1926

*   *   *

[C1]

1   ~~This/~~ ~~Here/~~ That is no country for old men—the young
    ~~Pass by me/~~ That travel singing of their loves, the trees
    ~~Break/~~ Clad in such foliage that it seems a song
    The shadow of the birds upon the seas
X The herring in the seas,
X The fish in shoals
X The leaping fish, the fields all summer long
X Praise [several words undeciphered], but no great monument
X Praise Plenty's horn, but no great monument
    ~~The leaping fish/~~ The crowding fish commend all summer long
    Deceiving [?] ~~abundance/~~ Plenty, but no monument
    Commends the never aging intellect
    The salmon rivers, the ~~fish/~~ mackerel crowded seas
    ~~Flesh/~~ ~~All/~~ Fish flesh and fowl, all spring all summer long
X ~~What/~~ Commemorate what is begot and dies.
    But praise what is begotten, born and dies
X And no man raises up a monument
X To the unbegotten intellect
X And man has made no mighty monument
X To praise the unbegotten intellect

[This page was entirely cancelled.]

*   *   *

[C2]

X   the trees.
3 X Those dying generations at their song
    X The salmon leap, the mackerel crowded seas
1   That is no country for old men; the young
2   In one another's arms, birds in the trees
3   Those dying generations at their song,
4   The salmon falls, the mackerel crowded seas
        Fish flesh and fowl, all spring and summer long
        Extoll what is begotten, born and dies
        And man has made no monument to extoll
    X The unbegotten wisdom of the soul
        The unborn, undying, unbegotten soul

*   *   *

[C3]

X Wherefore being old
9   ~~The~~/ An aged man is but a paltry thing
X An old man is a paltry
~~A Paltry business to be old~~, unless
11 ~~My~~/ Soul clap ~~hands~~/ its hands and sing, and ~~then sing more~~/louder sing
                                                                              dress
                                                                              oar

X For
X For every tatter
X For every mortal born out of the dress
X As time wears out

X It is a paltry business to be old
12   For every tatter in its mortal dress

●   ●   ●

[C4]

9   An aged man is but a paltry thing
     Nature has cast him like a shoe unless
11   Soul clap its hands and sing, and louder sing
12   For every tatter in its mortal dress
X And ~~come upon~~/ except that mood in studying
     And there's no singing school like studying
     The monuments of ~~its old~~/ our magnificence
X And for that reason have
     And therefore have I sailed the seas and come
16   To the holy city of Byzantium

●   ●   ●

[C5]

X O saints amid the gold mosaic of a
X O saints and martyrs ~~amid~~/ in God's holy fire
18 X As in the gold mosaic of a wall
X Look down upon me sickened with desire

   X And fastened to this dying animal
   X Immovable, or moving in a gyre

17   O sages standing in God's holy fire
18   As in the gold mosaic of a wall
19   Come from the holy fire, perne in a gyre
20   And be the singing masters of my soul
      That knows not what it is, sick with desire
      And fastened to a dying animal
      Or send the dolphin's back and gather me
24   Into the artifice of eternity

*   *   *

[C6]

      The dolphin's journey done I shall not take
26   My bodily form from any natural thing
27   But such a form as Grecian goldsmiths make
28   Of hammered gold and gold enamelling
      At the emperor's order, for his lady's sake
      And set me on a golden bough to sing
31   To lords [and] ladies of Byzantium
      Of what is past or present or to come

*   *   *

The particular interest of draft A1 is that it shows Yeats starting to work on a poem. Few of his very early drafts have survived; no doubt Yeats destroyed most of them as he progressed beyond them. In such drafts Yeats assembles his materials, gropes his way toward the metrical form he will use, and begins to explore phrasing and to set rhymes. Here Yeats picks two representatives of that youth to which he must bid farewell: the infant Christ on Mary's knees, and those immortal mountain people who turn up so frequently in Yeats's poetry. These persisted through many drafts, though eventually Yeats abandoned both of them in the C drafts. In draft A1 Yeats makes very little progress toward form or language. He does not begin to establish his rhyme scheme, though two words at the ends of lines (knees, sung) will persist through the B1 draft, indeed persist as rhyme sounds, the sole survivors of this uncertain beginning, in the finished poem (trees, seas, dies; young, song, long). Though Yeats begins to pound out lines with five metrical feet—"There is still a love for those that can still sing"—this draft seems to my ear a curious mixture of prose and verse. The lines "And in the hills those —I know not/ What name to call them by—still hunt and love" seem to me prose. The most interesting thing in the A1 draft is the opening line "This is no country for old men." This beginning entirely disappears for many drafts. Yeats returned to it in the C drafts after wandering in the wilderness for a very long time; and when he did, got the opening of the poem right.

Draft A2 carries over from A1 the infant Christ and the mountain people. All of the trial lines finished are now definitely in iambic pentameter verse, and Yeats is beginning to establish his abab rhyme scheme (day, knees, play). When Yeats rewrote the B1 version of this stanza in B2 he again picked up phrases such as "Here all is young" which he had abandoned in the A3 draft.

In the A3 draft Yeats finishes assembling the materials he will use through the B versions of this stanza by adding to the infant Christ and the mountain people a description of the natural beauty of Ireland ("The changing colour of the hills and seas") and the contrast of all this with the old age of his persona. He establishes the stanza form of the finished poem (eight lines of iambic pentameter rhymed abababcc), and has the rhyme words he will use in B1 in place. Indeed, except for line 3, A3 and B1 are nearly identical.

In page A4 of the drafts the voyager is en route; he has apparently taken ship in Ireland and is sailing "south eastward towards Byzantium," though the mariners who man his ship seem to come from some Mediterranean country. There is only a hint of the eventual sharp contrast between the country of the young and Byzantium, which is the substance of stanzas I and III of the finished poem, in the draft lines "But now I sail among these mariners / From things becoming to the thing become." Yeats slowly works in detail; "mariners" become "sun browned friendly mariners," and Byzantine detail such as the marble steps and the boat landing is added to contrast with the Irish detail of A3. A5 begins with a revision of the last four lines of A4; then Yeats introduces the symbolic dolphin, that will persist through all the drafts of the poem. He tries but quickly abandons detail describing the voyage—"Creak of the sail's tackle," and becomes more urgent when he writes "I fly from nature to Byzantium." Surely this draft line is the seed from which the first three stanzas of the finished poem will grow slowly. At the end of this page Yeats begins to try out descriptive details that will evoke Byzantium for us, a process which he continues on A6. Eventually Yeats reserved such Byzantine detail as he uses for the third and fourth stanzas of his poem. In "gold and ivory of Byzantium" we are on our way to the golden bird. The dome of Hagia Sophia, introduced in A6, has disappeared from the finished poem, along with the ivory, the marble stairs, and Phidias' statue, but it will magnificently reappear along with the dolphin in "Byzantium." On A7 Yeats achieves the substance of stanza II as that will appear in the earliest version of the complete poem, the typescript with the title "Towards Byzantium." His imagined persona, "a poet of the Middle Ages," is clearly present for the first time when Yeats writes "This Danish merchant on a relic swears." The relic is certain evidence that Yeats is medievalizing, and "Danish merchant" suggests that Yeats recalled the Danish kingdom that had its center in medieval Dublin. Yeats quickly cuts away particularity, goes on to explore and largely abandon detail about Byzantium with which he had already experimented, and then introduces a new detail, a mosaic picture, in the draft line "On gold limbed saints and emperors." This is a shadow of an image used in stanza III of the finished poem.

On A8 Yeats describes his imagined mosaic in greater detail—the saints become an angel momentarily; he then lists a series of rhyme words which he never did use. On A9 stanza III begins to take shape. The figures in the imagined mosaic have become a procession of saints and apostles

> in the gold of a wall
> As though it were God's love.

They will refuse the protagonist's prayer:

> "I sicken with desire
> And fastened to a dying animal
> Cannot endure my life—O gather me
> Into the artifice of eternity."

The splendid final line of stanza III seems to have sprung full blown; while composing Yeats often invented especially felicitous phrases without false starts. During the process of this remarkable draft Yeats gets five of his eventual rhyme words into place—wall, desire, animal, me, eternity—and nearly completes lines 21-24.

A10 is the first draft of stanza IV; again, this takes shape quickly. Its principal image, the golden bird singing among golden leaves, is in place as is the description of the content of its song. Five rhyme words have been chosen—take, enameling, sing, come, Byzantium—though the final couplet will be transposed in the next draft. Line 28 is finished. At the top of A11 Yeats continues work on stanza IV and very nearly completes it. At the beginning he carries over the dolphin from the preceding draft and symbolizes the protagonist's journey from time to eternity by a ride on the dolphin's back; then he abandons this for "The sensual shears," presumably the shears of Atropos. In line 30 "And set in golden leaves to sing" becomes "And set upon a golden bough to sing"; placing the golden bird upon the talismanic golden bough is surely a felicitous change. What was a descriptive detail without associations becomes a complex image charged with associations. Seven of the eight rhyme words are in place; line 30 is nearly finished, lines 27, 28, 31, and 32 are finished.

On the lower half of the page Yeats returns to stanza III and makes good progress with it. The first two lines gain intensity when Yeats reverses the elements of his comparison: we are no longer merely contemplating a mosaic picture; the saints "stand amid God's sacred fire/As in the gold mosaic of a wall." The protagonist prays to these saints

> Consume this heart and make it what you were
> Unwavering, indifferent, and fanatical.

This prayer differs radically from that in the finished poem, where the "sages" are asked to "be the singing-masters of my soul." At the end of the page stanza III is less far along than stanza IV, but six rhyme words are in place and two lines are finished (18, 24).

Drafts B1 and B2 which follow, the typescript of the complete poem and a revision of the typescript, are adopted from the A drafts. At the end of the revision stanzas III and IV are virtually complete; Yeats has still not achieved any lines he will keep in stanzas I and II.

Yeats begins by picking up a phrase from A4 for his title; he then goes on in stanza I to describe the Ireland from which his protagonist will sail to Byzantium. This stanza is still very much in process. There are hints at the country of the young in "Are in their hunting and their gallantries" and "The changing colours of the hills and seas," and the old age theme begins to appear at the close of the draft. Stanza II begins as in A5, then Yeats cancels four lines and writes another version which slightly changes A7. In stanzas III and IV he makes a few important changes: he drops "and" from the fourth line of III and changes the imagery and improves the wording of the first two lines of IV:

> The sensual shears being past I shall not take
> No shifting form of nature's fashioning

becomes

> The sensuous dream being past I shall not take
> A guttering form of nature's fashioning.

In revising this typescript Yeats makes stanza I more precisely Irish than it has been or will be by his reference to Teig, and we see the "poet of the Middle Ages" giving way to WBY in the line "I have toiled and loved until I slept like these"; the revision ends with a portentous metaphor: "a snail / Scrawls upon the mirror of the soul." Yeats has rewritten every line, and yet he has still not achieved anything that he will keep. In revising stanza II Yeats again rewrote every line without achieving any final results. He drops his first references to the dolphin and the mosaic picture; by reserving these for stanza III he enhances the drama of their appearance. Again, as in stanza I, he is on the way to stanza II of the finished poem, especially in the closing couplet "Transfigurations of the intellect / Can cure this aging body of defect." The slight changes made in III and IV require no comment.

Stanzas I and II were still far from finished when Yeats dated his revision 26 September 1926. Apparently he left the poem in this form for some months, for his own dating of the finished poem is 1927. On page C1 Yeats is moving very rapidly toward the final version of stanza I. He abandons all specifically Irish allusion[6] in favor of a country of the young that is timeless and placeless. This he vividly describes in a series of images of sensuality: lovers, trees, birds, fish which all "praise what is begotten, born and dies," whereas "man has made no mighty monument / To praise the unbegotten intellect." On this page Yeats puts seven rhyme words in place, he nearly finishes lines 2 through 6, he completes his first line. Lines 7 and 8 are still far from finished, though their essential ingredients are present in the words "mighty monument" and "unbegotten intellect." Yeats nearly completed his first stanza on page C2. Though his magnificent seventh and eighth lines still elude him, he completes lines 1-4 and improves lines 5 and 6.

On pages C3 and C4 Yeats accomplished equal wonders with drafts of his new second stanza. There is no hint yet of the scarecrow of line 10, that already many-times-tried figure from Yeats's phantasmagoria, but in this partial draft Yeats does complete lines 9, 11, and 12. At line 11 Yeats greatly enhances the drama of his poem when he recollects Blake's vision of the soul of his dead brother carried up to heaven clapping its hands for joy.[7] On sheet C4 Yeats gets all his rhyme words in place, finishes lines 9, 11, 12, and 16, and nearly finishes the remaining lines. When we recall what a weak thing stanza II was in "Towards Byzantium," these pages show us Yeats's creative power at its height.

Much less required to be done to stanzas III and IV, though the changes Yeats makes are among the most interesting to be found in these drafts.

[6] Yeats had rather frequently to reduce the amount of Irish allusion in his works. In the scenario and early drafts of *The King of the Great Clock Tower*, for instance, the King is O'Rourke of Breifny whose grandfather had married Dervorgilla. The excision of O'Rourke helped to make the myth Yeats was writing universal.

[7] G. B. Saul notes (*Prolegomena*, Philadelphia, 1957, p. 123) that L. A. G. Strong commented on this allusion in *Personal Remarks* (New York, 1953), p. 32.

Yeats begins with an improved version of his first five lines which takes off directly from the revised typescript. Yeats breaks this off after introducing the word "gyre." Then he starts again, changes the saints to sages, and completes lines 17-20 in final form. When Yeats changed the saints to sages he again made his poem more universal; with this change he seems to abandon entirely his "poet of the Middle Ages." He now prays to the wise of all ages and cultures who have preceded him into eternity or, as Yeats would have said, "the other life," that they become "the singing masters of my soul." The introduction of the word "gyre" is also critically important, for it raises the question of the degree to which Yeats intended "Sailing to Byzantium" to be read as a "systemic" poem. The word "gyre" does not occur very frequently in Yeats's poetry. When it does, as in his late poem "The Gyres," it is usually emblematic of the cyclical process of history.[8] In the cancelled lines where Yeats first introduced "gyre" into the drafts of "Sailing to Byzantium," it was applied to the protagonist; he was "immovable, or moving in a gyre." This is Yeats's way of saying that he was involved in the historic process. Now Yeats has his protagonist beseech the sages to leave momentarily the holy fire which symbolizes their eternal ecstasy and enter the gyre again in order that they may "be the singing masters of my soul," may help him put off the "dying animal" and enter the "artifice of eternity," help him, that is, to become a golden bird singing on a golden bough. In lines 21-24 Yeats retains most of the wording used in the revised typescript.

On sheet C6 Yeats makes a slight revision of stanza IV. In line 25 he introduces a second allusion to the dolphin, and he finishes lines 26-28, replacing "A guttering form" by "My bodily form" and returning to an earlier reading "Grecian goldsmiths" in preference to "Grecian smithies." Lines 29-32 are nearly identical in the revised typescript and C6.

A good deal remained to be done to "Sailing to Byzantium" before it could be printed in *October Blast*. To begin, its happy title is nowhere to

---

[8] In revising "The Two Trees" for *Selected Poems*, 1929, Yeats introduced "gyring" into line 15. I think the change was suggested to him by the phrase "circle of our life" in the original:

> There, through bewildered branches, go
> Winged Loves borne on in gentle strife,
> Tossing and tossing to and fro
> The flaming circle of our life.
>   *Countess Kathleen* through *Poems*, 1929

> There the Loves—a circle—go,
> The flaming circle of our days,
> Gyring, spiring to and fro
> In those great ignorant leafy ways;
>   *Selected Poems*, 1929

Yeats identifies the gyre with the winding stair, always, I think, emblematic of the historical cycle, in his letter to Sturge Moore, 26 Sept. [1930] (*Correspondence*, p. 163) .

be found in the drafts. Yeats made changes in every stanza, and greatly improved his poem in the process.

Stanza I. Yeats improved the diction and, I think, the movement of lines 5 and 6 when he changed

> Fish flesh and fowl, all spring and summer long
> Extoll what is begotten, born and dies

to read

> Fish flesh or fowl, commend all summer long
> Whatever is begotten born and dies.

His new seventh and eighth lines must be discussed along with his revision of line 14. In the C drafts these read

> 7 And man has made no monument to extoll
> 8 The unborn, undying, unbegotten soul
> 14 The monuments of our magnificence

Yeats's new seventh line "Caught in that sensual music all neglect" beautifully summarizes the thought of lines 1-6, a summary needed before Yeats goes on to state his contrast in line 8. In the C drafts Yeats does use "monument" in stanzas I and II, but his repetition is much less effective than in the finished poem. The repetition is not exact ("monument / monuments"), and these essential words, anticipatory of the entire development of the poem, are buried in the lines where they occur. In revising Yeats transferred "monument" to the beginning of line 8, making it plural, and sharpened his contrast of change with permanence: "Monuments of unageing intellect." With the revision of line 14 to read "Monuments of its own magnificence," "monuments" becomes a key or pivotal word in stanzas I and II. This revision had another result. In the C4 draft of stanza II five of the eight lines are, to my ear, in regular iambic pentameter (9, 12, 13, 14, 15), an incidence unusually high for Yeats's later poetry. The revision breaks up this tick-tock.

Stanza II. In line 10 Yeats replaced the cast shoe image with a scarecrow image, perhaps because "Nature has cast him like a shoe" makes Nature awkwardly horsy. In line 13 Yeats introduced the reading "Nor is there singing school but studying," which is less colloquial and syntactically tighter than "And there's no singing school like studying" found in the C drafts. Again, as with the change in line 14 discussed above, Yeats reduces the number of regular iambic lines. In line 15 he put an inversion into normal order: "have I sailed" becomes "I have sailed."

Stanza III. Yeats's revision of this stanza was radical. In the C5 draft lines 20-24 went

> And be the singing masters of my soul
> That knows not what it is, sick with desire
> And fastened to a dying animal
> Or send the dolphin's back and gather me
> Into the artifice of eternity.

Before printing the poem in *October Blast* Yeats revised these lines to read

> And be the singing masters of my soul.
> Consume my heart away; sick with desire
> And fastened to this dying animal.
> It knows not what it is; and gather me
> Into the artifice of eternity.

Donald Davie has suggested to me that Yeats made this revision because he came to feel a need to start "a new musical (i.e., metrical and syntactical) unit with 'sick with desire.' " What Yeats does is to break down one flowing syntactical unit into four syntactical units, the phrasing of all these units is made more crisp and pungent, and they are separated by heavier syntactical stops. When Yeats does this, he sets up a powerful counterpoint between the metrical unit, the line, and the syntactical unit, the clause. His revision also changed the thought of these lines. In the C version it is the soul "That knows not what it is"; in the finished poem the human heart knows not what it is. To achieve this more audacious statement, Yeats introduces the new thought "Consume my heart away" in line 21 and drops "knows not what it is" two lines. The syntactically weak subordinate clause "That knows not what it is" becomes a main clause "It knows not what it is." The consequence of these changes was momentous, for when "knows not what it is" was dropped two lines it displaced the dolphin, present from the first uncertain beginnings of the poem.

Stanza IV. The dolphin once gone, Yeats had to drop his second allusion to it. In line 25 "The dolphin's journey done I shall not take" becomes "Once out of nature I shall never take," a clear and dramatic summary of the action of the poem up to this point and a very tight articulation with line 24. Yeats re-wrote line 29 ("At the emperor's order, for his lady's sake / To keep a drowsy emperor awake") and had, I think, a minor and a major reason for doing so. The minor reason was to avoid the repetition of "lady's" with "ladies" in line 31, made awkward by the different grammatical form of the words. More important, the dropped phrase, since it clearly expresses a chivalric idea, was a final touch of medievalizing that had to go lest it interfere with the timelessness of the finished poem. The change in line 30 shows how important revisions that seem slight can be:

> And set me on a golden bough to sing

becomes

> Or set upon a golden bough to sing.

"Set me" has the unfortunate effect of reminding us that the protagonist is still a mortal man praying for a new incarnation; in the revised line the reincarnation has miraculously occurred. Finally, in the last line of his poem Yeats returns to the reading found in B1 and B2; "Of what is past or present or to come / Of what is past, or passing, or to come." The most surprising thing about these drafts is the persistence of the dolphin and its final disappearance. I believe that "Byzantium" grew in part from this suppression of the dolphin. The phrasing of the second poem is in several places anticipated in phrases dropped during the drafting of the first (e.g., "Grecian smithies"); its principal action is anticipated in such draft lines as

> Or send the dolphin's back, and gather me
> Into the artifice of eternity.

The explanation of Yeats's return to Byzantium is partly to be found in an exchange of letters with Sturge Moore. On 16 April 1930, Moore wrote, "Your *Sailing to Byzantium*, magnificent as the first three stanzas are, lets me down in the fourth, as such a goldsmith's bird is as much nature as a man's body, especially if it only sings like Homer and Shakespeare of what is past or passing or to come to Lords and Ladies." Yeats wrote the original prose version of "Byzantium" on 30 April 1930, almost immediately on receiving Moore's letter; he had a complete version done by 11 June. On 4 October 1930, Yeats wrote to Moore of "Byzantium": "The poem originates from a criticism of yours. You objected to the last verse of *Sailing to Byzantium* because a bird made by a goldsmith was just as natural as anything else. That showed me that the idea needed exposition." Yeats completed the poem in September, but continued to improve it. When Moore was designing a cover for *The Winding Stair*, he inquired about the dolphin: "Is your dolphin to be so large that the whole of humanity can ride on its back?" Yeats replied: "One dolphin, one man. Do you know Raphael's statue of the Dolphin carrying one of the Holy Innocents to Heaven?" We should remember, however, that Yeats wrote at the end of the prose version of "Byzantium", that the idea of a second Byzantium poem had been in his head for some time.

The Drafts of "Byzantium"

The successive drafts of "Byzantium" were composed in a bound manuscript book, from which I have transcribed them. Even though the pages on which Yeats wrote were fixed by the binding, the order of drafts is not always easy to determine. Yeats usually began on the right hand page of a two page opening, reserving the left hand page for revision and rewriting. Revisions written in pencil occur throughout the drafts. I believe that these are late, and that they were done at one time, so I note them. When there is no note to the contrary, the drafts are in ink.

[Page 1 of the MS. At the top of the page Yeats established his rhyme scheme: AABBCDDC.]

X When all that roaring rout of rascals are a bed
X When every roaring rascal is a bed
X When the last brawler's tumbled into bed
X When the emperor's brawling soldiers are a bed
X When the last brawler tumbles into bed
   When the emperor's brawling soldiers are a bed
X When the last
X The last robber
X The last benighted robber or assassin fled
X When the last
X The last robber or his
X The night thieves latest victim/ last benighted traveler dead or fled
X Silence fallen
X When starlit purple [?]
X When deathlike sleep destroys/ beats down the harlot's song
X And the great cathedral gong
   And silence falls on the cathedral gong
   And the drunken harlot's song

*   *   *

[The page opposite the first, from which lines 1-4 appear to have been copied clean.]

I

When the emperor's brawling soldiers are a bed
The last benighted victim dead or fled;
When silence falls on the cathedral gong
And the drunken harlot's song
A cloudy silence, or a silence lit
Whether by star or moon
I tread the emperor's town,
All my intricacies grown clear and sweet

[Added in pencil.]

All the tumultuous floods of day recede
Soldiers, robbers, victims are in their beds
3   Night resonance recedes—night walker's song
After cathedral gong
X I tread among the dark intricacies
X But a
I traverse all the town's intricacies
X A starry glittering
X All the town becomes
Under the starlight dome;
And things there become,
X Blood begotten shades and images
X A mystery of shades and images
X Mummies or blood begotten images
Mummies, or / and shades or stony / and hallowed images

*   *   *

[Page 2 of the MS]

cloth
path
light as a breath
X His breathless snores and seems to beckon me
His breathless body moves and summons / beckons me;
X I call / name it that harsh mystery
Death and life, or call it sweet life in death
X Death in life, or that dear life in death

And I adore that mystery
Harsh death in life, or that dear life in death

Before me bends ~~a something, man or shade or man~~/ an image man or
    shade
10   Shade more than man, more image than a shade,
  X Treads on the intricate
  X And though it is all wound in mummy cloth
  X And though it seems all wound in mummy cloth
  X It treads on the intricate path
  X And being wound in the intricate
  X And wound in the intricate mummy cloth
  X It knows the winding of the path
      What if the limbs are wound in mummy cloth
      That know the winding of the path
      What if the body's dry the mouths lack breath

[The next five lines have been added at the side of the page, in pencil.]

      Limbs that have been bound in mummy cloth
      Are more content with a winding path
13   A mouth that has no moisture and no breath
      May better summon me
      To adore

      That summon or beckon me
      I adore that mystery
  X Called death in life, or
      And call it death in life, or life in death
      That I call death or li [Added in pencil]

15   I hail the superhuman
  X Or death in life
      And call it etc.

         *   *   *

[Page 3 of the MS]

17   Miracle, bird or golden handiwork
18   More miracle than bird or handiwork
  X Sings to the starlight
  X Set hidden [?] by golden leaf
  X [Partial line, undeciphered]
  X What mighty hand ~~or~~/ and imagined out of metal

      In scorn   stood   imbued
  X In mockery of nature's blood and petal

X In mockery of nature's mire and blood
X In mockery   metal
X Mocking blind nature's mire and blood
X A great
X What great artificer [?]
X What mind decreed or hammer shaped the metal,
X Of golden

~~Sings all~~/ ~~Carols~~/ Mutters night long out of a golden bough
~~Or sings~~/ What the birds of Hades know
X Or roused by star or moonlight mocks
X Or wakened by the moonlight ~~sings aloud~~/ scorns
   Or by the star or moonlight wakened mocks aloud
X Under a golden or a silver petal
X Under a golden
X Out of the glory of its changeless metal
X In mockery of leaf and petal
X Mockery of man
22   ~~A~~/ ~~Liv~~/ In glory of changeless metal
     Living leaf or petal
     And man's intricacy of mire and blood.

[The following from the side of the page]

X Or else by the stars or moon em
   Mutters upon a starlight golden bough
   What the birds of Hades know
   Or by the moon embittered scorns aloud
22   In glory of changeless metal

*   *   *

[Page 4 of the MS]

And there is a certain square where tall flames wind and unwind
And in the flames dance spirits, by ~~that~~/ their agony made pure
And though they are all folded up in flame
It cannot singe a sleeve

                          live
                          ~~fla~~
                          sleeve
X Flames upon the marble
X A flame on the cathedral pavement flits
   At midnight on the marble pavement flits

X A certain flame
X Flames that no ~~wood/ fuel/~~ faggot feeds, no hand has lit
    A flame ~~that/~~ nor faggot feeds, ~~no mortal/~~ nor taper lights
    Nor breath of wind disturbs and to ~~this/~~ that flame
X ~~Can/ May the/~~ Do all/ the unrighteous spirits come
  ~~And/~~ May all unpurged spirits come
  And all their blood begotten passion leave

[Three lines in pencil, cued in from the facing page]

   ~~All/ The/~~ May blood besotted spirits come.
X And all that blood's imagination leave,
   And all blood's fury in that flame may leave
   ~~And the agony of a danr/~~ agony of trancel
   That is a measured dance
   O agony of the ~~fire /~~ flame that cannot singe a sleeve!

              *   *   *

[Page 5 of the MS]

33 X A straddle on the dolphin's mire and blood
   X Come the thin shades
   X The
   X The blood besotted
33   A straddle on the dolphin's mire and blood
   X Where the
   X Come spirits where
     ~~These spirits/~~ The crowds approach; the marble breaks the flood;
   X The lettered marble of the emperor;
   X The enchanted ~~marble/~~ pavement of the emperor;
   X Shadowy feet upon the floor,
   X Innumerable ~~feet,/~~ passion heavy feet
   X Intricacy of the dancing floor

   X The intricate pavement of the emperor,
   X Flame upon the dancing floor
   X Simplicity

   The bronze and marble of the emperor
   Simplicity of the dancing floor

   X A crowd of spirits
   X Breaks
   X The fin tortured

X The dolphin torn
X The dolphin tortured tide breaks
X That dolphin tortured flood breaks into spray
X That gong tormented current breaks ~~in spray~~/ in foam
X The dolphin torn, the gong tormented sea.

*   *   *

[Opposite page 5 of the MS]

X Breaks
   Breaks the bleak glittering intricacy
X Breaks

                    X breaks into ~~foam~~/spray
                         X Breaks

X Blood blind images yet
X Blood blind images that yet
X Where blind images beget
X Where the blind images beget

X ~~Where blind~~/ Break images ~~can~~/ that yet
X Blinder images beget
X The dolphin torn, the gong tormented sea.

   Where blind images can yet
   Blinder images beget
   The dolphin torn and gong tormented sea.

*   *   *

[Page 6 of MS, with passages cued in from the facing page inserted]

I

1   ~~All the foul~~/loud/ The unpurged images of day recede
      ~~Soldier, robber and victim are~~/ The emperor's drunken soldiers are a bed
      Night's resonance recedes, night walker's song
      After cathedral gong;
5   A starlit or a moonlit dome disdains[9]

[9] Throughout the drafts, and in the Cuala Press *Words for Music*, the spelling "distains" is found. Yeats would not have distinguished disdains/distains in pronunciation, according to Mrs. Yeats, and she regards "distains" as a misspelling that got into print because the Cuala Press set from Yeats's MS. Whether Yeats corrected "distains" to "disdains" or changed "distains" to "disdains," it seems certain that he and no other introduced the present reading in Macmillan's *The Winding Stair*. The *Variorum Edition* shows that the texts of poems included in *Words for Music* were very carefully corrected for the Macmillan book. No one but Yeats could have done this correcting.

6   Aĺl thàt man is,
7   All the intricacies/ mere complexities
      All the mire and blood/ mere blood and/ mire and blood of human veins

II

9   Before me treads/ floats an image, man or shade
10   ꞌ Shade more than man, more image than a shade;
     X An image that was wound/ bound in mummy cloth
     X Best knows/ Recalls or can recall that winding path;
13 X A mouth that has no moisture and no breath
     X Cries out the summons
     X Can stoutly summon   X Man's blood may/ can
     X Can merrily summon   X Can all blood summon
15 X I hail the superhuman

[Cued in from the opposite page]

     X Can best/ Unbinds the bobbin of the path
     X All   a breathing mouth can
                                         X All breathing clay
                                         Xꞌ Mire and blood can summon
11   A bobbin that is/ Hades a bobbin/ For Hades' bobbin bound in mummy
         cloth
12   Can unravel/ May unwind the winding path
13   A mouth that has no moisture and no breath
     Breathing mouths may summon
15   I hail the superhuman

[Back to original page]

16   And/ I call it death in life and life in death.

III

17   Miracle, bird, or golden handiwork
18   More miracle than bird or handiwork
     X Mutters upon a starlit golden bough   Planted on a starlit golden bough
20 X All that the birds of Hades know   Can like the cocks of Hades crow
21   Or by the moon embittered scorn aloud
22 X In glory of changeless/ measured [?] metal
     X Living leaf or petal
     X And/ Man's intricacy/ Or blind/ measureless imagery of mire and blood.

[Cued in from the facing page]

22   In ~~all simplicity of/ All that~~/ glory of changeless metal
  X ~~Common~~/ Bird or leaf or petal
  X Living leaf or petal
  X ~~And~~/ Every complexity of mire and blood
23   · Common bird or petal
      And all complexities of mire and blood

[Back to original page]

IV

At midnight on the ~~marble~~/ emperor's pavement flits
A flame nor faggot feeds nor taper lights
Nor breath disturbs, X ~~a self/ to that~~/ flame begotten **flame**
           X and to that flame born flame
             a flame begotten flame
  X There images and spirits come
  X Images and spirits come
  X ~~All~~/ There imaged spirits thither **come**
  X ~~And~~/ There all that blood-begotten fury **leave**
  X O agony of trance
  X That is a measured dance
  X O agony of flame that cannot singe a sleeve

[Cued in from the facing page]

28   Where blood begotten spirits come
29   And all complexities of fury leave.
30   Dying into a dance
31   An agony of trace
32   An agony of flame that cannot singe a sleeve.

               •   •   •

[Page 7 of the MS]

V

33   A straddle on the dolphin's mire and blood
      ~~The images~~/ Those crowds approach, the ~~marble~~/ metal breaks **the flood;**
35 X ~~Precious metals~~/ The golden smithies of the emperor;
    X ~~Integrity/ Simplicity~~/ Integrity of the dancing floor
    X Breaks the bleak ~~glittering intricacies~~/ aimless flood of imagery
      The precious metal of the emperor;
      Marble of the dancing floor

Breaks that ~~bitter bleak complexity~~/ bright flood, that bleak complexity
~~Where~~/ Images ~~can~~/ that yet
Worse images beget
40   That dolphin torn, that gong tormented sea.
                                        June 11 [1930]

[The revised version of stanza v given below was written into a blank
space on this page some time after Yeats had completed the next draft of
"Byzantium."]

33   A straddle on the Dolphin's mire and blood
      Those crowds approach; smithies break the flood,
35   The golden smithies of the emperor;
36 ·   Marbles of the dancing floor
      Break ~~bleak~~/ bitter, bleak, aimless complexities,
38   Those images that yet
      More images beget
40   That dolphin torn, that gong tormented sea.

                        *   *   *

[Page 8 of the MS]

                        Byzantium

                            I

1   The unpurged images of day recede;
2   The emperor's drunken soldiery are a bed;
      Night's resonance recedes, night-walker's song
4   ~~And after that the~~/ After great cathedral gong,
5 ·   A starlit or a moonlit dome disdains
6   Àll thàt man is,
7   All mere complexities,
8   ~~All that stupidity and~~/ ~~All mere mire and blood of human veins~~/ The fury
      and the mire of human veins.

                            II

9   Before me floats an image, man or shade,
10   Shade more than man, more image than a shade;
11   For Hades' bobbin bound in mummy cloth
12   May unwind the winding path;
13   A mouth that has no moisture and no breath
      Breathing mouths may summon.

15   I hail the superhuman;
     I call it death in life or life in death.

III

17   Miracle, bird, or golden handiwork,
18   More miracle than bird or handiwork,
19   Planted on a starlit golden bough,
20   Can like the cocks of Hades crow
21   Or by the moon embittered scorn aloud,
22   In glory of changeless metal,
23   Common bird or petal
24   And all complexities of mire or blood.

IV

     At midnight on the emperor's pavement flits
     A flame nor faggot feeds nor taper lights
     Nor breath disturbs, a flame begotten flame,
28   Where blood begotten spirits come
29   And all complexities of fury leave,
30   Dying into a dance,
31   An agony of trance,
32   An agony of flame that cannot singe a sleeve.

*   *   *

[Yeats completed this draft on the facing page, transcribed below]

V

33   A straddle on the dolphin's mire and blood
     Those crowds approach; smithies break the flood,
35   The golden smithies of the emperor;
36   Marbles of the dancing floor
 X   Break bitter, bleak, aimless/ stupid aimless furies of complexity,
38   Those images that yet
     More/ Fresh/ More images beget,
40   That dolphin torn, that gong tormented sea.
 X   Break the bleak fury or blind complexity
 X   Of images that yet
39 X Fresh images beget
37   Break bleak/ blind/ bitter furies of complexity
38   Those images that yet
39   Fresh images beget.
40   [That dolphin torn, that gong tormented sea.]

*   *   *

Inserted loose in the manuscript book from which I have been transcribing is a still later MS of "Byzantium," written on two sheets of paper. In it Yeats made several changes. Stanza IV was revised as follows:

25   At midnight on the emperor's pavement flit
26   Flames that no faggot feeds nor steel has lit
27   Nor storm disturbs, flames begotten of flame,
28   Where blood begotten spirits come, etc.

Then, in stanza V, Yeats made a change that describes the movement of the blood begotten spirits *towards* the emperor's pavement, that is towards paradise, less clearly than earlier versions.

33   A straddle on the dolphin's mire and blood
34   Spirit after spirit! The smithies break the flood, . . .

In stanza II throughout the drafts the reading

A mouth that has no moisture and no breath
Breathing mouths may summon

has persisted. Though I thought this reading might perhaps have authority, Mrs. Yeats told me it had none, that she had heard Yeats speak the poem so often saying "breathless" that she was certain he intended "breathless."

Yeats's attack in the drafts of "Byzantium" is at once quick and precise. After writing the prose version of the poem Yeats added that the subject had been in his head for some time. A study of the drafts shows that indeed it must have been, for the progression of images even in the first draft is essentially that found in the finished poem. Yeats also decided before beginning work on the poem to use once again the stanza used for "In Memory of Major Robert Gregory," "A Prayer for My Daughter," and for the middle section of "The Tower." This has the rhyme scheme AABBCDDC which Yeats set at the head of the "Byzantium" manuscript. In "Byzantium" Yeats did make one slight change in the stanza by reducing the number of metrical feet in lines 6 and 7 from four to three.[10] No doubt the fact that Yeats had already thoroughly explored this stanza partly accounts for the precision of his attack.

[10] Marion Witt discussed this stanza in "The Making of an Elegy," *MP*, XLVIII (November 1950), pp. 115-116. Frank Kermode in *Romantic Image* (London, 1957), pp. 38-40, notes that Yeats borrowed the stanza from Cowley's "Ode on the Death of Mr. William Harvey."

On page 1 and the page opposite to it Yeats drafts his first stanza. At the outset he is troubled by excessive detail, an unusual event in Yeats's drafts; he introduces quite a company of sensualists before settling on the soldiery and nightwalker of the finished poem: "roaring rout of rascals / every roaring rascal / last brawler / emperor's brawling soldiers" give place to robbers, assassins, benighted travelers. Then silence falls alike on "the cathedral gong / And the drunken harlot's song." In the drafts on the opposite page Yeats retains the soldiers, the benighted victim, the harlot's song, and the cathedral gong; he then sets the night scene and introduces an "I-persona."

> I tread the emperor's town
> All my intricacies grown clear and sweet.

"Intricacies" is the key word in the first draft of "Byzantium"; in the second draft it is replaced by "complexities," the key word of the finished poem. Eventually Yeats will withhold his I-persona until line 15. In the pencil drafts which follow Yeats makes a start on the magnificent line with which the finished poem opens in "All the tumultuous floods of day recede," he transfers "intricacies" from the protagonist to the town, and first introduces the starlit dome of Hagia Sophia. The last four lines of the draft look forward toward the rest of the poem; indeed the last of them, "Mummies and shades and hallowed images," gives too much away. In spite of excess detail that needs to be cut (robbers, victims, mummies, shades, and hallowed images), this is a remarkable first draft. Four rhyme words are in place (recede, beds, song, gong), and line 3 is done.

Page 2 introduces the walking mummy of the prose version. Yeats first establishes the rhyme words he will use in lines 11-13, then he makes two false starts in which the entire stanza, as it were, is compressed into two lines. Then in "Before me bends an image man or shade / Shade more than man, more image than a shade" he gets the essence of lines 9-10. He goes on to drafts of 11-14 and has considerable trouble though he does assemble all the materials finally used save "Hades' bobbin." In the first drafts of line 14 the mummy summons the protagonist, that is the poet, relieved of his accidence but still a living man; this perhaps explains why in all the successive drafts of this line Yeats uses the phrase "breathing mouths." Lines 15-16 are nearly complete. At the end of this draft seven rhyme words are in place; lines 10, 13, and 15 are done.

As Yeats returns to the golden bird of "Sailing to Byzantium" on page 3, his speed and assurance seem almost miraculous. He completes lines 17-18 instantly—no doubt he had composed them in his head and is merely writing them down—then has a little trouble with the lines that follow. Once the golden bird mocks nature's mire and blood, the whole stanza has been telescoped, so to speak. Mire and blood need to be reserved for the end of the stanza. Yeats fills out his stanza with description of the bird and its setting, even for a moment inventing an artificer of the bird, whom he quickly drops. Again, by the end of the draft the third stanza is nearly finished: all the rhyme sounds and seven of the rhyme words are in place, lines 17, 18, and 22 are done.

Page 4 opens with a prose outline of the fourth stanza. In my experience of Yeats's MSS, this is an unique event; writing prose versions of poems was part of Yeats's standard practice, but in no other instance known to me does he begin actual composition of a section of a poem with a prose version. Yeats goes on to list possible rhyme words, then begins his drafts. His materials fall into place quickly. The spirits summoned to the purifying dance are first "unrighteous," then "unpurged," then "blood besotted." In the second draft Yeats transfers "unpurged" to his first line with magnificent effect. Yeats finishes none of his lines in this draft, though he does set seven of his rhyme words—lit, flame, come, leave, trance, dance, sleeve. Yeats will sharpen and tighten his phrasing through several further drafts, but the basic work of composition is done.

In the first draft of his final stanza on page 5 Yeats's procedure is equally sure and direct. He writes down line 33, no doubt composed in his head, and goes on to explore details of the Byzantine art works he will use. At first he is content with the mosaic pavement mentioned in the prose version; its "marble" becomes successively "lettered marble," "enchanted pavement," "intricate pavement." Then when he writes "The bronze and marble of the emperor" he is on his way to his second and indirect allusion to the golden bird. Even more interesting is the series of cancelled draft lines in which Yeats works toward his splendid final line; his experiments lead through "fin tortured," "dolphin torn," "dolphin tortured," and "gong tormented" to the inevitability of "The dolphin torn, the gong tormented sea." Yeats ends the draft by experimenting with lines 37-39. The success of this first draft will at once be apparent when a clean copy of the final stanza is assembled:

> A straddle on the dolphin's mire and blood
> The crowds approach; the marble breaks the flood;
> The bronze and marble of the emperor
> Simplicity of the dancing floor
> Breaks the bleak glittering intricacy
> Where blind images can yet
> Blinder images beget
> The dolphin torn and gong tormented sea.

Yeats's second draft, on pages 6 and 7 of the MS, shows what a great writer at the height of his powers can do. For example, the first line in draft 1 reads "All the tumultuous floods of day recede"; now Yeats tries "foul images," "loud images," and then recalls "unpurged" from the first draft of stanza IV and completes his splendid first line. In line 2 he first takes over the "Soldier, robber, victim" of the first draft, then happily reduces these to a single instance, the drunken soldiers. Yeats keeps lines 3 and 4, then invents lines 5 and 6 in final form out of a mere mention of the starlit dome in draft 1. In line 7 when Yeats changes "intricacies" to "complexities" he changes the key word in his poem. By the time he finishes this draft Yeats has all his rhyme words in place, lines 1, 5, 6, and 7 are done, and the rest nearly done.

In the second draft of stanza II Yeats finishes line 9 by changing "bends an image" to "treads an image," then to "floats an image." He copies line 10 and then goes on to many drafts of lines 11-12; the enigmatic phrase "Hades' bobbin" develops slowly, but once it is achieved the next line, "May unwind the winding path," comes quickly. Lines 13-16 take the form they will keep throughout the drafts; only line 14 required much change. "May better summon me" of draft 1 becomes successively "Cries out the summons," "Can stoutly summon," "Can merrily summon," "Man's blood can [summon]," "Can all blood summon," "All breathing clay [can summon]," "Mire and blood can summon," "Breathing mouths may summon." At the end of the draft all lines except line 14 are finished. Stanza III required relatively little work. Yeats follows draft 1 closely, but introduces many improvements in diction. In draft 1 line 19 reads "Mutters upon a starlit golden bough"; Yeats changes this to "Planted on a starlit golden bough." "Mutters" somewhat deflates the golden bird, but "planted" carries the deflation further. In line 24 Yeats changes "intricacy" to "complexities," a change implicit in the changed seventh line. At the end of the draft lines 17, 18, 20-23 are done, lines 19 and 24 nearly done.

In revising stanza IV Yeats changes every line but the 26th. In line 25 "marble pavement" becomes "emperor's pavement"; in draft 1 line 28 reads "May all unpurged spirits come"; since Yeats has now introduced "unpurged" into line 1, he puts line 28 through a series of characteristic changes before settling on the reading found in the finished poem, "Where blood begotten spirits come." Lines 28-32 are finished; lines 25-27 require slight revision still.

Stanza V still required a good deal of work. Yeats makes a substantive change when he introduces a second Byzantine art work by adding an allusion to the golden bird. In line 35 Yeats, no doubt unconsciously, introduces in "smithies" a word which he had rejected in the last stanza of "Sailing to Byzantium." In draft II Yeats completes lines 33, 35, and 40, though he has cancelled line 35 in the form it will have in the finished poem. All the rhyme words are in place. The draft is dated June 11 [1930]. Yeats wrote the first prose version of "Byzantium" on April 30.

He revised that, presumably after some lapse of time, before beginning his drafts; yet the poem is essentially complete in the second draft just studied. Yeats completed "Byzantium" far more quickly than was usual when he was working on a major poem.

The third and fourth drafts require little comment. In the third draft Yeats changed "soldiers" to "soldiery" in line 2. He introduced "great" into line 4 to give it four feet; it now conforms with the fourth lines of the other stanzas. The second, third, and fourth stanzas show little change. The fifth stanza did require more revision. Yeats decided to retain a form of line 35 which he had cancelled in draft II; line 37 was still giving trouble, which was resolved on the third try. In line 39 "worse images" became "fresh images." By the end of the fourth draft "Byzantium" had very nearly taken the form in which we know the poem.

The materials presented above can help us to make our own readings of the Byzantium poems, and to value properly the many interpretations that have been published. The main lines of my own readings are: Both poems are deeply concerned with Unity of Being, and with the achievement of Unity of Being through art. In "Sailing to Byzantium" the protagonist achieves the temporal aspect of Unity of Being by leaving the country of the young, dominated by sensuality, and sailing to Byzantium, symbol of the spiritual life. "Byzantium" explores Unity of Being in its eternal aspect. At the outset of the poem unpurged images of sensuality give way to a serene image of spirituality, the moonlit dome of Hagia Sophia. Death the summoner, personified as a walking mummy, calls the souls of the departed to paradise. The golden bird is again examined, but alone it is not a sufficient symbol of Yeats's paradise. A sufficient symbol is found when the ghosts of the dead swim through the sensual seas on the backs of dolphins, warm-blooded mammals, toward the mosaic pavement where they dance in the purifying flames. We have moved from complexity to ultimate simplicity; sense and spirit have become one inextricable beam; Unity of Being is an ideal valid both in Time and Eternity.

Byzantium

by D. J. Gordon and Ian Fletcher

And therefore I have sailed the seas and come
To the holy city of Byzantium.

I

As an historical act the composition of the Byzantium poems is a
great leap, a sudden capture: an act possible only to an artist whose
imagination works in the dimension of history and with its monuments
and records, and strictly comparable to the appropriation of the Japa-
nese Noh. The conditions had to be observed: the historians or gram-
marians had to prepare the material: it had to be fairly easily accessible
to anyone who wanted to find it; and it had to give the poet the answers
he, at that moment, wanted. Given the conditions, and an imagination
of this sort, the result was an expropriation of a whole culture, its translation into images, intensely personal, synthetic; yet grounded on impersonal observation; and in one of their aspects acts of historical judge-
ment; and capable of transmitting and sealing a historical view; and so
becoming part of the story.

The jump is—and to present it in this way is hardly to oversimplify—
to "And therefore I have sailed the seas and come / To the holy city of
Byzantium" from Voltaire's declaration that Byzantine history was "a
worthless repository of declamation, and miracles disgraceful to the
human mind." Or from Gibbon's assurance, when he reduces Santa
Sophia:

> A magnificent temple is a laudable monument of national taste and religion,
> and the enthusiast who entered the dome of St. Sophia might be tempted to

suppose that it was the residence, or even the workmanship, of the Deity.
Yet how dull is the artifice, how insignificant the labour, if it be compared
with the formation of the vilest insect that crawls upon the surface of the
temple.

Or dismisses the throne of Solomon:

[The Emperor's] fanciful magnificence employed the skill and patience of
such artists as the times could afford: but the taste of Athens would have
despised their frivolous and costly labours; a golden tree, with its leaves and
branches, which sheltered a multitude of birds, warbling their artificial notes
and two lions of massy gold, and of the natural size, who looked and roared
like their brethren of the forest. . . .

Or confidently rejects a thousand years:

In the revolution of ten centuries, not a single discovery was made to exalt
the dignity or promote the happiness of mankind. . . .

A judgment to be echoed, with less justification because on far less
secure premises, by the nineteenth century rationalist historians, so that
even a Lecky could write:

of that Byzantine Empire, the universal verdict of history is that it consti-
tutes with scarcely an exception, the most thoroughly vicious form that civilization has assumed.

II

Yeats's first direct contact with Byzantine art was at Ravenna in 1907,
when he made a tour of Northern Italy with Lady Gregory and her son.
This visit would not appear to have left a decisive impression on his
work: his interest was concentrated on Italian painting, particularly that
of the Renaissance; and the cultivated tourist was still likely to visit
Ravenna for Dante's sake. His main guidebook was Reinach's *Apollo*
(1907) which has little on the subject of Byzantine art. It was rather the
historical studies he engaged in after 1918 that turned his attention to the
subject.

What particularly fascinated him now was the search for cyclic patterns in history. He was reading such books as Burkitt's *Early Eastern
Christianity* (1904), W. G. Holmes's elementary *The Age of Justinian
and Theodora* (1905/1907) with its description of the Golden Throne of
the Emperors; Mrs. Arthur Strong's *Apotheosis and the After Life* (1915),
and Strzygowski's *Origin of Christian Church Art* (1923)—"searching out

signs of the whirling gyres of the historical cone as we see it and hoping
that by this study I may see deeper into what is to come." This search
issued in *A Vision* (1925), that strange construct, which has troubled his
admirers so much, an amalgam of history, psychology, and eschatology,
in which Byzantium as historical, no less than as an artistic entity, has
an important role.

Such new-found interest in the historical Byzantium made Yeats wish
to visit the more easily accessible monuments of its art. And so he and
Mrs. Yeats planned—in company with Mr. and Mrs. Ezra Pound—a visit
to Sicily to see the great mosaics at Palermo and Cefalu. It would appear
that the visit took place in January 1925. During this time Yeats was
still working on *A Vision*, and the section *Dove and Swan* in which his
famous account of Byzantium appeared, concludes with a note: "finished
at Syracuse in 1925." (The dating may be romantic, but in any case shows
what Yeats considered the appropriate site for this composition.) From
Sicily, Mr. and Mrs. Yeats went for a short time to Capri and then on to
Rome by the end of February 1925. In Rome, they concentrated on seeing the finest examples of Early Christian art. The whole tour lasted for
about six weeks. Yeats brought back with him photographs of those monuments which had most interested him. Particularly notable is the mosaic
at La Zisa, Palermo, with its two palm-trees between peacocks, flanking
formalized fruit-bearing trees with birds in the branches, emblems of
immortality. On the apse at San Clemente in Rome the Redeemer is
shown on a cross with its base in foliage and birds perching on its arms.
In an article on *The Sacred Dance* by G. R. S. Mead (*The Quest*, 1910)
which Yeats knew, San Clemente is singled out as possessing a choir
raised to form a ceremonial dancing-floor; Mead was arguing that there
had been liturgical provision for a dance symbolising the dance of the
blessed in Paradise. The mosaics on the tribune of San Prassede provide
striking counterparts of the sages in their golden fire.

Before the visit to Ravenna in 1907, Yeats must have been aware of
the idea of Byzantium as it recurred in books and discussions. The late
nineteenth century had inherited an image of Byzantium as the history
of decadence—a culture frozen at a late stage in its development. But a
new school of Byzantine scholars became active in France in the 1880s—
the fathers, in fact, of our present notion of Byzantium. The great
English representatives of this new scholarship were J. B. Bury, whose
History of the Later Roman Empire appeared in 1889, and O. M. Dalton,
whose *Byzantine Art* was published in 1911—Yeats bought a copy of this
some years later. Texier and Pullan's study of Byzantine church architecture in Asia Minor dates from 1864; and in 1894 the first serious study
of Santa Sophia, by Lethaby and Swainson, appeared; and the Nineties
saw the beginnings of Westminster Cathedral. But through the nineteenth
century in England serious interest in Byzantine art was to be found in

such an obvious book as Lindsay's *History of Christian Art*; and Ruskin's studies of St. Mark's opened a new field to many. Such activity in the world of scholarship was paralleled in literature: J. E. Neale's novel *The Fall of Constantinople* (1857) represented the irenic concern of the Tractarians; but the writers of the decadence tended to cling to their over-simplified notions of Byzantine history. Symptomatic are such plays as Wills's *Claudian* (1884), of which Yeats writes in 1889; Sardou's *Theodora*, translated into English in 1885; Michael Field's *Equal Love* (1896), high minded and highly colored, which was published in the issue of *The Pageant* that contained a short story by Yeats: historical novels such as Frederic Harrison's *Theophano* (1904) and *Nicephorus* (1906) and, in France, Sar Péladan's play *Le Prince de Byzance* (1893).

In England, the circles which Yeats frequented were familiar with Byzantine art and specially with Ravenna. Burne-Jones visited the town in 1873 to see its "heavenly churches," and himself designed mosaics: the revival of mosaic no less than cloisonnée, enamel with golden frames, another typically Byzantine mode of art, was part of that general "revival" of the arts of design centering round Morris and his followers. F. G. Stephens lectured on Byzantine Art in Liverpool in 1878. Both Oscar Wilde and Arthur Symons visited and wrote about Ravenna. Although Wilde's *Ravenna* does not refer to the mosaics, elsewhere, in a passage in *The Decay of Lying*, which he had read to Yeats on a memorable Christmas, he writes of Byzantine art in terms which closely approach Yeats's own later conception of it:

> The whole history of the arts in Europe is the record of the struggle between Orientalism, with its frank rejection of imitation, its love of artistic convention, its dislike of the actual representation of any object in Nature, and our own imitative spirit. Wherever the former has been paramount, as in Byzantium, Sicily or Spain. . . . we have had beautiful and imaginative work in which the visible things of life are transmuted into artistic conventions and the things that life has not are invented and fashioned for her delight.

Yeats's intimate friend, Arthur Symons, described Ravenna in his *Cities of Italy* (1907) and Constantinople in his *Cities* (1903), where there is an emphatic account of the impressiveness of Santa Sophia. Symons also has a poem of about the same date on the mosaics at Sant' Apollinare Nuovo. But, as Dr. Giorgio Melchiori observes in his brilliant analysis of the Byzantine poems, there is a passage in Yeats's early story "Rosa Alchemica" describing the mosaics of the apostles against their golden ground in the Battistero degli Ortodossi at Ravenna. The circular walk of the apostles round the dome recalls the "perne in a gyre" of "Sailing to Byzantium." The fact that these mosaics are in the dome, not along the walls, as at Sant' Apollinare, would seem to relate them more firmly to "Byzantium." The context in "Rosa Alchemica" includes a description of the Alchemists' refining fire "and of a dancer under a dome of *flame-like* figures, which concludes in a half-dream." Yet whatever Yeats may have gathered about Byzantium and its art from the literary field, it was his later historical reading and the visit to Sicily and Rome that conditioned his choice of Byzantium as a composite symbol.

Whatever Yeats had found and read about Byzantium in his English sources, in earlier years, had been fragmentary, and often trivial. His appropriation of Byzantium as symbol is a genuine conquest. The sort of feelings he came to have about Byzantium and Byzantine art and Santa Sophia were present in the early writers, in the eloquence of a Procopius or the dark poetic language (the phrase is Gibbon's) of Paul the Silentiary (whose accounts he must surely have found, perhaps in the Lethaby and Swainson); and could be found in a modern form, in 1911, unexpectedly perhaps, in Dalton's learned textbook:

> . . . Its forms do indeed evoke and quicken the sense of life, but it is a life elect and spiritual, and not the tumultuous flow of human existence. They are without the solidity of organisms which rejoice or suffer; they seem to need no sun and cast no shadow, emerging mysteriously from some radiance of their own. . . .

> It is greatest, it is most itself, when it frankly renounces nature; its highest level is perhaps attained where, as in the best mosaic, a grave schematic treatment is imposed, where no illusion of receding distance, no preoccupation with anatomy, is suffered to distract the eye from the central mystery of the symbol. The figures that ennoble these walls often seem independent of earth; they owe much of their grandeur to their detachment. They exert their compelling and almost magical power just because they stand on the very line between that which lives and that which is abstracted.

In England it was in the early nineteen-twenties that the story began which has made Byzantine art so popular with the purveyors of those elaborate picture books which have taken the place of the early nineteenth century annuals; and the story of the forces that made the reception of a non-naturalistic art eventually possible need not be rehearsed. Yeats was acting, as poets can, as antenna of his age: his crystallisation has become one of the meanings of Byzantium.

III

Byzantine art becomes no less than a symbol for Art itself, for in no other mode is the opposition between Art and Nature so strikingly expressed. The conventional forms of Byzantine mosaic seem to deny the nature from which they derive. Those images, in fact, were designed to express the Divine, the supernatural, the transcendent realm which opposes the flux of time and nature. The personal application of the symbol is intensified by Yeats's obsession with old age, change, decay, and death, and with the wisdom that outlasts them. The symbol, then, expresses the permanence of the artist in the perfection of his artifices; but it contains more than this, for Byzantium, at its highest point, represented for Yeats a civilization in which all forms of thought, art, and life interpenetrated one another, and where the artist "spoke to the multitude and the few alike." Byzantium is not only the city of perfected art. It is also a city dedicated to the Holy Wisdom, ruled by an Emperor, who himself is half divine, intermediary between God and Man, who sits in the throne of Solomon between the Lions and the Golden Tree. For this wisdom is the wisdom of both East and West: Byzantium was the meeting place of the two cultures that have formed the Western world. The whole city, with its great dome and its mosaics which defy nature and assert transcendence, and its theologically rooted and synthetic culture, can serve the poet as an image of the Heavenly City and the state of the soul when it is "out of nature."

"Byzantium" begins with the Emperor's dome. This, like the dome of Santa Sophia, is Heaven, perfection, Eternity, a reversal of Shelley's "dome of many-coloured glass," opposed to the natural world, the world of daylight, of passions, and flux, that is struck through by the liturgical gong, an intimation of a transcendent order. But the dome has other meanings. Dr. Melchiori suggests that the dome is the equivalent of Blake's cosmic egg and the sphere, the perfect shape, and that Byzantium has succeeded to Blake's city of art, Golgonooza. The dome, an inclusive form, could be used as a symbol of the union of arts and activities which should characterize a good society, that favorite preoccupation of Yeats and his generation. A little magazine, to which Yeats contributed frequently between 1897 and 1900, was called *The Dome*, precisely because it was a "union of the arts" magazine. In January 1899 the editor invited readers to contribute designs for a fantastic memorial college of arts in a ruined town; the winning design, not unnaturally, included a dome. But in 1924 Yeats was to see the union of the arts manifested in another type of architecture. He associates the Stadhus of Stockholm with its stylized mosaics and his favourite *art nouveau* decoration with Byzantium. The Stadhus, he wrote, "is decorated by many artists working in harmony with one another and with the design of the building as a whole, and yet all in seeming perfect freedom." He refers to the mosaic-covered walls of the Golden Room, to the wrought-iron work and bronzes "naked as if they had come down from a Roman heaven . . . all that multitude and unity could hardly have been possible had not love of Stockholm and belief in its future so filled men of different minds, classes and occupations, that they almost attained the supreme miracle, the dream that haunted all religions." This was to be closely echoed in Yeats's description of Byzantium in *A Vision*.

The Golden Tree with its Golden Bird in the poems exemplifies admirably the syncretistic nature of Yeats's Byzantine symbols. The golden bird is described as *set* on the golden bough, one of several ironic qualifications in the poem, confirmed by its role of keeping the drowsy Emperor awake. The bird is an automaton, like Andersen's mechanical bird with its cold songs that outsing the nightingale; and Yeats may have been recalling Wilde's "over our heads will float the Blue Bird singing of beautiful and impossible things, of things that are lovely and never happen, of things that are not and should be." The similarities of cadence are striking and so too is the reversed effect: Yeats's bird can only sing of actual happenings in a phenomenal world, whose ecstatic absurdity is no longer possible in the Heaven of Art. The birds in the Throne of Solomon seemed to have sung through air being forced out of an airtight compartment by the introduction of water (*v.* G. Brett, "The Automata of the Byzantine Throne of Solomon," *Speculum*, 1954).

Yeats knew also from his reading in Strzygowski and in Goblet D'Alviella's *Migration of Symbols* (1894)—one of his sacred texts—of the stylized tree-pattern as it appears in Near Eastern and Byzantine art, and his authorities informed him that this could be identified with the Hebrew Tree of Life. Yeats chose to identify the Golden Tree of the Emperor with this all-important symbol, and it is tempting to think that he may have seen in the mosaic of the apse of San Clemente at Rome, with its cross springing from a stylized tree, yet another example of this form. He felt that he possessed sufficient historical evidence to justify such an identification and it was particularly important for him to do so, for in this way the image of Byzantium can be associated with the hermetic imagery of the Golden Dawn, the magical society in which Yeats was prominent for many years and whose rituals provided him with imagery that he never forgot. One of the fundamental symbols of the Order was in fact the Tree of Life, derived from Kabbalistic sources and expressed in geometrical form. The Tree of Life or Minutum Mundum expresses the degrees of being and the way of ascent through the ten Sephiroth to the *Ain Soph,* that final wisdom which is the ground of being. The Golden Bird, and this once more is hermetic imagery, represents the purified soul. Byzantium in the second poem has moved out of history: it has become the City of the Dead and the poet is concerned with the fate of the soul after death. The method is still to add hermetic and pagan images to Byzantine images. The image and the shade of the second stanza have been related to the *ka* and *bai,* the impersonal double and the soul, often represented as bird-shaped, but with human head and often human arms, of Egyptian after life. Cumont's *After Life in Roman Paganism* (1922)—Yeats knew of Cumont's work —has a number of striking parallels of word and idea with "Byzantium": the astrological sun and moon imagery, the journey of the departed soul across water, Hermes's role as summoner to rebirth, and the distinction between "image" and "shade." The cock of Hades is associated with Hermes as summoner, and this, as well as the dolphins, appears in Mrs. Strong. The cock on sarcophagi was intended first as an emblem of protection against evil spirits, later became an image of rebirth and is frequently associated with the sun. In Regardie's *Golden Dawn*, Hermes's cock perches on the Tree of Life and it appears with the God in the Tarot pack.

A further example of this syncretistic method appears in the introduction of the Dolphin, who carries the souls of the dead. Yeats knew this detail in Mrs. Strong, though in Angelo de Gubernatis' *Zoological Mythology* (1872) which he often used there is a more explicit account. Dolphins ridden by winged children are not unusual in Roman sarcophagi, and dolphins are found with peacocks in the decoration of San Vitale; dolphins with putti were a favorite motif with Renaissance sculptors. And when he went to Sweden to receive the Nobel prize in 1923, Yeats, as Dr. Melchiori reminds us, saw Carl Milles' *Sol Glitter,* a naiad riding a dolphin.

It is because Byzantium can include so much that Yeats can use it so powerfully; his synthetic or syncretistic method makes for the richness of the symbol; the sustained rhetoric guarantees its power. But of course this method, with the need it imposes for analysis of the kind sketched above, makes for difficulty and uncertainty—and of the second poem there is no completely acceptable account. Images of a lifetime are present; but there is no assurance that they still carry the meanings they had in earlier contexts. What is asserted with clarity, unforgettably, is Byzantium itself: and the stylization of nature's violence and disorder.

A Vision

by A. G. Stock

A Vision, with its doubtful origins, its bizarre terminology, and the unfashionable drift of its philosophy, is an awkward book to swallow. One naturally asks what Yeats himself thought about its sources and in what sense he believed in its contents. If the answer to neither question is quite simple it is not because Yeats was being needlessly obscure; but he was moving in an uncertain borderland for which ordinary language is not shaped. As he pointed out, "belief" for the modern mind is not a word with precise, invariable meaning. Even people who accept a common creed may believe it in different ways with different implications, and it is almost impossible to tell the exact truth about one's own beliefs in language that cannot be misunderstood.

It would take an unusually dogmatic mind to be positive that telepathy, mediumship, automatic writing, and the like can never happen, that every recorded instance is either pure chance or pure fraud or a mixture of the two; but to admit the phenomena is not to agree about the explanation or the value to be given to them. Their existence appears to imply something incompatible with a great body of assumptions valid for common life and for scientific reasoning, and this in itself fascinates one kind of mind and makes another kind prefer to leave them alone. Yeats had been fascinated by them since very early youth: he had set out by doubting most of the generally received notions of mind and matter, time and space, and was sure that much in his own experience justified his doubts. In the making of *A Vision*, it seems clear at least that in some way not usual in ordinary intercourse the separation between his own mind and his wife's had broken down. He was not, however, silly enough to make out on this account that the book ought to be accepted as a miraculously inspired gospel. To introduce the first edition he invented a story, which was not and fairly obviously was not intended to be convincing to the most childlike credulity, explaining how he came by the material. This, as he explained in the second edition, was because his wife did not wish to acknowledge her share in it, nor he himself to claim it as his creation in the same sense as his poems. In the second edition he gave a full account of its origin.

He gives the facts, and the construction he puts on them is implied in his phrases. He speaks of "communicators" who are very clear about their doctrine, anxious to teach it to him, impatient of his ignorance and his mistakes, and still more impatient when he questions them in terms learnt from other philosophies. They appear to be bodiless minds, aware of minds and of thoughts, but unaware of the world of sense except as it is reflected in the minds of living men.

> Once when they had given their signal in a restaurant, they explained that, because we had spoken of a garden, they thought we were in it.[1]

And yet the sensible world has meaning for them; at another time they call a halt in the work to listen to the hoot of an owl, because "sounds like that give us great pleasure." Sounds like that gave Yeats great pleasure too, for his poetry is full of them; they may well have listened through his ears.

They are hypersensitive to communicated thought, and afraid of being influenced by it:

> They once told me not to speak of any part of the system, except of the incarnations which were almost fully expounded, because if I did that the people I talked to would talk to other people, and the communicators would mistake the misunderstanding for their own thought.[2]

They have a queer inner certainty of something which has to be communicated to the outer world, but this outer world is a confusion and a menace to them because they can only be aware of it through the intervention of embodied minds.

Besides the communicators there are "frustrators" who slip in at times to confuse him with misleading teaching. But unless he himself is suspicious enough to ask point-blank, the communicators will not tell him when the frustrators have been at work. Only once, when some masquerading frustrator has been explaining "a geometrical model of the soul's state after death, which could be turned upon a lathe," the communicators burst out with a reprimand as if goaded beyond endurance by seeing the symbols they have given him reduced to absurd mechanical toys.

---

[1] *A Vision*, p. 10.   [2] *Ibid.*, p. 11.

The sudden indignant interruption suggested a mind under a dream constraint, which it could throw off if desire were strong enough, as we can sometimes throw off a nightmare.[3]

Throughout his writings, Yeats regarded the reasoning that systemizes mechanically for system's sake as a danger to the intuitive perception of truth. He was aware of his own bent for just such reasoning, and disapproved of it; it looks as if the communicators only anticipated what would have been his considered feeling about the ingenious gadget.

He tells us little more about the frustrators' actual messages. But if this hint is enough to go upon they were perhaps working with one side of his mind, the mechanically logical side, to the exclusion of the intuitive perception for which as a poet he must always be alert. In the completed structure of *A Vision* both obviously have their place, but its essence is in the second; logical coherence is only an instrument for expounding and ordering the intuitive perception and if it went beyond this would make nonsense of the whole.

He could not say positively why the frustrators desired to mislead or the communicators to instruct him. The teaching did not seem to be given out of regard for him. They were indifferent what else he did with it provided he put their meaning into a correct form; it was as if they needed his power of expression for some purpose not his. Nor would he say positively whether he took them to be separate beings, or separate parts of his own being, or different voices from a confused being other than himself; only, for the most part, treating them as separate beings was the clearest way to write about them.

In fact he could not easily have explained more. One thing Yeats certainly believed was that the source of all things is in mind, that human minds are in some way a part of that source and the world they look out on in some way an emanation or reflection of it. He believed in consequence that the mind, turned away from the phenomenal world, might have more direct access to ultimate reality and thence even a reinforced power over the phenomenal world itself. For this world, in its relation to reality, was what ultimately interested him: he was not disposed to cry "Om! Om!" and let it go to blazes.

Many people, in Europe as well as Asia, may be ready to accept the theory in the abstract. But ordinary thinking for which ordinary language is framed begins from quite different assumptions, so habitual that they are used without even being consciously remembered, far less questioned. To throw them over is like passing from a known science to another with a totally different set of concepts, or learning a language

[3] *Ibid.*, p. 14.

with a different etymology and grammatical structure. Within the new terms you cannot talk about the same things in the same way, and though you can think about some things with a precision which was impossible before, the uninitiated cannot follow your process of thought. The old criteria for distinguishing between sensible and nonsensical statements do not apply. Not that the distinction ceases to exist, but to make it with confidence you must learn the appropriate discipline.

Yeats had done this in years of exacting occult studies, but few of his readers and critics find it worth while to follow him. Moving in a world of thought where matter is liable to dissolve into mind and the values normally given to subjective and objective perceptions break down, he could not give "straight" answers to questions about whose mind is the source of what and in what sense minds are separate and in what sense one; but he did not therefore accept as authoritative any nonsense which purported to come from a supernatural source. He judged in terms of his own learning.

He compared the voices to dreams. He believed that dreams were not mere reflections from the actual, but projections from the reality underlying it, and at the same time they were plastic and deceitful. The two statements are not contradictory, and to accept them both perhaps brings us nearer to most people's experience of dreams than to deny either.

Sometimes the philosophic voices themselves have become vague and trivial or have in some other way reminded us of dreams. Furthermore their doctrine supports the resemblance, for one said in the first month of communication, "We are often but created forms," and another, that spirits do not tell a man what is true but create such conditions, such a crisis of fate, that the man is compelled to listen to his Daimon. And again and again they have insisted that the whole system is the creation of my wife's Daimon and of mine and that it is as startling to them as to us. Mere "spirits," my teachers say, are the objective, a reflection and distortion; reality itself is found by the Daimon in what they call, in commemoration of the Third Person of the Trinity, the Ghostly Self. The blessed spirits must be sought within the self which is common to all.

Much that has happened, much that has been said, suggests that the communicators are the personalities of a dream shared by my wife, myself, occasionally by others. . . . In partly accepting and partly rejecting that explanation for reasons I cannot now discuss, in affirming a Communion of the Living and the Dead, I remember that Swedenborg has described all those between the celestial state and death as plastic, fantastic, and deceitful, the dramatis personae of our dreams; that Cornelius Agrippa attributed to Orpheus these words: "The Gates of Death must not be unlocked, within is a people of dreams." [4]

[4] *Ibid.*, pp. 22-23.

Readers may rephrase this for themselves and rationalize it according to the postulates of their own thinking, and in doing so will perhaps discover what they themselves think about the ghostly communicators. They are not likely to arrive at a more accurate statement of Yeats's own view.

But he did believe intensely in the teaching of *A Vision*, and if "by their fruits shall ye know them" is sound logic he was right, for writing it increased his power as a poet enormously. Turning from *Responsibilities* to *The Tower*, it is impossible to think that he had been wasting his brains in the interval. He meant so much by it that he went on writing and revising it till within a year or two of his death, and wrote to Edmund Dulac in 1937:

> I do not know what my book will be to others—nothing perhaps. To me it means a last act of defence against the chaos of the world, and I hope for ten years to write out of my renewed security.[5]

The thinking which he put into it so ardently is neither metaphysical nor scientific, but mythological. His language about the soul begs all the questions which a metaphysician would be bound to reason out. In writing of history he does not try to investigate facts; he takes them from whatever authorities have appealed to him and interprets them by a thesis. But he creates and arranges images so as to express his sense of values, and this is the genius of mythology. A myth is a myth not because it is false to physical or historical fact but because, true or false, it offers just such an expressive image. If we believe absolutely in its values we accept it as true, in a sense to which mere factual accuracy can only be an endorsement. In this sense, without reference to their historical authenticity, the crucifixion of Christ and the meditation of Buddha and Demeter's search for Persephone are all alike myths. In this sense the evolution of man and the class struggle have perhaps taken shape as myths in our own time, but each of these expresses values which Yeats abhorred.

A Vision is his own myth, a statement of values completely true for himself, though, as his words to Dulac admit, possibly for no one else. The apparatus of Faculties and Principles and whirling gyres amounts to a complicated algebraical formula which arranges in intelligible order the whole of his knowledge and experience.

Hardly anything is set down "as fact." He assumes one concept—the soul, or Daimon, existing in eternity, and though he does not define it very explicitly the meaning is clear enough for anyone but a meta-

[5] From Ellmann, *Yeats, The Man and the Masks*, p. 294. The words perhaps take on further meaning in the light of his description of a civilization as "a struggle to keep self-control."

physician. He conceives each individual Daimon as an aspect of the all-inclusive One, the ground of all being. This underlying One is acknowledged, but neither in *A Vision* nor in his poems as a whole is it the thing chiefly emphasized. It is a knowledge on which, at rare moments in his poetry, he sinks back restfully, but he thinks of them as moments rather of exhaustion than of achievement. One of the clearest is in the 1921 volume, in the middle of civil war:

> For one throb of the artery,
> While on that old grey stone I sat
> Under the old wind-broken tree,
> I knew that One is animate,
> Mankind inanimate fantasy.[6]

But this knowledge is not what he seeks. The Daimon is man's link with God, through which all souls are in some sense joined to one another, and the bent of his mind made this belief a starting-point for exploring magic and telepathy rather than for the beatitude of contemplation. The mystic's ecstasy in merging himself with the One is not his quest; more important, more exciting, is the uniqueness of the individual soul's experience. He does not think of life in the world as a fall. The creative artist can hardly do so, for to him the formless gains, not loses, by taking on form. It is the Daimon's deliberate choice, for since time and space are necessary conditions of consciousness the soul's experience is a part of the self-knowledge of God.

Yeats's father, who was a rationalist, held that the greatest thing in the world was human personality. In his own transcendental terms, Yeats is not far from his father's position.

For a mind to which the soul's experience and its immortality are so much more interesting than knowledge of the Absolute, reincarnation is almost a necessary idea. It appears to be a part of pagan Irish tradition and may be latent in the Irish imagination, for it will sometimes crop up like an irrepressible survival in the talk of quite orthodox Christians. Yeats had accepted it naturally, and in his early youth the Brahmin Mohini Chatterjee tried to make him think of it as an exercise for the tranquillizing of desire.

> Somebody asked him if we should pray, but even prayer was too full of hope, of desire, of life, to have any part in that acquiescence that is the beginning of wisdom, and he answered that one should say, before sleeping, "I have lived many lives. I have been a slave and a prince. Many a beloved has sat upon my knees and I have sat upon the knees of many a beloved. Everything that has been shall be again." [7]

[6] *Collected Poems*, p. 214.
[7] "The Pathway" (*Collected Works*, vol. VIII).

But though the doctrine itself was after Yeats's heart, his early poem "Fergus and the Druid" shows that even then he was not satisfied with this use of it. He was not at all sure that he wanted to lose the active passion of life in contemplative serenity. In 1929, after writing *A Vision* had cleared his thoughts, he recalled the Brahmin's words with a gloss of his own:

> That he might set at rest
> A boy's turbulent days
> Mohini Chatterjee
> Spoke these, or words like these.
> I add in commentary,
> "Old lovers yet may have
> All that time denied—
> Grave is heaped on grave
> That they be satisfied." [8]

Ten years later he speaks of reincarnation in "Under Ben Bulben" as if he had learnt it from Ireland, not India:

> Many times man lives and dies
> Between his two eternities,
> That of race and that of soul,
> And ancient Ireland knew it all. [9]

This poem ends in an epitaph, but in it, as in all his last poems, his gaze is turned fiercely lifeward and he thinks of time as the incarnation of eternity. To return again and again to the flesh is not a punishment as in Indian philosophy, but the soul's deliberate choice.

Long before, in his preface to Lady Gregory's *Gods and Fighting Men* he had written:

> It sometimes seems as if there were a kind of day and night of religion, and that a period where the influences are those that shape the world is followed by a period where the greater power is in influences that would lure the soul out of the world, out of the body. [10]

This is an earlier form of the thought which grew into "Dove or Swan." It is the chief of the antinomies summed up in his symbolic gyres, a dual movement reflected in the magnifying glass of history. History for him was a partial interpretation of the human soul: men make it, not by planning, but inevitably as they make their shadows, by being where

[8] *Collected Poems*, p. 279.   [9] *Collected Poems*, p. 398.   [10] *Plays*, p. xix.

and what they are. In so far as prophecy was possible it was not by understanding the mechanistic forces which the Marxist uses as his key, but by understanding the complexity of the human soul and its rhythms. And because he took account of this complexity he could maintain a strange, detached tolerance side by side with fierce partisanship.

Within the soul the lifeward-turning impulse is what he calls the antithetical. It makes a man aspire to mirror in himself all that he can conceive of wisdom and beauty and power, and live to his utmost intensity. In history he sees it as dominant in the pagan ideal world, where the gods are within nature, where perfection is manifold and pride and passion and conflict are not evil; a world for heroes and poets, but harsh to the weak. The opposing primary movement is the soul's self-transcendence, the impulse to service and self-forgetfulness. It sees God beyond the world and sees man as nothing, unless he is the instrument of a power greater than himself. Pride is its deadly sin, but it shelters the weak under a canopy of brotherly love and teaches men to despise all that distinguishes themselves individually and to venerate only what is universal. In history its reign was heralded when the Virgin Mary sang, "He hath put down the mighty from their seat, and hath exalted the humble and meek," and divinity took the form of the most helpless thing on earth.

But since these opposites are in the soul itself the world swings perpetually between them—in the lives of men, in religious and secular thought, in the greater and lesser cycles of civilization. Embodied in time the soul of man is not a simple essence, and while one part enjoys its carnival another part, feeding on scraps, grows quietly among the shadows till it steps forward and breaks up its opposite, reintegrating the dismembered pieces into an unimaginably new pattern of its own. An aristocratic age cracks when it has hardened into hierarchical forms, emptied of the indwelling divinity which once inspired them:

> What if the glory of escutcheoned doors,
> And buildings that a haughtier age designed. . . .
> What if those things the greatest of mankind
> Consider most to magnify, or to bless,
> But take our greatness with our bitterness? [11]

A democratic age ends by losing its awareness of the God before whom all men are equally everything and nothing, and exalts equality for equality's sake in dead administrative efficiency. There is no evolution towards an all-inclusive perfection in his scheme, there is only the gyre, each circuit of which is the denial of another. And yet, with ages as with

---

[11] *Collected Poems*, p. 226.

incarnations of men, the present builds out of the fragments of a super-seded past, and for its new design it may draw much or little, according to its wisdom and vision, from the accumulated skill of the old builders. In interpreting history Yeats seems to have felt that he was preserving half-forgotten values from the far past, doomed to be still further ob-literated before the far future tried to recreate them.

He was not religious, if religion is a striving for absorption out of the world into the universality of God. His father had told him this.

> You can only pretend it. Your interest is in mundane things, and heaven to you is this world made better, whether beyond the stars or not.[12]

By contrast, and not with unqualified approval, he saw the genuine re-ligious mystic in his son's friend and fellow-poet A. E.:

> He has no love, no admiration for the individual man. He is too religious to care for really mortal things, or rather, for he does care, to admire and love them.

The distinction was a true one. To A. E., visionary, democrat, and practical builder of the Irish co-operative movement, it was the common humanity in men that mattered: to Yeats it was the distinction of in-dividual personality. In his wheel of incarnations Yeats puts A. E. with the saints and the great scientists and selfless workers for mankind in the primary phases where the celestial sun is king; for saint and scientist alike renounce the choices of the personal will to lay themselves open to a truth from beyond it. The great poets belong to the moon, with the passionate heroes they celebrate. But he might have answered his father that the moon also is religion, though of a different kind. In the doctrine as he formulated it there are elements from many sources, but the proportions of the complete design are neither Christian, Hindu, nor Buddhist, but pagan; both the supernaturalism and the love of life are of a pagan kind. It is as if Oisin had lived on unconverted somewhere in Europe, and as the centuries passed had enlarged and adapted his original Druidic faith, taking into it whatever could be integrated of Greek or Christian or oriental thought. From the beginning Yeats had been on Oisin's side, and in old age he could still declare

Homer is my example and his unchristened heart.[13]

[12] See Joseph Hone, *W. B. Yeats, 1865-1939*, pp. 46-47, for this and the following quotation.
[13] *Collected Poems*, p. 286. But cf. Virginia Moore's very different reading of this line in *The Unicorn*, chap. IX.

In one passage of *A Vision* he relates his scheme to that of Plotinus, whose universe is arranged on levels of diminishing reality from the timeless One to the fleeting world of sense. It is necessary, he points out, that primary man who looks beyond himself should see it thus; it is equally necessary that gyres and not planes should express anti-thetical man's vision of a many-centered universe with the absolute at the heart of every circle. Plotted on a graph the phases of his gyres go round and round, so that there is no reason in logic or geometry, but only in emotion, to prefer the full moon to the dark. On his own show-ing indeed, Yeats too must enter a primary phase in some future in-carnation. It is imaginable that by then the world will have come round to the antithetical and be pursuing such a vision of heroic anarchy as he longed for in his poems, while he slaves in patient humility in some hospital for the destitute, caring too much for the image of God in man to waste his energy on poetry. Or rather, of course, it will not be William Yeats who lives thus, but the timeless Daimon behind the transitory man who projects himself into life after life, foreseeing and choosing, between lives, what the next shall be, till he has taken in all experience. But here and now the writer of *A Vision* is antithetical man; he must pursue his own unity of being and admire all proud and lonely things, must set himself against the levelling spirit of his primary age. Through his symbol he acknowledges the right to exist, and even the necessity, of ideals he does not share, and at the same time fights for his personal ideal with the whole energy of his spirit; accepts the certainty of defeat, and makes defeat and victory equally unimportant in the endless cycle of change. This, though it is not listed in any register, is a religion both exhilarating and exacting.

The world's great myths and symbols are an attempt not so much to comprehend the directionlessness of infinity—if they were, the phase-less sphere would be enough for all—as to find a standpoint in it, and trace a pattern to which thought and experience may conform. The patterns differ but the fabric is the same for all: all have to take account of the fluid world, and of human action and passion, and of the con-sciousness of eternity which is behind these. But it is time rather than eternity that presses most heavily on the greater part of mankind for most of their lives. Throughout history, religion and philosophy have sought to tranquillize the passions by detaching men from their personal, temporal preoccupations. The great teachers and sages reach beyond the personal to a detachment which does not nullify joy and pain, but makes them indifferently acceptable. There is a lower level on which religion is turned into a quest for immunity from the shocks of experience, in partial or complete withdrawal from passionate life. Not to love or hate much is not to be exposed to deep suffering, and so

> Lips that would kiss
> Form prayers to broken stone[14]

—and the serenity of emotions thus anaesthetized is a spurious copy of the serenity of a deeper insight.

Yeats was not in search of this kind of security. Poetry had admitted him to an eternal world before the actual world took hold of him, and he was more in danger of resting there than of losing sight of it. As a young man he knew and was troubled by this; in "The Man Who Dreamed of Faeryland," one of the best of his early poems, he recognizes the power to withdraw from life as a gift not wholly blessed:

> He stood among a crowd at Dromahair;
> His heart hung all upon a silken dress,
> And he had known at last some tenderness,
> Before earth took him to her stony care;
> But when a man poured fish into a pile,
> It seemed they raised their little silver heads,
> And sang what gold morning or evening sheds
> Upon a woven world-forgotten isle
> Where people love beside the ravelled seas;
> That Time can never mar a lover's vows
> Under that woven changeless roof of boughs:
> The singing shook him out of his new ease.[15]

In some of his early letters to Katharine Tynan he is uneasy, both as man and poet, because he is too much wrapped up in his dreams; intensity of feeling for life is eluding him.

> I have woven about me a web of thoughts. I wish to break through it, to see the world again.
>   Yesterday I went to see, in a city hotel, an acquaintance who has had sudden and great misfortunes, come in the last few days to a crisis. . . . I saw his hands and eyes moving restlessly and that his face was more shrunken than when I saw him some months before. Of course all this pained me at the time but I know (now that he is out of my sight) that if I heard that he was dead I would not think twice about it. So thick has the web got.[16]

And when he was preparing *The Wanderings of Oisin* for press he wrote to her that his poetry so far was "the cry of the heart against necessity," and that he hoped some day to write poetry of insight and

---

[14] T. S. Eliot, "The Hollow Men."   [15] *Collected Poems*, p. 49.   [16] *Letters*, p. 58.

knowledge. It is startling to find him, at twenty-three, so clearly aware of his limitations.

Evidently he was not content, even when he seemed to be so, to let the love of poetry beckon him out of the world as the love of God may beckon a saint. In middle age he wrote in an essay:

The imaginative writer differs from the saint in that he identifies himself— to the neglect of his own soul, alas!—with the soul of the world, and frees himself from all that is impermanent in that soul, an ascetic not of women and wine but of the newspapers. That which is permanent in the soul of the world, on the other hand, the great passions that trouble all and have but a brief recurring life of flower and seed in any man, is the renunciation of the saint, who seeks not an eternal art but his own eternity.[17]

And a poem in *The Winding Stair* sums it up succinctly:

> The intellect of man is forced to choose
> Perfection of the life, or of the work,
> And if it take the second must refuse
> A heavenly mansion, raging in the dark.[18]

The gyres make passionate experience as real and significant as the inescapable consciousness of eternity. Both are in his poetry, but the second was visible in it from the beginning: it is the first that grows in power and significance and freedom of expression. He needed and used his philosophy rather to drive him into life than to raise him above it, and this is where he chiefly differed from the contemplative mystics.

There are critics who write apologetically of *A Vision*, as if it were an embarrassment to admirers of Yeats' poetry. This seems to me needless; it is not only a storehouse but a great achievement in its own right. The claim that visionary revelations are valid, and are worth years of disciplined concentration to receive, will be called sense or nonsense according to different readers' prejudices, but this is not the main point. Dante and Milton would probably have made it, and that does not prevent their writings from being understood by sceptics. On the whole, however, the modern world clings to rationalist prejudices and prefers its own language for the medium of instruction. And it is hard to translate between the languages of supernaturalism and of modern rationalism, since few people are equally at home with both. Overtones of meaning are easily lost in translation, false implications easily slipped in; and like other language problems, this one raises passions over the language itself which obscure the importance of the things said in it, and thus estrange minds fundamentally akin. There are devout believers in the super-

---

[17] "The Two Kinds of Asceticism" (*Collected Works*, vol. VIII).
[18] *Collected Poems*, p. 278.

natural whose faith only extends into an inescapable eternity the dreary profit-and-loss mentality of a materialistic shopkeeper; there are also atheists and rationalists who transcend their egoism as completely as the most visionary of mystics.

Yeats at any rate believed that the whole man was needed to discover truth. He put himself through a discipline which welded together all his scattered perceptions and turned a dreamer's mind into hard crystal, and sought with intense, sustained concentration for a view of the universe which would hold his whole experience of life in one perspective with his whole sense of justice. In whatever form they came to him his conclusions could hardly be negligible. The judgments of *A Vision* are a tremendous intellectual summing-up of a view of life that is fearless and joyous, without blinking the fact of evil and the necessity of conflict. It includes the conception of eternity and the immortality of the soul, but unlike so many transcendental philosophies, it does not thin down the significance of flesh-and-blood experience. Perhaps its most striking quality is that, personal as it is, and full of combative energy, it recognizes diversity, and acknowledges for every man a vision, a quest, and a salvation that are his alone. It also looks at history stretching into the far past and the far future, gives full value to civilization and tradition, and yet contemplates the destruction of both without losing faith in the creative energy of the spirit that has built and will build again. All this is harmonized in the intricate pattern of a cosmic dance, unity and multiplicity at once.

To recognize its moral and intellectual balance is not to treat the book as the sacred scripture of a revealed religion. Yeats himself, except perhaps in moments of dizzy exhilaration, did not think it would make converts or set the world to rights. It is what he called it, one man's defence against the chaos of the world, and this is its real strength.

It is a common complaint that the modern world lacks a coherent philosophy; that science has destroyed religious belief, and uncertain belief has destroyed the sureness of aim and proportion without which the greatest creative art is impossible. Mr. T. S. Eliot has pointed out the strength that Aquinas gave to Dante, and suggests that even Shakespeare might have done greater work, not less passionate but more serene in its total effect, had his age been capable of a statement as inclusive as the *Summa Theologica*. It was not, nor is our own, and a philosophic synthesis cannot be faked and foisted on men whose actual values it does not fit. A poet is neither missionary nor philosopher; he cannot simultaneously reason out his principles and create from them; but he needs principles too self-evident to himself to be questionable, and an audience to whom he can make himself understood without stopping to expound them. Whether that audience is half the world or the fit few that Milton asked for, it is the only one that concerns him.

Yeats had dreamed in his youth of being a great popular poet, of writing epic and dramatic cycles to give back to Ireland, perhaps through Ireland to the world, an integrated vision of perfection; but he never dreamed of accommodating his sense of truth to the world's. He discovered that art could not be popular unless it expressed a vision shared between artist and audience.

> I did not see [he says] until Synge began to write, that we must renounce the deliberate creation of a kind of Holy City in the imagination, and express the individual.[19]

Even to do that in more than random flashes of insight, he had to work down to a "Summa Theologica" hidden like a skeleton in the body of his own poetry, the frame which gave power to the wings. *A Vision* relates together ideas and images scattered through his previous writings, bringing out latent meanings which may sometimes have escaped him when he wrote them. In everything he wrote after it his thought moved with new swiftness and precision, as if he had a survey map of the country of his mind. To articulate it he drew on his life's experience, his reading of history, his Hermetic studies, and ten years of hard work at philosophy after the outline had been drawn, not "constraining one by another," but unifying them in a new whole.

It is not an inviting book: as he truly observed, the symbols are harsh, like those of a dream that has not been worked over by the waking mind. They are also tediously repetitive:

> Yet every symbol, except when it lies in vast periods of time and so beyond our experience, has evoked for me some form of human destiny, and that form, once evoked, has appeared everywhere, as if there were but one destiny, as my own form might appear in a roomful of mirrors.[20]

Just so a devout man will meditate on some text from his scriptures till it becomes a key to interpret things past, present, and to come. He could dig poetry out of it as from a mine. Here, for instance, from an unpromising chapter entitled "Various Tabulations," is

XVI. TABLE OF THE QUARTERS (ANTITHETICAL)

	Inward Contests	*Automatism*	*Condition of Will*
1st Quarter	with body	Instinctive	Instinctive
2nd Quarter	with heart	Imitative	Emotional
3rd Quarter	with mind	Creative	Intellectual
4th Quarter	with soul	Obedient	Moral

[19] *Autobiographies*, pp. 493-94.   [20] *A Vision*, p. 213.

Such tabulations laid out one after another are dry, irritating, un-illuminating, anatomization in place of living discourse. But turn to the ninth "Supernatural Song" in *A Full Moon in March*, and see with how little change the dead matter springs to life:

> He with body waged a fight,
> But body won; it walks upright.
>
> Then he struggled with the heart;
> Innocence and peace depart.
>
> Then he struggled with the mind;
> His proud heart he left behind.
>
> Now his wars on God begin;
> At stroke of midnight God shall win.[21]

If the text is thus alive with inspiration for Yeats himself, why should it not serve as spiritual food for a band of disciples, and become the scripture of a church? I think the answer is in the very structure of the teaching. It is based on a discipline of arduous submission, not to an authority beyond himself (which is what the book would be to a disciple) but to his own inmost self: a skeleton cannot be shared. Even the basic antinomy of "primary" and "antithetical," though it is a workable way of sorting out experience, is not the only way. Another man, less conscious than Yeats, or differently conscious, of divided aims and powers would probably need a different formula, and if he had Yeats's concentration of purpose would find his own, and see the world reflected in it. The constant presupposition is the Daimon, and the doctrine only makes sense to those who believe in their Daimon. "For spirits," as the communicators told him, "do not tell a man what is true, but create such conditions, such a crisis of fate, that the man is compelled to listen to his Daimon" —and if he listens his Daimon will say to him alone what no one else will perfectly understand.

This reinforces what I have said or implied already—that Yeats was no sort of Christian. The statement can be disputed and is hard to defend absolutely: there are many kinds of Christians, and he not only believed in supernatural power but acknowledged the divinity of Christ more unequivocally than some of them. Yet he could not be called a follower of Christ, for it was not in Christian teaching, whether scripturally or traditionally interpreted, that he sought the all-inclusive liberating truth. He sought it within rather than beyond the subjective self; life-giving sap drawn up through the roots rather than rain falling from heaven on the leaves. By pushing the metaphor further one might

---

[21] *Collected Poems*, p. 332.

say that all the waters of life are from one primal fountain, or say in Yeats's own terms that in the phaseless sphere there is no distinction between primary and antithetical. But the distinction does exist in consciousness and alters values, and it seems to me to have a crucial bearing on the meaning of Christian humility. Yeats's own writing seldom echoes that emphasis on shared suffering and shared salvation which, if the ideals of one faith can be distinguished from those of another, is what marks out Christianity. In his play *Calvary*[22] there is a latent antagonism to the thought of Christ as universal redeemer. "God has not died for the white heron"; and the heron's lonely self-sufficiency, though it wanes with the moon, consoles him more than the sacrifice of God.

This aloofness pervades the whole of his thought and sets him as far from Christianity, or indeed from any of the great religious folds, as from atheism or materialism. He demonstrates that a man can walk alone. In our age of collective security this is a portent all the more significant because so few desire to see it.

[22] *Plays*, p. 447.

Yeats' Romanticism

by Allen Tate

I

The profundity of Yeats's vision of the modern world and the width of its perspective have kept me until this occasion from writing anything about the poetry of our time which I most admire. The responsibility enjoins the final effort of understanding—an effort that even now I have not been able to make. The lesser poets invite the pride of the critic to its own affirmation; the greater poets—and Yeats is among them—ask us to understand not only their minds but our own; they ask us in fact to have minds of a related caliber to theirs. And criticism must necessarily remain in the presence of the great poets a business for the anthill: the smaller minds pooling their efforts. For the power of a Yeats will be given to the study of other poets only incidentally, for shock and technique and for the test of its own reach: this kind of power has its own task to perform.

Ours is the smaller task. The magnitude of Yeats is already visible in the failure of the partial, though frequently valuable, insights that the critics have given us in the past twenty years. There is enough in Yeats for countless studies from many points of view, yet I suspect that we shall languish far this side of the complete version of Yeats until we cease to look into him for qualities that neither Yeats nor any other poet can give us; until we cease to censure him for possessing "attitudes" and "beliefs" which we do not share. Mr. Edmund Wilson's essay on Yeats in the influential study of Symbolism *Axel's Castle* asks the poet for a political and economic philosophy; or, if this is unfair to Mr. Wilson, perhaps it could be fairly said that Mr. Wilson, when he was writing the essay, was looking for a political and economic philosophy, and inevitably saw in Yeats and the other heirs of Symbolism an evasion of the reality that he, Mr. Wilson, was looking for. (If you are looking for pins

"Yeats' Romanticism." From *Collected Essays* (Denver: Alan Swallow, 1959), pp. 227-236, by Allen Tate. Copyright © 1941, 1959 by Allen Tate. First published in *The Southern Review*, VII (Winter 1941). Reprinted by permission of the publisher, Alan Swallow. This essay bears the subtitle "Notes and Suggestions."

you do not want needles, though both will prick you.) Mr. Louis Mac-
Neice's book-length study of Yeats says shrewd things about the poetry,
but on the whole we get the impression that Yeats had bad luck in not
belonging to the younger group of English poets, who had a monopoly
on "reality." (The word is Mr. MacNeice's.) Those were the days when
not to be a communist was to be fascist, which is what Mr. MacNeice
makes Yeats out to be. (Yeats liked the ancient "nobility," of which, for
Mr. MacNeice, Wall Street and the City offer examples.)

I cite these two writers on Yeats because in them we get summed up
the case for Yeats's Romanticism, the view that he was an escapist re-
tiring from problems, forces, and theories "relevant" to the modern world.
While it is true that Yeats, like every poet in English since the end of
the eighteenth century, began with a Romantic use of language in the
early poems, he ended up very differently, and he is no more to be fixed
as a Romantic than Shakespeare as a Senecan because he wrote passages
of Senecan rhetoric. If one of the historic marks of Romanticism is the
division between sensibility and intellect, Yeats's career may be seen as
un-Romantic (I do not know the opposite term) because he closed the
gap. His critics would then be the Romantics. I do not think that these
squabbles are profitable. It is still true that Yeats had a more inclusive
mind than any of his critics has had.

II

Two years before Yeats died he wrote to Dorothy Wellesley:

> At this moment all the specialists are about to run together in our new
> Alexandria, thought is about to be unified as its own free act, and the
> shadow in Germany and elsewhere is an attempted unity by force. In my
> life I have never felt so acutely the presence of a spiritual virtue and that is
> accompanied by intensified desire.

Scattered throughout Yeats's prose there are similar passages, but this
one is only from a letter, and it lacks the imaginative reach and synthesis
of the great passages towards the end of *A Vision*, where I recall particularly the fine paragraph on early Byzantium and Section III of "Dove
or Swan" in which Yeats describes the annunciation to Leda which
brought in the classical civilization, as the annunciation to the Virgin
brought in the Christian. Of Byzantium he says:

> I think that in early Byzantium, maybe never before or since in recorded
> history, religious, aesthetic, and practical life were one, that architect and
> artificers—though not, it may be, poets, for language had been the instru-

ment of controversy and must have gone abstract—spoke to the multitude and the few alike. The painter, the mosaic worker, the worker in gold and silver, the illuminator of sacred books, were almost impersonal, almost perhaps without the consciousness of individual design, absorbed in their subject-matter and that the vision of a whole people.

Mr. Cleanth Brooks has shown that the great sonnet "Leda and the Swan" is no pretty picture out of mythology, that it gets its power from the powerful forces of the imagination behind it. Section III of "Dove or Swan" begins:

> I imagine the annunciation which founded Greece as made to Leda, remembering that they showed in a Spartan temple, strung up to the roof as a holy relic, an unhatched egg of hers; and that from one of her eggs came Love and from the other War. But all things are from antithesis, and when in my ignorance I try to imagine what older civilization that annunciation rejected I can but see bird and woman blotting out some corner of the Babylonian mathematical starlight.

In these three passages I believe that we get the main threads of Yeats's thought expressed in language which refers to the famous "system" but which is nevertheless sufficiently clear to persons who have not mastered the system or who even know nothing of it. Study of the Great Wheel with its gyres and cones might give us extensive references for certain ideas in the passage from the letter. We should learn that we are now in the twenty-third phase of our historical cycle, in which thought is abstract and unity of life must be imposed by force, and that culture is Alexandrian. The picture of a perfect culture that he gives us in Byzantium (which in the poem of that name becomes something more than mere historical insight), where men enjoy full unity of being, has too many features in common with familiar Western ideas to be seen as an eccentric piece of utopianism. Byzantium is a new pastoral symbol and will be taken as that by anybody who sees more in the pastoral tradition than ideal shepherds and abstract sheep. The annunciation to Leda offers historical and philosophical difficulties; yet in spite of Yeats's frequently expressed belief that he had found a new historical vision, the conception is not historical in any sense that we understand today. It is a symbol established in analogical terms; that is, our literal grasp of it depends upon prior knowledge of the Annunciation to the Virgin. The "Babylonian mathematical starlight" is self-evidently clear without Yeats's scattered glosses on it: it is darkness and abstraction, quantitative relations without imagination; and I doubt that Yeats's definitions make it much clearer than that. If Leda rejected it, we only learn from Yeats's "system" that the coming of Christ brought it back in; for an entire cultural cycle can be predominantly antithetical or predominantly primary, at the same time that it goes through the twenty-eight phases from primary to antithetical back to primary again.

In the letter to Dorothy Wellesley occurs a sentence which sounds casual, even literally confessional; there is no harm done if we take it at that level; there is merely a loss of insight such as we get in Mr. Mac-Neice's *The Poetry of W. B. Yeats,* in which Yeats's myth is dismissed as "arid" and "unsound." In the midst of the "attempted unity by force," he writes: "In my own life I have never felt so acutely the presence of a spiritual virtue and that is accompanied by intensified desire." The literal student of *A Vision,* coming upon statements like this, may well wonder what has become of the determinism of the system, which, with an almost perverse ingenuity, seems to fix the individual in a system of coordinates from which he cannot escape. Mr. Cleanth Brooks believes that some measure of free will lies in Yeats's conception of the False Mask, which some unpredictable force in the individual may lead him to choose instead of the True Mask. I believe this is only part of the explanation.

Does not the true explanation lie in there being *no* explanation in terms of the system? Even if we see Yeats as he saw himself, a man of Phase 17 living in Phase 23 of our civilization, the discrepancy merely introduces a complication which the system can easily take account of. Mr. MacNeice at this point enlightens us almost in spite of himself: "Freedom for Yeats, as for Engels, was a recognition of necessity—but not of economic necessity, which he considered a vulgarism." Yes; and he would have considered psychological necessity, or any inner determinism no less than an outer, economic determinism, a vulgarism also. But in the phrase the "recognition of necessity" we get a clue to Yeats's own relation to his system and to what seems to me the right way to estimate its value. He only wanted what all men want, a world larger than himself to live in; for the modern world as he saw it was, in human terms, too small for the human spirit, though quantitatively large if looked at with the scientist. If we say, then, that he wanted a *dramatic* recognition of necessity, we shall have to look at the system not as arid or unsound or eccentric, which it well may be in itself, but through Yeats's eyes, which are the eyes of his poetry.

If we begin with the poetry we shall quickly see that there is some source of power or illumination which is also in us, waiting to be aroused; and that this is true of even the greater number of the fine poems in which the imagery appears upon later study to lean upon the eccentric system. I would say, then, that even the terms of the system, when they appear in the richer texture of the poems, share a certain large margin of significance with a wider context than they have in the system itself. May we say that Yeats's *A Vision,* however private and almost childishly eclectic it may seem, has somewhat the same relation to a central tradition as the far more rigid structure of *The Divine Comedy* has to the

Christian myth? I dare say that Mr. Eliot would not chide Dante for accepting a "lower mythology." Perhaps the central tradition in Dante and Yeats lies in a force that criticism cannot specifically isolate, the force that moved both poets to the dramatic recognition of necessity; yet the visible structure of the necessity itself is perhaps not the source of that power. I do not say that Yeats is comparable in stature to Dante; only that both poets strove for a visible structure of action which is indeed necessary to what they said, but which does not explain what they said. I believe that Mr. Eliot should undertake to explain why Arnold's Higher Mythology produced poetry less interesting than Yeats's Lower Mythology, which becomes in Yeats's verse the vehicle of insights and imaginative syntheses as profound as those which Arnold talked about but never, as a poet, fully achieved. Myths differ in range and intensity, but not, I take it, as high and low; for they are in the end what poets can make of them.

If Yeats could feel in the midst of the Alexandrian rigidity and disorder the "presence of a spiritual virtue," was he denying the inclusiveness of the system; or could he have seen his senile vigor and insight in terms of the system? Possibly the latter; but it makes little difference.

III

A Vision has been described by more than one critic as a philosophy; I speak of it here as a "system"; but I doubt that it is a system of philosophy. What kind of system is it? Yeats frequently stated his own purpose, but even that is a little obscure: to put myth back into philosophy. This phrase may roughly describe the result, but it could not stand for the process; it attributes to the early philosophers a deliberation of which they would have been incapable. The language of Plotinus, whose *Enneads* Yeats read late in life, is compounded of primitive symbolism, the esoteric fragments of classical myth, and the terms of Greek technical metaphysics; but there is no calculated intention of instilling myth into philosophy.

In what sense is *A Vision* a myth? There are fragments of many myths brought in to give dramatic and sensuous body to the framework, which attains to the limit of visualization that a complex geometrical picture can provide.

A broad view of this picture, with its gyres and cones, to say nothing of the Daimons and the Principles whose relation to the Faculties defies my understanding, gleans at least two remarkable features. I merely note them:

(1) ". . . the subjective cone is called that of the *antithetical tincture* because it is achieved and defended by continual conflict with its op-

posite; the objective cone is called that of the *primary tincture* because whereas subjectivity—in Empedocles 'Discord' as I think—tends to separate man from man, objectivity brings us back to the mass where we began." From this simple definition—verbally simple, but very obscure—we get the first picture of the intersecting cones; and from this the whole structure is elaborated.

It is clear visually with the aid of the diagrams; but when Yeats complicates it with his Principles and Daimons, and extends the symbol of the gyres to cover historical eras, visualization breaks down. It is an extended metaphor which increasingly tends to dissolve in the particulars which it tries to bring together into unity.

When we come to the magnificent passages on history in "Dove or Swan," all the intricacies of the geometrical metaphor disappear; and the simple figure of historical cycles, which Yeats evidently supposed came out of his gyres, is sufficient to sustain his meaning. Again Yeats's "system" overlaps a body of insight common to us all.

I would suggest, then, for the study of the relation of Yeats's "system" to his vision of man, both historical and individual, this formula: As the system broadens out and merges with the traditional insights of our culture, it tends to disappear in its specific, technical aspects. What disappears is not a philosophy, but only a vast metaphorical structure. In the great elegy, "In Memory of Major Robert Gregory," we get this couplet:

> But as the outrageous stars incline
> By opposition, square and trine;

which is the only astrological figure in the poem. Yet it must not be assumed that Yeats on this occasion turned off the system; it must be there. Why does it not overtly appear? It has been absorbed into the concrete substance of the poem; the material to be symbolized replaces the symbol, and contains its own meaning. I would select this poem out of all others of our time as the most completely expressed: it has a perfect articulation and lucidity which cannot be found in any other modern poem in English.

(2) In his early poems Yeats is concerned with the myths of ancient Ireland. We may find unreadable today a poem like *The Wanderings of Oisin* or plays like *Deirdre* or *The Land of Heart's Desire*. The later poems are less dependent upon fable and fully developed mythical plots for their structures. And yet Yeats entered his later poetic phase at about the same time he began to be interested in his system, in putting myth back into philosophy. Did this mean that he was taking myth out of his poetry?

Thus the second remarkable feature of the system, as I see it, is that it is not a mythology at all, but rather an extended metaphor, as I have already pointed out, which permits him to establish relations between the tag-ends of myths eclectically gathered from all over the world. For example, there is nothing in the geometrical structure of the system which inherently provides for the annunciation to Leda; it is an arbitrary association of two fields of imagery; but once it is established, it is not hard to pass on through analogy to the Annunciation to the Virgin.

IV

Thus it is difficult for me to follow those critics who accept Yeats's various utterances that he was concerned with a certain relation of philosophy to myth. Any statement about "life" must have philosophical implications, just as any genuine philosophical statement must have, because of the nature of language, mythical implications. Yeats's doctrine of the conflict of opposites says nothing about the fundamental nature of reality; it is rather a dramatic framework through which is made visible the perpetual oscillation of man between extreme introspection and extreme loss of the self in the world of action. The intricacies of Yeats's system provide for many of the permutations of this relation; but it cannot foresee them all; and we are constantly brought back to the individual man, not as a symbolic counter, but as a personality rich and unpredictable. Yeats's preference for the nobleman, the peasant, and the craftsman does not betray, as Mr. MacNeice's somewhat provincial contention holds, the "budding fascist"; it is a "version of pastoral" which permits Yeats to see his characters acting above the ordinary dignity of men, in a concrete relation to life undiluted by calculation and abstraction. I can only repeat here that the "system" is perpetually absorbed into action. If Yeats were only an allegorist, the meaning of his poetry could be ascertained by getting hold of the right key. The poetry would serve to illustrate the "system," as the poetry of the Prophetic Books fleshes out the homemade system of Blake.

V

Mr. Eliot's view, that Yeats got off the central tradition into a "minor mythology," and Mr. Blackmur's view, that he took "magic" (as opposed to religion) as far as any poet could, seem to me to be related versions of the same fallacy. Which is: that there must be a direct and effective correlation between the previously established truth of the poet's ideas and the value of the poetry. (I am oversimplifying Blackmur's view, but not Eliot's.) In this difficulty it is always useful to ask: *Where* are the poet's ideas? Good sense in this matter ought to tell us that while the ideas doubtless exist in some form outside the poetry, as they exist for Yeats in the letters, the essays, and *A Vision*, we must nevertheless test them in the poems themselves, and not "refute" a poem in which the gyres supply certain images by showing that gyres are amateur philosophy.

> Turning and turning in the widening gyre
> The falcon cannot hear the falconer. . . .

—the opening lines of "The Second Coming": and they make enough sense apart from our knowledge of the system; the gyre here can be visualized as the circling flight of the bird constantly widening until it has lost contact with the point, the center, to which it ought to be able to return. As a symbol of disunity it is no more esoteric than Eliot's "Gull against the wind," at the end of "Gerontion," which is a casual, not traditional or systematic, symbol of disunity. Both Mr. Blackmur and Mr. Brooks—Mr. Brooks more than Mr. Blackmur—show us the systematic implications of the symbols of the poem "Byzantium." The presence of the system at its most formidable cannot be denied to this poem. I should like to see, nevertheless, an analysis of it in which no special knowledge is used; I should like to see it examined with the ordinary critical equipment of the educated critic; I should be surprised if the result were very different from Mr. Brooks's reading of the poem. The symbols are "made good" in the poem; they are drawn into a wider convention (Mr. Blackmur calls it the "heaven of man's mind") than they would imply if taken separately.

I conclude these notes with the remark: the study of Yeats in the coming generation is likely to overdo the scholarly procedure, and the result will be the occultation of a poetry which I believe is nearer the center of our main traditions of sensibility and thought than the poetry of Eliot or of Pound. Yeats's special qualities will instigate special studies of great ingenuity, but the more direct and more difficult problem of the poetry itself will probably be delayed. This is only to say that Yeats's Romanticism will be created by his critics.

Reality

by Richard Ellmann

> They have put a golden stopper into the mouth of the bottle. Pull
> it, Lord! Let out reality.
> —*Upanishads* (translated by Yeats and Purohit Swami)

> I pray
> That I, all foliage gone,
> May shoot into my joy.
> —YEATS, *The Herne's Egg*

During the last years of his life Yeats struggled to come to even
closer grips with reality. Looking back over his career he was conscious
of much "evasion" and "turning away," and knew how elaborate was
the machinery which he had invented, especially in his prose and in his
day-to-day experience, to prevent frontal attack. In his moments of doubt
even the *Vision* seemed a gigantic protective mask, and like Melville's
Ahab, he sometimes wanted to break through all masks. Frank O'Connor
has described Yeats's relations with other men as "a circuitous and brilliant
strategy performing complicated manoeuvres about non-existent ar-
mies." [1] Few of the poet's friends were aware that this proud, aggressive
man, immortality in his pocket, had evolved the strategy out of timidity.
Yeats knew it well, however, and in 1933 admitted that, though he had
overcome his shyness a little, "I am still struggling with it and cannot
free myself from the belief that it comes from lack of courage, that the
problem is not artistic but moral." [2] Although of late years he had spoken
more directly he was still unsatisfied and felt that he had played his
inner being false by dressing it in costume and metaphor instead of ex-
pressing it directly. Then too he had submerged some of his individuality
in nationalist work, in the Abbey Theatre, in the Senate, and had more

"Reality." Chapter XVIII of *Yeats: The Man and the Masks* (New York: The Mac-
millan Company, 1948) pp. 273-286, by Richard Ellmann. Copyright 1948 by The
Macmillan Company. Reprinted by permission of The Macmillan Company and Faber
& Faber Ltd.

[1] MS of article by Frank O'Connor, in his possession.

[2] *Letters to the New Island*, xii-xiii.

profoundly betrayed it by introspection and cautiousness. Now he must raze the scaffolding and reveal what he had concealed. Sometimes he was content to think that his real self was in his verse. "My character is so little myself," he put in a manuscript book, "that all my life it has thwarted me. It has affected my poems, my true self, no more than the character of a dancer affects the movements of a dance." [3] Usually in the past he had attributed his writings to his mask, but now he suggests that the mask is his uncreative ordinary self which has so often accommodated itself to the demands of convention. Other times even his poems seemed an unsatisfactory expression of that fanatic whom he had tamed to speak an alien tongue, a conventional patter. In a letter of December 17, 1937, he writes of *On the Boiler*, the new occasional publication he is planning: "I must lay aside the pleasant patter I have built up for years, & seek the brutality, the ill breeding, the barbarism of truth." [4] To do so he revealed for the first time the violence of his early quarrels with his father:

When I was in my 'teens I admired my father above all men; from him I learnt to admire Balzac and to set certain passages in Shakespeare above all else in literature, but when I was twenty-three or twenty-four I read Ruskin's "Unto This Last" of which I do not remember a word, and we began to quarrel, for he was John Stuart Mill's disciple. Once he threw me against a picture with such violence that I broke the glass with the back of my head. But it was not only with my father that I quarreled, nor were economics the only theme. There was no dominant opinion I could accept. Then finding out that I (having no clear case—my opponent's case had been clarifying itself for centuries) had become both boor and bore I invented a patter, allowing myself an easy man's insincerity, and for honesty's sake a little malice, and now it seems that I can talk nothing else. But I think I have succeeded, and that none of my friends know that I am a fanatic. . . . But now I must, if I can, put away my patter, speak to the young men before the ox treads on my tongue.[5]

Again and again he tries to tear off the polite, superficial part of himself,

> Leave nothing but the nothings that belong
> To this bare soul, let all men judge that can
> Whether it be an animal or a man.[6]

[3] Hone, 443.

[4] Unpublished letter to Ethel Mannin. This and other letters to Miss Mannin quoted in this chapter are in her possession.

[5] *On the Boiler* (Dublin, Cuala, 1941), 14-15.

[6] "Parnell's Funeral," *The King of the Great Clock Tower* (New York, Macmillan, 1935), 24.

He lies down "where all the ladders start, / In the foul rag-and-bone shop of the heart." [7] He chooses new models; now he is Timon, Lear, or Blake beating against the wall "till Truth obeyed his call";[8] he is a fool, a foolish passionate man,[9] a wild old man,[10] a mad old man.[11] He dreams of Swift and of Parnell, their lives raped by the stupid world. In his last prose work he imagines himself as a half-mad ship's carpenter who mounts *On the Boiler* to denounce his neighbors. He tries to return to the elemental passions as if they were the *prima materia* of the world:

> You think it horrible that lust and rage
> Should dance attendance upon my old age;
> They were not such a plague when I was young;
> What else have I to spur me into song? [12]

Lust and rage are here not the lasciviousness and irascibility of an old man's brain grown febrile, as some critics have said, but pure passions, spontaneous and complete as peasant life. To suit his subject matter Yeats pares his style, too, down to the bone, and writes simple ballads about Cromwell, Parnell, and Roger Casement which ring far truer than the ballads about Moll Magee and Father Gilligan which he had written in his youth. It had taken him a lifetime to acquire this kind of simplicity. To help him he seeks out new friendships with people like Dorothy Wellesley, whose imagination played like his with the basic patterns of life; with F. R. Higgins, who looked on life with the eye of a ballad maker; with Margot Ruddock, whose verse like her mind had sudden bursts of radiant illumination; with Ethel Mannin, whose naturalness he had always striven for; and with Frank O'Connor, who attracted him by his warm, laughing realism. He sought out young men to manage the Abbey Theatre, and, lest the mechanical age outrun him, he gave radio talks for the British Broadcasting Corporation.

These last years suggest the violence of some Hellenistic statue, with Yeats "ravening, raging, and uprooting that he may come / Into the desolation of reality." [13] After Lady Gregory's death in May, 1932, his own health went from bad to worse, until he could not climb the stairs without gasping and stopping continually for breath. He might not have had sufficient energy for his last years of work had not a friend half-jestingly mentioned to him, early in 1934, the Steinach operation for rejuvenation. Yeats was intensely excited and hopeful; to a man who had

[7] "The Circus Animals' Desertion," *Last Poems*, 81.
[8] "An Acre of Grass," *Last Poems*, 17.
[9] *The King of the Great Clock Tower*, vii.
[10] "The Wild Old Wicked Man," *Last Poems*, 32.
[11] "Why Should Not Old Men Be Mad?" *Last Poems*, 76.
[12] "The Spur," *Last Poems*, 37.
[13] "Meru," *The King of the Great Clock Tower*, 44.

remade himself over and over during his lifetime, rejuvenation by any means made an intense appeal. In May, 1934, a distinguished London surgeon performed the operation, and Yeats almost immediately got a great burst of energy such as he had not had for years. His health remained very unsteady, but his attitude towards his maladies was changed. After having written little verse since Lady Gregory's death except the rather mechanical play *The King of the Great Clock Tower* and the philosophical lyric about "Meru," he broke loose after the operation with the little philosophical songs of the Hermit Ribh, which must rank among his best work, and before his death wrote four more plays, including his finest, *Purgatory*, and another book of verse.

In all these writings *reality* is the key word; it is the state which the poet wishes to attain and, in another sense, the state which he must interpret. He must speak, as D. H. Lawrence (whose works he was now reading with pleasure) would put it, from the solar plexus, and say finally what he had always meant to say, and perhaps even more than that, about every aspect of life. Conventional morality and all conventional attitudes were thrust aside. Yeats's bluntness was not always well timed; on several occasions during these years he was abashed to find he had blamed or praised the wrong people, and had to rewrite his poems accordingly. Sometimes, and especially in *On the Boiler*, he deliberately made his statements extravagant. But while his sincerity had its absurd side, it did drive or enable him to think his thoughts through.

During these years he arrived at his final conclusions about politics. He began badly in 1933 by involving himself slightly with a group of Irish fascists who wore blue shirts and at one time seemed likely to threaten the De Valera government. Their leader was General O'Duffy, whom Yeats met not many times, as has been said, but only once. Yeats recognized from the first, as his letters prove, that O'Duffy was a demagogic, fictile man, but hoped that he might develop leaderlike qualities which he never did. Eventually O'Duffy went off with an Irish brigade to fight for Franco in the Spanish civil war. Yeats, like most of his fellow countrymen, was by this time thoroughly disaffected, and hoped O'Duffy would not return from Spain a hero. The general happily did not prove a very helpful acquisition to the Falange.

Although Yeats was often seen in a blue shirt at this time, he had been wearing blue shirts since 1925 or 1926, and the reason was not political but esthetic. If he learned the habit from anyone, it was from William Morris. His brief encounter with O'Duffy must have shown that they were more at odds than in accord. What Yeats wanted was a political party which would espouse Unity of Being and turn it into "a discipline, a way of life," even a "sacred drama." [14] In February, 1934, still toying

[14] *The King of the Great Clock Tower, Commentaries and Poems* (Dublin, Cuala, 1934), 37.

with the unofficial army, he wrote some marching songs for O'Duffy's men which included such lines as:

> What's equality?—Muck in the yard:
> Historic Nations grow
> From above to below.[15]

But by August of the same year he had realized his error and rewrote the poems so that nobody could sing them; and in addition, to show that his earlier utterances had been transitory, he made another poem to embody his growing disaffection with all politics:

> What if the Church and the State
> Are the mob that howls at the door! [16]

In 1935 Yeats still urged in conversation the despotic rule of the educated classes, but as the terror of Fascism and Nazism increased he ceased to speak in favor of any existing government. His friend Ethel Mannin, the novelist, and Ernst Toller tried on one occasion to persuade him to take a definite position against totalitarianism. They asked him to recommend Ossietsky, whom the Nazis had imprisoned, for the Nobel Peace Prize.[17] Yeats refused, and in letters defending himself indicated his disaffection with every known governmental system:

> Do not try to make a politician of me, even in Ireland I shall never I think be that again—as my sense of reality deepens, & I think it does with age, my horror at the cruelty of governments grows greater, & if I did what you want I would seem to hold one form of government more responsible than any other & that would betray my convictions. Communist, Fascist, nationalist, clerical, anti-clerical are all responsible according to the number of their victims. I have not been silent, I have used the only vehicle I possess—verse. If you have my poems by you look up a poem called "The Second Coming." It was written some sixteen or seventeen years ago & fortold what is happening. I have written of the same thing again & again since. . . . I am not callous, every nerve trembles with horror at what is happening in Europe "the ceremony of innocence is drowned." [18]

He did not finally explain his political position until *On the Boiler* (written in 1938), which is chiefly a declaration that politics are irrelevant. He advocates eugenics and individualism and says that nothing else matters:

---

[15] "Three Songs to the Same Tune," *Spectator*, 152 (Feb. 23, 1934), 276.
[16] *The King of the Great Clock Tower* (New York, Macmillan), 39.
[17] Ethel Mannin, *Privileged Spectator* (London, Hutchinson, 1939), 80-84.
[18] Unpublished letter, April 7, 1936.

I was six years in the Irish Senate; I am not ignorant of politics elsewhere, and on other grounds I have some right to speak. I say to those that shall rule here: If ever Ireland again seems molten wax, reverse the process of revolution. Do not try to pour Ireland into any political system. Think first how many able men the country has, how many it can hope to have in the near future, and mold your system upon those men. It does not matter how you get them, but get them. Republics, Kingdoms, Soviets, Corporate States, Parliaments, are trash, as Hugo said of something else "not worth one blade of grass that God gives for the nest of the linnet." These men, whether six or six thousand, are the core of Ireland, are Ireland itself.[19]

One can imagine that, had Yeats lived on during the second World War, he would have had little to say about its issues, and would merely have repeated with more conviction a remark he made somewhat at random about the first war, "We should not attribute a very high degree of reality to the Great War." [20] He would have taken the position more confidently because he thought he had come at last to "a coherent grasp of reality," [21] and was now wholly preoccupied with it.

It will be remembered that *A Vision* had prophesied that after 1927 "Men will no longer separate the idea of God from that of human genius, human productivity in all its forms." Until late in 1931 the closest approach Yeats had discovered to his own way of thinking about reality was in Berkeley, and Berkeley did not associate God's imagination and power with man's as closely as Yeats would have wished. But in 1931 he found confirmation in an unexpected quarter. He made the acquaintance of an Indian swami, Shri Purohit, and learned that in the wisdom literature of the East the accepted belief was that "the individual self, eater of the fruit of action, is the universal Self, maker of past and future." [22] At the highest moments of consciousness the individual self, detached from action, was aware of this identity. In the efforts which the Indian holy man makes to get rid of all that prevents this knowledge Yeats found his own image of the artist who purges away the inessential to get down to the bedrock of passion. That the total meaning of the Upanishads was different from this did not escape him, but he imagined some reconciliation between East and West; as he wrote Ethel Mannin, "I want to plunge myself into impersonal poetry, to get rid of the bitterness, irritation & hatred, my work in Ireland has brought into my soul, I want to make a last song, sweet & exultant, a sort of European *Geeta,* or rather my *Geeta* not doctrine but song." [23] For four years Yeats and Purohit

[19] *On the Boiler*, 13.

[20] Unpublished note among MSS of first edition of *A Vision*.

[21] Unpublished letter to Mrs. Shakespear, Feb. 21, 1933.

[22] Shree Purohit Swami and Yeats, *The Ten Principal Upanishads* (London, Faber, 1937), 34.

[23] Unpublished letter to Ethel Mannin, June 24, 1935.

were closely associated, until in 1936 the swami returned to India. During their friendship Yeats wrote introductions to the swami's autobiography, to a partial autobiography by the swami's master, and to the swami's translation and annotation of Patanjali's *Aphorisms of Yoga*. In 1936 poet and holy man went to Majorca to translate the Upanishads.

Stimulated by this friendship, Yeats seriously considered devoting his remaining years to philosophical verse; in 1933 and 1934 he wrote a group of philosophical poems but then used his theories less directly. He was surprised and delighted, while preparing an anthology of modern verse for the Oxford University Press, to discover that other poets were dealing with similar themes. He read with excitement Dorothy Welles-ley's "Matrix," which had lines like, "The spiritual, the carnal, are one," when he himself had written only shortly before, "Natural and super-natural with the self-same ring are wed." [24] In Turner, another of the poets whom he praised extravagantly in the introduction to his anthology, he read, "I had watched the ascension and decline of the Moon / And did not realize that it moved only in my own mind." Yeats rejoiced to find companions on the route, and predicted that they must go even further, "that soul must become its own betrayer, its own deliverer, the one activity, the mirror turn lamp." [25]

Because of this all-encompassing belief in soul, self, or imagination, words which Yeats uses interchangeably, many of his later poems assert more peremptorily than before the virtual identity between images produced by the imagination and actual people and events. Yeats liked to tell Frank Harris's story of Ruskin's picking up a phantom cat, opening the window, and throwing the cat outside. In *The King of the Great Clock Tower*, *The Death of Cuchulain*, "The Circus Animals' Desertion," and elsewhere he calls all his characters together as if to say, here is the universe which I have created and peopled and made as real as anything in the world:

> Are those things that men adore and loathe
> Their sole reality?
> What stood in the Post Office
> With Pearse and Connolly?
>
> .   .   .   .
>
> Who thought Cuchulain till it seemed
> He stood where they had stood? [26]
>
> Did that play of mine send out
> Certain men the English shot? [27]

[24] "Ribh Denounces Patrick," *The King of the Great Clock Tower*, 41.
[25] Yeats, "Introduction," *Oxford Book of Modern Verse*, xxxiii.
[26] *The Death of Cuchulain*, *Last Poems*, 125-26.
[27] "The Man and the Echo," *Last Poems*, 83.

When Pearse summoned Cuchulain to his side,
What stalked through the Post Office? [28]

Not only are the symbols like men, but conversely the men are like symbols or actors:

Come gather round me, players all:
Come praise Nineteen-Sixteen,
Those from the pit and gallery
Or from the painted scene
That fought in the Post Office
Or round the City Hall. . . .

Who was the first man shot that day?
The player Connolly,
Close to the City Hall he died;
Carriage and voice had he;
He lacked those years that go with skill,
But later might have been
A famous, a brilliant figure
Before the painted scene.[29]

A man is welded to his image, a player to his role; when we speak of the *drama* of a heroic action our language is no more figurative than when we speak of its *reality*. Yeats does not escape his own symbols, but is caught up into them also, and in the poem "High Talk" he describes himself as Malachi Stilt-Jack, and insists that the stilts are part of him as much as his body is, and that, on the other hand, both are also metaphor: "All metaphor, Malachi, stilts and all." All that he has thought and created is part of him, substantial as his flesh.

But even after Yeats had hammered home the power of the human imagination, one question was left. What is the relation between the human self and the universal Self of the Upanishads, or, to put it another way, what limitations upon man's omnipotence exist? What is the relation, for example, between life and death, or between man and God? Once Yeats had said that man had created death, but that was a momentary cry of defiance; he thought a great deal more about this subject now that he was preparing the second edition of *A Vision*, and came to the conclusion that life stood in relation to death or to destiny or to God as his two gyres stood to one another. "To me," he wrote Ethel Mannin, "all things are made of the conflict of two states of consciousness, beings

[28] "The Statues," *Last Poems*, 57.
[29] "Three Songs to the One Burden," *Last Poems*, 54.

or persons which die each others life live each others death. That is true of life & death themselves." [30]

Rarely had he pushed his thoughts so far before. The new the *Vision,* when it appeared in 1937, put a great deal of emphasis upon the Thirteenth Cycle, "which may deliver us from the twelve cycles of time and space," [31] a doctrine that in 1925 he had hardly touched upon. The idea of thirteen cycles seems to have come from Christ and the Twelve Apostles; and the Thirteenth Cycle, with its absurdly mechanical title, has many qualities of divinity. "Within it live all souls that have been set free," Yeats says.[32]

But not until the last pages of the book does the Thirteenth Cycle assume its real importance. There Yeats describes how, having fully evolved and knit together the symbol of *A Vision,* he draws himself up into the symbol, as he could well do now that it was wholly personalized as a system and systematized as an expression of personality. He declares, "It seemed as if I should know all . . . and find everything in the symbol," and then makes a startling shift to a kind of theology:

> But nothing comes—though this moment was to reward me for all my toil. Perhaps I am too old. . . . Then I understand. I have already said all that can be said. The particulars are the work of the *thirteenth sphere* or cycle which is in every man and called by every man his freedom. Doubtless, for it can do all things and knows all things, it knows what it will do with its own freedom but it has kept the secret.[33]

Only at this point do we realize that Yeats, after building up a system over three hundred pages, in the last two pages sets up that system's anti-self. All the determinism or quasi-determinism of *A Vision* is abruptly confronted with the Thirteenth Cycle which is able to alter everything, and suddenly free will, liberty, and deity pour back into the universe. The revolt against his father's scepticism and against his own was complete at last, though it brought him to no church. God had forced His way ineluctably into Yeats's mind:

> Then my delivered soul itself shall learn
> A darker knowledge and in hatred turn
> From every thought of God mankind has had,
> Thought is a garment and the soul's a bride
> That cannot in that trash and tinsel hide:
> In hating God she may creep close to God.
>
> At stroke of midnight soul cannot endure
> A bodily or mental furniture.

[30] Unpublished letter, Oct. 20, 1938.   [31] *A Vision* (1938), 210.
[32] *Idem.*   [33] *A Vision* (1938), 301-2.

What can she take until her Master give!
Where can she look until He make the show!
What can she know until He bid her know!
How can she live till in her blood He live! [34]

Looking back over Yeats's work we can see that such a God was always likely to come out of it; the "Eternal Darkness" and the "great journey-man" were among His antecedents, but until now He had been as much as possible disregarded and His power undermined. He is the God of unwilling belief.[35]

Whether Yeats meant that the Thirteenth Cycle could "do all things" or could merely influence the "particulars" he does not seem to have decided. In the passage from the *Vision* it is noticeable that he takes both positions. Either way his theories were considerably disrupted by their enlargement. Some of his resultant uneasiness may be observed in an essay which he wrote on Shelley, where he says that the plot in *Prometheus Unbound* was made incoherent because Shelley, in defiance of his theories, made Demogorgon terrible instead of benevolent:

> Demo-gorgon made his plot incoherent, its interpretation impossible, it was thrust there by that something which again and again forced him to balance the object of desire conceived as miraculous and superhuman, with nightmare.[36]

Yeats's God also disturbs the plot. No doubt he was thinking of this element in his thought when, in October, 1938, he wrote Ethel Mannin that the *Vision* was his "public philosophy," while his "private philosophy" remained unpublished because he only half understood it.[37] Had he lived, he would probably have tried to systematize more formally the relation between God and man.

But such systematization was not necessary for two plays which he wrote between 1936 and his death in 1939, where his new theology is introduced. The hero of *The Herne's Egg* (1936-37), "the strangest, wildest thing" [38] he had ever written, deliberately and knowingly commits sacrilege against the Great Herne by raping his priestess. The deity

---

[34] *The King of the Great Clock Tower*, 42-43.

[35] In one of his last essays, Yeats makes the significant remark: "I think profound philosophy must come from terror. An abyss opens under our feet; inherited convictions, the pre-suppositions of our thoughts, those Fathers of the Church Lionel Johnson expounded, drop into the abyss. Whether we will or no we must ask the ancient questions: Is there reality anywhere? Is there a God? Is there a Soul?" "Modern Poetry: A Broadcast," *Essays 1931 to 1936*, 21. Cf. *A Vision* (1938), 301.

[36] "Prometheus Unbound," *Essays 1931 to 1936*, 57.

[37] Unpublished letter, Oct. 9, 1938.

[38] Unpublished letter to Ethel Mannin, Dec. 19, 1935.

never appears on the stage but at the climactic moment manifests himself convincingly by thunder. As a result of the desecration the hero is doomed to die at a fool's hand, but rather than allow the prophecy to be fulfilled, and combatting the supernal power to the last, he kills himself. Cuchulain, in Yeats's last play *The Death of Cuchulain* (1938-39), recognizes that to go forth to battle will probably be fatal and suspects that his adversary is this time not an army of men but death itself; yet, though he could avoid the combat, he goes forward flaunting his individuality against inevitability. All that is known fights with all that is unknown; God is Himself man's opponent, and the final struggle is with Him, whether He keep His own shape or take that of death or destiny. As Yeats wrote in a little poem called "The Four Ages of Man,"

> He with body waged a fight,
> But body won; it walks upright.
>
> Then he struggled with the heart;
> Innocence and peace depart.
>
> Then he struggled with the mind;
> His proud heart he left behind.
>
> Now his wars on God begin;
> At stroke of midnight God shall win.[39]

The war on God is the ultimate heroism, and like all heroism in Yeats ends in defeat.

For the poet who had at last made room for God in his cosmogony, the stroke of midnight was fast approaching. In 1937 Yeats found breathing and walking so difficult that, though he had previously anticipated death with terror, he now told his wife that it was harder for him to live than to die. He tried to recover his health in the south of France, but while he was staying at Cap Martin late in the winter of 1938 he fell terribly ill. On January 21, 1939, he wrote his last poem, "The Black Tower," in which the soldiers still guard the king's tower because they are sworn to do so, though they are sure, or virtually sure, that he will never come again. The following day he said in a letter to a friend:

> I know for certain that my time will not be long. I have put away everything that can be put away that I may speak what I have to speak & I find my expression is a part of "study."
>
> In two or three weeks—I am now idle that I may rest after writing much verse—I will begin to write my most fundamental thoughts & the arrange-

[39] *The King of the Great Clock Tower*, 43.

ment of thought which I am convinced will complete my studies, I am happy and I think full of an energy I had despaired of. It seems to me that I have found what I wanted. When I try to put all into a phrase I say "Man can embody truth but he cannot know it." I must embody it in the completion of my life. The abstract is not life and everywhere drags out its contradictions. You can refute Hegel but not the Saint or the Song of Sixpence.[40]

The life of a saint was a life turned to image, and the Song of Sixpence too was an image condensed out of vapors. This letter was Yeats's final justification of his lifelong effort to cast all his experience into symbol. Four days after writing it he suffered a relapse, but gathered enough strength to dictate some revisions to his wife. Then he passed into a coma and on January 28 he was dead.

He had written his epitaph in verse for a grave at Drumcliff churchyard near Sligo, but technicalities for the time being prevented transportation of the body to Ireland. So, as he had himself suggested, he was carried up the long, high, winding mountain road to the cemetery at Roquebrune for a temporary resting place. The procession ascending the winding path was a last use of one of the poet's symbols.

His death was not immediately announced, so one wreath did not arrive till after the funeral was over and everyone had left. It was from James Joyce, a fellow symbolist who believed with equal intensity in natural things.[41]

[40] Letter to Lady Elizabeth Pelham, in Hone, 510. Corrected by reference to her copy.
[41] Allan Wade, who came to Roquebrune shortly after the funeral, has supplied me with this information.

Chronology of Important Dates

1865, June 13	William Butler Yeats born, first of the four children born to John Butler Yeats and Susan Pollexfen Yeats.
1875-80	Yeats at Godolphin School, Hammersmith, England. Holidays in Sligo, Ireland.
1882	First poems composed.
1884	Registers at Metropolitan School of Art, Dublin.
1885	First lyrics published in March issue of *Dublin University Review*.
1886	Art studies abandoned in favor of career as professional writer.
1887	Family returns to London. Mother suffers stroke which leaves her feeble-minded. Yeats joins Blavatsky Lodge of Theosophical Society in London, publishes first poems in English magazines.
1888	Meets William Morris, G. B. Shaw, W. E. Henley, and Oscar Wilde. Compiles *Fairy and Folk Tales*.
1889	Publishes first book of poems, *The Wanderings of Oisin and other Poems*. John O'Leary introduces Yeats to Maud Gonne.
1890	Joins Hermetic Order of the Golden Dawn.
1891	Founding member of Rhymers' Club and Irish Literary Society (London).
1892	Founding member, Irish Literary Society (Dublin). *The Countess Kathleen and Various Legends and Lyrics* published.
1893	*The Celtic Twilight* and three-volume *Works of William Blake* published.
1894	Meets Mrs. Olivia Shakespear through her cousin Lionel Johnson. Begins revision of all early poetry for first collected volume. *The Land of Heart's Desire* written, *The Shadowy Waters* begun.
1895	Editor: *A Book of Irish Verse*. *Collected Poems* published.
1897	*The Secret Rose* published. First summer at Lady Gregory's home, Coole Park.
1899	Rehearses plays for first performances of Irish Literary Theatre. *The Wind Among the Reeds* wins *Academy* prize as best book of poetry of the year.

The *Chronology of Important Dates* is abridged from the chronology in *A Reader's Guide to William Butler Yeats* (New York: Farrar, Straus, and Cudahy, Inc., 1959) by John Unterecker. Copyright © 1959 by John Unterecker. Reprinted by permission of The Noonday Press and the author.

1900   Death of mother.

1902   Founding of Irish National Theatre Society: Yeats, president. *Cathleen ni Hoolihan* produced.

1903   *In the Seven Woods, Ideas of Good and Evil* published. First American lecture tour (40 lectures) financial success.

1905   *The Shadowy Waters* produced in London, immediately re-written.

1906   Named director of Abbey Theatre with Lady Gregory and Synge. *Poems 1899-1905* published.

1907   Yeats defends Synge at *Playboy* riots. Tour of Italian cities with Lady Gregory and her son Robert.

1908   Eight-volume *Collected Edition* finished, complete revision of early work. Visits Maud Gonne in Paris, studies French.

1909   Meets Ezra Pound.

1910   Civil List pension (£150 per year) awarded with proviso that Yeats is free to indulge in any Irish political activity.

1911   *Plays For an Irish Theatre* published. Meets George Hyde-Lees through Mrs. Shakespear, visits Paris with Lady Gregory.

1912   Yeats lectures at Harvard on "The Theatre of Beauty." Yeats forms second Abbey company in Dublin. Ezra Pound with Yeats, reads aloud in evenings, teaches Yeats to fence.

1913   Pound acts as Yeats's secretary. *Poems Written in Discouragement* (Cuala) published.

1914   American lecture tour. *Responsibilities* published.

1915   Winter in Sussex with Ezra and Dorothy Shakespear Pound. Interest in Nōh plays stimulated by Pound. *At the Hawk's Well* written, produced in London with masks by Dulac, dances by Michio Ito. Yeats refuses offer of knighthood.

1916   Easter Rising in Dublin. John MacBride (Maud Gonne's husband) executed. Yeats visits Maud Gonne in France, buys Bally-lee tower.

1917   Proposes to Maud Gonne's adopted daughter Iseult at Cole-ville; proposal rejected. Marries George Hyde-Lees. Mrs. Yeats's automatic writing begins on honeymoon in Sussex. *The Wild Swans at Coole* published.

1918   *The Only Jealousy of Emer* written.

1919   February 24: daughter, Anne Butler Yeats, born. Yeats and family move into Ballylee.

1920   American tour with Mrs. Yeats. Sees father in New York for last time. *Michael Robartes and the Dancer* published.

1921, August 22   Son, William Michael Yeats, born.

1922   February 2: death of father, John Butler Yeats. *The Trembling of the Veil* published. Yeats invited to become member of Irish Senate, attends faithfully. D.Litt. conferred by Trinity College.

1923, November   Nobel Prize for literature awarded. Accepts in person, writes *The Bounty of Sweden.*

1925   Irish Senate speech on divorce. First version of *A Vision* printed.

1926   *Oedipus the King* adapted for Abbey.

1927   *Oedipus at Colonus* completed. Major speeches in Senate. Lung congestion and influenza lead to collapse, ordered to take complete rest.

1928   Moves to Rapallo with family. Term as Senator ends; because of poor health, refuses to stand for re-election. Begins *A Packet for Ezra Pound. The Tower* published.

1929   *Fighting the Waves* produced in Dublin with Ninette de Valois dancing. December 21: collapse in Rapallo from Malta fever.

1930   *The Words on the Window-Pane* written.

1931   May: D.Litt. degree from Oxford. August: last summer visit with Lady Gregory at Coole.

1932   Yeats organizes Irish Academy of Letters. Last American lecture tour, profits for Irish Academy.

1933   Cambridge degree awarded. *The King of the Great Clock Tower* written.

1934   Steinach rejuvenation operation performed, Yeats regarding it as successful. *Wheels and Butterflies* published.

1935   Lung congestion returns. *A Full Moon in March* published. Seventieth birthday banquet. *The Herne's Egg* begun. First *Broadsides* published.

1936   Ill with "breathlessness." BBC lecture on Modern Poetry.

1937   Four BBC broadcasts. *Essays 1931-1936* published.

1938   Moves to south of France. *On the Boiler* written. August: Last speech at Abbey Theatre on opening of *Purgatory.* December: *Death of Cuchulain* begun.

1939   Sudden illness, Thursday, January 26. Death, Saturday, January 28. Burial: Roquebrune, France.

1948, September   Yeats's body returned to Ireland on Irish corvette *Macha.* Body piped ashore at Galway. Mrs. Yeats, Yeats's children, and Yeats's brother Jack accompany funeral procession to Sligo. Military guard of honor at Sligo: government representative, Mr. Sean MacBride, Minister for External Affairs (Maud Gonne's son). Burial at Drumcliffe "under bare Ben Bulben's head" with stone inscribed as directed in "Under Ben Bulben."

Notes on the Editor and Authors

JOHN UNTERECKER, the editor of this anthology, teaches at Columbia University. A poet and a critic, he is best known as author of *A Reader's Guide to William Butler Yeats*. His biography of Hart Crane will soon be published.

W. H. AUDEN, poet and critic, has won an international reputation for the urbane eloquence of his lyrics and poetic dramas.

R. P. BLACKMUR, a distinguished poet and critic, teaches at Princeton University. Many of his most significant essays are contained in *Language as Gesture* (1953).

CURTIS BRADFORD is Oakes Ames Professor of English at Grinnell College. He worked with the Yeats manuscripts in Dublin in 1954-55 and again in the summer of 1960. His soon-to-be-published *Yeats at Work* studies at length the successive manuscripts of selected poems, plays, and prose works.

T. S. ELIOT, world-famous as a poet, is responsible for shaping, through his eloquent criticism, the literary tastes of a whole generation of readers.

RICHARD ELLMANN is best known for his achievements in such critical biographies as his monumental *James Joyce*. He teaches at Northwestern University.

IAN FLETCHER is Lecturer at the University of Reading.

D. J. GORDON is Professor of English at the University of Reading.

HUGH KENNER teaches at the University of California (Santa Barbara). His books include *The Poetry of Ezra Pound* and *Wyndham Lewis*. He is editor of the Twentieth Century Views' *T. S. Eliot* volume.

FRANK KERMODE, author of *The Romantic Image,* teaches at the University of Manchester.

GIORGIO MELCHIORI, author of *The Tightrope Walkers,* has established himself as a major critic of Yeats with the publication of his *The Whole Mystery of Art*.

A. G. STOCK has drawn on her own Irish background in writing her persuasive study of Yeats's development, *W. B. Yeats: His Poetry and Thought*. She is Sir G.O. Banerjee Professor of English at the University of Calcutta.

ALLEN TATE, a brilliant poet and eloquent critic, teaches at the University of Minnesota. His *Collected Essays* was published in 1959.

WILLIAM YORK TINDALL is best known for his *Forces in Modern British Literature, 1885-1956* and for his penetrating critical studies of James Joyce, Dylan Thomas, and D. H. Lawrence. He teaches at Columbia University.

ALEX ZWERDLING teaches at the University of California (Berkeley). The article reprinted here is part of a forthcoming longer study, *Yeats and the Heroic Ideal*.

Selected Bibliography

For the student seriously interested in Yeats, minimum equipment is the most recent editions of the *Collected Poems* and the *Collected Plays*. Almost as indispensable are the chatty *Autobiography* and Allan Wade's superb edition of Yeats's *Letters*. *Mythologies, Essays and Introductions,* and *A Vision* are helpful in offering Yeats's own passing comments on poems and plays. All of these books are published in America by The Macmillan Company and are regularly kept in print. *Autobiographies* (Anchor), *A Vision* (Macmillan), and an edition of *Selected Poems* edited by M. L. Rosenthal (Macmillan) are available as paperbacks. *The Senate Speeches of W. B. Yeats* (Bloomington: Indiana University Press, 1960) shows Yeats as practicing, practical, and witty statesman.

Since Yeats frequently revised printed drafts of his poems, Allt and Alspach's invaluable *The Variorum Edition of the Poems of W. B. Yeats* (New York: The Macmillan Company, 1957) is a book which will prove illuminating to any reader not familiar with Yeats's habits as a self critic.

Joseph Hone's *W. B. Yeats, 1865-1939* (New York: The Macmillan Company, 1943) is the only full-fledged biography, though a great deal of otherwise unavailable biographical information can be located in A. Norman Jeffares' *W. B. Yeats, Man and Poet* (New Haven: Yale University Press, 1949), T. R. Henn's *The Lonely Tower* (London: Methuen, 1950), Virginia Moore's *The Unicorn* (New York: The Macmillan Company, 1954), and Richard Ellmann's splendid biographical studies *Yeats: The Man and the Masks* (New York: The Macmillan Company, 1948; also published as an Everyman paperback) and *The Identity of Yeats* (New York: Oxford, 1954).

Useful general introductions to the poems can be found in my own *A Reader's Guide to William Butler Yeats* (New York: The Noonday Press, 1959; also available as a Noonday paperback) and A. G. Stock's *W. B. Yeats: His Poetry and Thought* (Cambridge, England: Cambridge University Press, 1961).

Special studies of particular merit include Donald A. Stauffer's brilliant treatment of Yeats's imagery, *The Golden Nightingale* (New York: The Macmillan Company, 1949), F. A. C. Wilson's *W. B. Yeats and Tradition* (New York: The Macmillan Company, 1958), Giorgio Melchiori's *The Whole Mystery of Art* (New York: The Macmillan Company, 1961), Thomas Parkinson's *W. B. Yeats, Self-Critic* (Berkeley: University of California Press, 1951), and Frank Kermode's *The Romantic Image* (New York: The Macmillan Company, 1957).

The enormous bibliography of periodical literature about Yeats includes hundreds of essays and perhaps thousands of reviews. A generous selection of the best of the essays then available was reprinted in Hall and Steinmann's *The Permanence of Yeats* (New York: The Macmillan Company, 1950).

The second edition of Allan Wade's *A Bibliography of the Writings of W. B. Yeats* (London: Hart-Davis, 1957) is both comprehensive and accurate in cata-

loguing Yeats's extensive publications. This great bibliography is in part sup-
plemented by George Brandon Saul's *Prolegomena to the Study of Yeats's Poems*
(Philadelphia: University of Pennsylvania Press, 1957), a book which locates
much significant critical comment.

TWENTIETH CENTURY VIEWS

Forthcoming Titles